ATATÜRK: FOUNDER OF A MODERN STATE

Kemal Atatürk teaching the new latin alphabet to the people, Istanbul, 1928.

Atatürk
Founder of a Modern State

ALI KAZANCIGIL *and*
ERGUN ÖZBUDUN
editors

ARCHON BOOKS
Hamden, Connecticut 1981

First published 1981 in London by C. Hurst & Co.
and in the U.S.A. as an Archon Book
an imprint of
The Shoe String Press, Inc.
995 Sherman Avenue
Hamden, Connecticut 06514

ISBN 0-208-01968-5

Printed in Great Britain

Library of Congress Cataloging in Publication Data
Main entry under title:

Atatürk, the founder of a modern state.

   Bibliography: p.
   Includes index.
   1. Atatürk, Kemal, 1881-1938--Addresses, essays,
lectures. 2. Turkey--Politics and government--1918-
1960--Addresses, essays, lectures. I. Özbudun, Ergun.
II. Kazancigil, Ali.
DR592.K4A855 1981   956.1'024'0924   81-19094
ISBN 0-208-01968-5   AACR2

Photographs (cover and frontispiece) reproduced by courtesy of
the Turkish Ministry of Foreign Affairs.

Contents

v

Note on pronunciation

It is hoped that the following guidance may be useful to readers unacquainted with Turkish.

c   *j* as in *jar*

ç   *ch* as in *child*

g   soft *g*, lengthens the preceding vowel

i   *ee* as in seed

ı   like *u* in *radium*

ö   like German *ö*

ü   like German *ü*

ş   like *sh* in *shop*

Introduction

ERGUN ÖZBUDUN and ALI KAZANCIGIL*

Like all great men in history, Mustafa Kemal Atatürk can be viewed from a number of different perspectives: as the founder of a state, as a nation-builder, as a creator of political institutions, as a moderniser of his society, as an extraordinarily capable political leader, as a successful military commander, as an educator of his nation, as one of the first successful anti-imperialist leaders of the Third World, as a statesman who deeply believed in and contributed to world peace.

In this volume, we have chosen to emphasise Atatürk as the founder of a modern state, hence the title of the book. Our choice has been motivated by two reasons. First, we believe that many aspects of Kemal Atatürk's life and work can be coherently examined around this main theme. Thus his role in the modernisation of Turkey cannot really be separated from his state-building role, as the creation of a modern state has been a pre-requisite for the modernisation of the Turkish society. Similarly, Atatürk's policy of friendly relations with all nations, analysed by Danilov in this volume, undoubtedly helped him to concentrate on the task of building and consolidating the new Turkish state. Secondly, following the spirit of Unesco's participation in the commemoration of the Atatürk centennial in 1981, we were interested in bringing out the universal significance of Kemalism.[1]

In what ways does Kemalism represent a path for national development? Around the mid-1960s Harold D. Lasswell and Daniel Lerner could maintain: 'Kemal Atatürk was the nearest approximation to a genius of modernisation that any "emerging nation" had seen in this quarter-century.'[2] But societal change and development are seen today in the Third World as a culture-bound and pluralist process, contrary to the earlier mono-directional, western-centred model. So at a time when the certitudes of 1950s and 1960s concerning socio-economic and political modernisation are being severely challenged, and the image of the systemic unity of the world (economically and technologically) is being increasingly counterbalanced by the image of its civilisational and cultural diversity, are there a number of lessons which the Third World nations can draw from the Kemalist experience?

* The opinions expressed in this Introduction and in 'The Ottoman-Turkish state and Kemalism' (pages 37−55) do not necessarily represent the official views of Unesco.

1

We think that Atatürk's achievements in the founding of the modern Turkish state deserve special emphasis, since in much of the Third World today there appears to be a wide gap between state-building and political institutionalisation and the process of social and economic change.[3] As a consequence of this over-riding concern, we tried to present the Kemalist experiment in a comparative and historical perspective. While many of the contributions to the present volume have an implicit comparative concern, the one by Hayashi has been specifically designed as a two-nation comparison between the Turkish and the Japanese models of modernisation, the two cases of early modernisation in the non-Western world. Also on the comparative side are the articles by Eisenstadt and Özbudun. The former analyses the Turkish revolution within the framework of his theories on revolutions and the transformation of societies;[5] the latter describes the Kemalist political regime in the light of the theories of authoritarian regimes and of regime changes and transitions.

As regards the historical perspective, again many of the contributions — notably those by Ahmad, Karal, Kazancıgil and Mardin — emphasise the historical setting within which the Kemalist revolution emerged. More specifically, these articles analyse the elements of continuity and change between the late Ottoman empire (particularly the Young Turk period of 1908–18) and the Kemalist republic. We feel such an historical perspective to be especially useful, since works on the great men in history usually tend to emphasise the unique personality characteristics of the leader and to lose sight of the societal factors which operate as either constraining or facilitating conditions.[6]

There are important reasons for analysing Kemalism in an historical perspective. Two diametrically opposed views on Kemalism agree on the assumption that it represents a total break with the Ottoman past. The first, held by certain doctrinaire Kemalists in Turkey, as well as by foreign observers with a cursory knowledge of the country, sees it as a sudden and total transformation from a theocratic empire into a modern nation-state, in which the secular-nationalist doctrine replaced Islam as the cultural foundation and overall ideology of the Turkish polity. The second, held mostly by the Islamic and Third World critics of Kemalism, views it as an effort to impose an alien and enforced secularisation upon an Islamic society, an effort which was bound to fail because it isolated itself from the cultural heritage of the people, and therefore failed to mobilise its energy.[7]

We feel, however, that both interpretations are historical oversimplifications. Even if we leave aside the question of whether the

Ottoman empire really conformed to the standard image of a 'theo-cratic state',[8] it should be underlined that the empire underwent a century-long period of gradual modernisation and secularisation. Many Western laws and practices had been adopted and a basically secular educational system had been established by the end of the nineteenth century. Granted that the dualism between secular laws and the *Sharia*, between secular education and religious education persisted until the reforms of Atatürk; yet the trend towards mod-ernisation and secularisation was quite clear. Kemalism represented an intensification, radicalisation and culmination of this trend. It was not an alien model simply borrowed from abroad, but the result of a lengthy historical process of continuous interaction between the Ottoman empire and the West — or put differently, it was the endogenous response of certain Ottoman élites to events which threatened to destroy the independence of the state — and this response was conditioned by certain characteristics and traditions of the Ottoman-Turkish polity, as well as by the impact of the nine-teenth- and early twentieth-centuries capitalist world-economy and interstate system upon the Ottoman social formation.

Elements of continuity between the Ottoman and Turkish polities are numerous, particularly at the level of value systems, cultural codes and symbols of collective identity as the basis of the legitimacy and institutionalisation of the state. However, continuities between the Young Turks (1908–18) and the Kemalists are, in particular, marked with some important exceptions as in foreign affairs, where the rational and peaceful policies of the Kemalist period contrasted with the adventurous dreams of Young Turk leaders which had so many tragic consequences. Important steps were taken in this brief and turbulent period towards the centralisation and rationalisation of the governmental structures, secularisation of laws and educa-tion, and the emergence of a national economy.[9] One also observes a close resemblance between the social background characteristics of the Young Turk political élite, whose criteria of recruitment were Turkishness, education, youth and belonging to the 'official' class, and the political élite of the Kemalist era.[10] It was due to Kemal Atatürk's genius and vision as a political leader, however, that such policies and trends were carried to their logical conclusions cul-minating in the establishment of a modern, secular, republican state.

One of the features that distinguish the Kemalist revolution from other modernising movements in the Islamic world is the extent to which secularism was emphasised in republican Turkey. Turkey remains today the only Islamic country whose Constitution stipu-lates that secularism is one of the basic organisational principles of the state (Constitution of 1961, Art. 2), and where the legal system (including such areas as personal status, family law and inheritance, which in all Islamic countries proved highly resistant to secularising trends) is completely secularised. Laws contain no discriminatory provisions based on religion, and the Constitution specifically rules out such discrimination. Religious instruction at public schools can only be optional. Finally, as the most telling aspect of Kemalist secularism, the Constitution (together with other laws) strictly forbids, under penal sanctions, political and associational activity with the aim of establishing a political, social, economic or legal order based even partly on religious principles (Constitution, Arts. 19 and 57; Penal Code, Art. 163).

This emphasis on secularism stems from Atatürk's rationalist and positivist outlook, aptly described by Mardin in this volume. If it were possible to reduce Kemalism to a single dimension, it would not be wrong to single out rationalism, since it was a rationalist and positivist mentality that underlay nearly all Atatürk's speeches, thought, actions and reforms. Regarding the relationship between rationality and religion in general, but more specifically within the context of Islamic societies, Kemalism maintained that rationalisation necessarily involves secularisation. In this perspective, Islam, having been born simultaneously as a religion and as a state, in contrast to many other world religions, regulates a large area of social, economic, political and legal relations, out of which emerged an elaborate· system of Islamic law called the *Sharia* (or *Şeriat* in Turkish). Consequently, it is deemed highly problematic for Islamic societies to modernise their social and political structures without a substantial measure of secularisation. True, some attempts have been made both in the early centuries of Islam (especially by the *Mutazila* sect) and in the late nineteenth and early twentieth centuries (especially by such thinkers as Jamal-ad-Din al-Afghani, Muhammad Abduh and Rashid Rida) to reconcile dogma and reason, to interpret Koranic prescriptions in such a way as to be compatible with modernisation. These efforts, however, did not produce a genuine reform movement in Islamic countries,[11] because the thoughts of the reformers remained 'within the bounds set by Islamic dogma . . . the postulated synthesis of dogma and ratio remains a postulate; it is unattainable.'[12]

It should however be added that there are a number of Islamic thinkers who refuted the argument according to which there can be no progress and modernisation without secularisation in Islamic societies. For instance, the Moroccan Allal el-Fassi or, even more explicitly, the Egyptian Khalid M. Khalid tried to give an Islamic content to the concept of progress and modernity contrary to 'reformist' Islamic thinkers who aimed at re-interpreting Koranic prescriptions so as to make them compatible with progress and modernity as defined by the European tradition.

The emphasis which Atatürk placed on secularism seemed excessive to some of his critics. However, despite the radical nature of Kemalist secularism, it should be stressed that it never intended, explicitly or implicitly, to eradicate Islam in Turkey. It was anti-clerical, to be sure, but not anti-religious. It aimed at individualisation or privatisation of Islam, attempting to make it a matter of individual conscience rather than the fundamental organising principle of the society. Consistent with this, freedom of religion at the individual level was always respected, while organised political manifestations of Islam were strictly forbidden. Judged by these criteria, the ultimate aim of Kemalism seems to have been accomplished, since a majority of believing and practicing Turkish Muslims are now distinguishing between their religious beliefs and their public and political lives — as evidenced by their electoral behaviour. Indeed, during the 1970s, fundamentalist Islamic political parties have been able to carry only a small minority of votes at the elections.

It should be pointed out that, in a deeper sense, the aim of the Kemalist conception of secularism was to broaden the autonomy of the individual in society and to liberate him from the collective constraints of a stifling community tradition (Mardin in this volume), in a culture where individualism had no historical and philosophical roots. In short, Kemalism had much more in common with the rationalist and libertarian philosophy of the Enlightenment than with the anti-liberal ideologies of the twentieth century.

Kemalism was what Barrington Moore called a 'revolution from above',[13] and definitely not a social revolution. But then, the latter type of revolution is very rare in history, the latest example being the Iranian. The great majority of nations which gained their independence over the last quarter of a century are trying hard to institutionalise their political systems, to strengthen their states 'from above'. In the Third World, 'In most cases it may not be exaggerated to assert that, instead of the state being as classical theories — i.e. those originating in the centre — supposed, some sort of reflection of civil society, it was, to a large extent on the contrary, the state apparatus that shaped the basic features of our societies'.[14] This volume does not aim at presenting Kemalism as a 'model' but at stimulating a debate around issues concerning state-building and institutionalisation in nations undergoing a very rapid political and socio-cultural change. In this way, the study of Kemalism 'should contribute to the study of the various development and modernisation processes'.[15]

NOTES

1. Unesco's General Conference, at its twentieth session in 1978, adopted a resolution (Resolutions, Vol. 1, 3/1.5 and 2, 3/4) concerning the celebration of the hundredth anniversary of the birth of Atatürk. The resolution referred to Atatürk as 'an exceptional reformer in all the fields coming within Unesco's competence, . . . the leader of one of the earliest struggles against colonialism and imperialism, an outstanding example in promoting the spirit of mutual understanding between peoples and lasting peace between the nations of the world'. In 1979, the Executive Board of the Organisation adopted at its 108th session a decision (Doc. 108 Ex/Decisions, 15 Nov. 1979, 4.1.V) concerning an 'Atatürk international centenary symposium . . . [to] contribute to the study of the various development and modernisation processes in member-states'. This symposium is planned to take place from 16–18 December 1981, at Unesco Headquarters, in Paris (Programme and Budget for 1981–1983, 21 C/5 approved, par. 3223).

2. In their 'Foreword' to Frederick W. Frey, *The Turkish Political Elite*, Cambridge, Hass., M.I.T. Press, 1965, x.

3. Samuel P. Huntington, *Political Order in Changing Societies*, New Haven and London, Yale University Press, 1968.

4. For an earlier attempt to compare the two cases of modernisation, see Robert E. Ward and Dankwart A. Rustow (eds.), *Political Modernisation in Japan and Turkey*, Princeton, N.J., Princeton University Press, 1964.

5. S. N. Eisenstadt, *Revolution and the Transformation of Societies*, New York, the Free Press, 1978.

6. Otto Kirchheimer, 'Confining Conditions and Revolutionary Break-throughs', *American Political Science Review*, 59 (Dec. 1965), 964–74.

7. For a criticism along these lines, see Hichem Djait, *L'Europe et l'Islam*, Paris, Seuil, 1978, 56.

8. To be sure, no Islamic state was a theocracy in the sense of being ruled by a priestly class. The Ottoman empire differed from the classical model of an Islamic state in another respect as well. According to the classical Islamic theory of the state, 'the ruler cannot be but the judge and the administrator; his power can be executive, administrative, and judicial, but not legislative. [. . .] God alone is the Great Legislator, since he has already given the Law [*Sharia*], divine, perfect, sufficient, unchangeable, written in the Koran for eternity in the last revelation necessary for humanity. Therefore, there is neither place nor need for a legislating State, and governing is not a process of legislation, but of administration and interpretation. The ruler is neither the creation nor the creator of the Law, but its instrument.' See William Zartman, 'Pouvoir et Etat dans l'Islam', *Pouvoirs*, 1980 (No. 12), 6. Contrary to this view of things, there was always an important place for legislation outside the sphere of *Şeriat*, in the Ottoman state. One only has to remember that one of the greatest Ottoman sultans, Süleyman I, has been referred to as 'Süleyman the Legislator' (*Kanunî*).

9. Sina Akşin, *Jön Türkler ve Ittihat ve Terakki*, Istanbul, Gerçek Yayınevi, 1980; Feroz Ahmad, *The Young Turks*, London, Oxford University Press, 1969.

10. On these criteria of recruitment, see Sina Akşin, 'Ittihat ve Terakki Üzerine', *Siyasal Bilgiler Fakültesi Dergisi*, 26 (March 1971), 169–72. On the republican political élite, see Frederick W. Frey, *op. cit.* On a comparison between the two, see Mehmet Turhan, 'Siyasal Elit Değişimi: Türkiye, Mısır, Israil Örnekleri', unpublished Ph.D. dissertation, Faculty of Law, Ankara University, 1981.

11. As Albert Hourani, notes, 'Islam needed a Luther: this indeed was a favourite theme of al-Afghani's, and perhaps he saw himself in the role' (*Arabic Thought in the Liberal Age, 1798–1939*, London, Oxford University Press, 1970, 122).

12. Bassam Tibi, 'Islam and Social Change in the Modern Middle East', *Law and State*, 22(1980), 98, 100. Malcolm Kerr, in his detailed and profound analysis of the political and legal theories of Muhammad Abduh and Rashid Rida, observes that these 'Islamic modernists' failed to provide satisfactory answers by which the twentieth-century revolutions in Islamic countries might 'be given a sense of moral direction'. Insofar as their answers 'inspired action, it was of the negative and destructive kind promoted by the Muslim Brotherhood, but more generally they inspired a passive, uneasy, ineffectual acceptance of European institutions and social practices, without providing them with any firm moral basis.' (*Islamic Reform The Political and Legal Theories of Muhammad 'Abduh and Rashid Ridā*, Berkeley and Los Angeles, University of California Press), 1966, 221 and *passim*.

13. Barrington Moore Jr., *The Social Origins of Dictatorship and Democracy: Lord and Peasant in the Making of the Modern World*, Boston, Beacon Press, 1966.

14. Guillermo O'Donnell, 'Comparative historical formations of the state apparatus and socio-economic change in the Third World', *International Social Science Journal* vol. XXXII, no. 4., 1980, 717.

15. Unesco, Doc. 108 Ex/Decisions, 4.1.V.

Part I:

Political Structures and Dynamics

The Principles of Kemalism

ENVER ZIYA KARAL

Kemalism and Kemalist principles are products of the Turkish revolution, which started with the Turkish Independance War and resulted in the formation of a national and secular Turkish state. This event, which occurred in the years following the collapse of the Ottoman empire, gave birth to 'Kemalism', named after leader of the movement, Mustafa Kemal Atatürk.

The term 'Kemalism' was first used by Western authors;[1] later, in Turkish, it was referred to as *Atatürkçülük*. With the passage of time, it was referred to as 'Kemalist Principles' basing the title on the principles forming the concept. According to Reşat Kaynar, 'Kemalism is the ideological principle of the *Turkish* Republic . . . Kemalism is not doctrinaire, but pragmatic.'[2] Kemalism is also classified as a collection of idealisms and principles, and 'a doctrinaire ideology' supported by action. A famous Turkish author, Falih Rıfkı Atay, who shared Atatürk's ideals, gained his confidence, and spent most of his life in the leader's close circle, defines Kemalism as a fundamental religious reform.[3] Yakub Kadri Karaosmanoğlu, who is considered one of the ideologues of Kemalism, and whom Atatürk warmly praised, claims: 'There is no such thing as the *Principles* of Kemalism. There is just one principle: to defeat the imperialistic intentions of the imperialist nations in Turkey. What has been done has been done with that aim.'[4] Rom Landau, author of various works on Atatürk, wrote: 'Kemalism, which is the fundamental of modern Turkey is neither a political and social system alone, nor a life philosophy. It is much more than that. It is giving understanding and meaning to the emergence of Turkey into modern science and development; to new technology, education, ethics, as well as to new faith and work-life. It is giving a new spirit to the position of humanity in universe.'[5]

There is no doubt that all the above are facets of Kemalism. However, it is possible to note deep contrasts between them. Thus it is very difficult to accept any unequivocal definition of what Kemalism is. As to the origin of the difficulty, a new look is required at the many publications on the personality, military qualities, and reforms of Atatürk. Those in Turkish are listed in *A Bibliography of Atatürk and his Reforms*,[6] published by the Turkish Ministry of Education. Those in other languages are to be found in *Atatürk and Turkey: a Bibliography 1918–1938*, published by the Near East

11

Section of the Library of Congress. It is evident from these publications that not many books have been written on Kemalism. It is possible to attribute the lack of writings on its principles to two causes: one is the view common to most Western authors that the Turkish revolution lacked a theoretical base, and the other is the fact that Atatürk himself omitted to give a systematic explanation of his thoughts and actions. The view of Western authors that, unlike the French revolution, the Turkish revolution had no preparatory phase of intellectual development, although it may be conceded to a degree, is by no means completely correct. It is a fact that the French revolution was born in a society already possessing concepts of nationality and a modern state, and was realised within a sequence of time. The Turkish revolution was launched in order to achieve the qualities of nationalism and a modern state in a fundamentally medieval, theocratic empire, and to throw off the pre-existing institutions and concepts. The revolution entered the path of development through an appreciation of developments in the Western world and beginning a westernisation movement. Therefore, there is no reason why one should not regard the westernisation movements as the scientific basis of the Turkish revolution. The supporting factors may be classified as interest in the literature, spirit and political philosophy of the West around the end of the nineteenth century.

The fact that Atatürk himself has offered no systematic explanations of his thoughts and actions in an ideological manner is closely related to the revolution's character. The fact is that the principles of the Revolution have been determined retrospectively, following the realisation of the reform movement. Atatürk found it essential to keep total secrecy regarding every aspect of every one of his reforms until the time came to announce it openly. This was a matter of security, and it was only by this method that he was able to do away with the institutions which existed throughout the Ottoman empire.

Because of this, we look in this article first at the main factors and concepts leading to Atatürk's revolution. An estimation of the Kemalist movement will follow. The vagueness apparent in the intellectual background of Kemalism received a striking illustration in the discussions at a seminar held in Istanbul on the fiftieth anniversary of the Turkish republic, on the 'Economic and Social Aspects of Kemalism'. Many scholars, although they had known Atatürk personally and closely, and had published books on his life and thought, claimed that he was a man incapable of reading books of political philosophy, and that feeling came before thought in his life.[7] This was not so.

Atatürk's family, being uneducated, had not been able to equip him with an academic background. His father died when he was seven, and his mother wanted him to receive a religious education and become a Muslim preacher. Atatürk chose, by his own will and decision a military education for himself, and pursued his own education apart from the classical education supplied by military schools. He learned French and German by his own efforts, and read the historical and literary works of the very few Turkish authors active at that time while he was in military school. He was influenced by the excitement and style of the patriotic poetry of Namık Kemal. He practically memorised the ideas of Tevfik Fikret on civilisation, women's education, humanism and secularism, and later reflected some of them in his speeches; he took great interest in the literary publications of Ziya Gökalp, mostly on the social life of the Turks in pre-Islamic times, and in the new literary movement which Gökalp started with his book '*Yeni Hayat*' (New Life) during the second Constitutional era. His 'What should be the direction of the New Reform Movement?' in *Içtihat*, the periodical of Abdullah Cevdet, was based on translations of French philosophers. And he revised the works of the poets Mehmet Emin, Celal Nuri and Mehmet Izzet.

He was particularly interested in the works of Jean-Jacques Rousseau, August Comte and Emile Durkheim. Among the historical writers he read and which inspired him, was Auguste Mignet. He closely examined biographies of Napoleon and of Desaix and Moreau, generals of the French Revolutionary period, and reached the verdict that Napoleon was unjust to them. He also read novels, and noted down many passages from various books of Marcel Prévant. For some reason, he did not record the name of a book on socialism on which he took many notes.[8] Atatürk was not particular about having a comfortable place for reading; he would study during hikes, on horseback, or under canvas while mobilised for war. He would take advantage of any spare time for reading. He would record the time he had been able to set aside for reading, and then the thoughts and ideas which a particular book inspired, along with adverse criticism. He discussed them with his friends. The following observations made by him during the preparation of the Turkish Constitution in 1920 in a conversation with Yusuf Kemal Tengirshenk, a professor of law, who served as minister successively of justice and of foreign affairs, on Auguste Comte are particularly interesting: 'The ideas of Auguste Comte were valuable in achieving the peace of the bourgeoisie. . . . If we are going to be westernised, let us go to the fundamentals of the West . . . to the definite sovereignty principles of the West. Sovereignty belongs to the nation. It cannot be segmented or divided. Not even an inch of it can be spared.'

Yusuf Kemal continued: 'I believe that in 1920s there was not one soldier who was familiar even with the name of Auguste Comte, let alone his ideas. But I witnessed the fact that Mustafa Kemal, during his debates on the Constitution, knew the subject more throughly than the professor of constitutional law, Celaleddin Arif.'[9]

Another factor reinforcing the intellectual work of Atatürk besides reading continuously was the attention he paid to the effects of nature on human beings. He believed that people were the products of nature, equipped with intelligence for survival: thus did he preserve himself from oriental fatalism. He did not even believe in luck; luck is only the approach of events which we have not been able to calculate beforehand.[10] His ideas of society and of life as a whole were not diverted to the traditional obligation to prepare oneself for another world, and for the happiness and joy expected there — a pure product of medieval thought. On the contrary, he believed that satisfaction and happiness should be attained during the individual's lifetime. 'A person should work not for himself, but for those who will come after him. If he should stop to think whether those following will appreciate his efforts, he is considered unsuccessful. The happiest men should be those who prefer their efforts to remain anonymous to the generations that follow.'[11]

Starting from this point, Atatürk's self-explanation in relation to the national ideal he was to follow to the end of his life was: 'I have passions — so many of them. These are not directed towards simplicities such as gaining a big fortune or achieving a great position. Fulfilment of my passions will provide much for my country, and I am seeking the fulfilment and satisfaction which the realisation of such a task will give me.'[12] At that time he did not reveal what he meant by his ideal, which he referred to simply as his 'great idea'; he said only that it was a national task. According to him, 'the power directing human beings is the ideal. . . . To gain the hearts and confidence of those one is to lead, one must first find out and share their hidden desires and thoughts.'[13] Atatürk believed in the transformation of thought into an ideal and its high moral personality. During the Balkan wars of 1912, when the assistant commander-in-chief of the army and navy, Izzet Paşa, announced that some men of religion were to be sent to the front line to boost the morale of the soldiers, he responded that morale was being given by the regimental *müftü* and officers. 'To send a delegation of such people will show that the war-power of our army is near to collapse, and will result in speculation about the poor state of our government. Therefore this attempt should be stopped.'[14]

Atatürk's giving of priority to the intellect resulted in the introduction of a new concept of ethics. For a long time, it was impossible to separate ethics from religion in both the western world and the orient. Atatürk claimed, referring to certain actions which we do not perform because they are declared to be unethical by religious authority, that such prohibitions are all man-made. According to him, ethics belong to society and the nation. Therefore they can only be seen in a sociological or national context. For Atatürk this concept of ethics was also the mainspring of political ideals. His classification of ethics as social or national was founded on the principle of the superiority of the state to the individual. In other words, it meant a separation from the philosophy of the Middle Ages, which had required individual sacrifice and immersion of oneself in mystical thoughts.[15]

The principal ideas which Atatürk tried to communicate to the public during the Turkish War of Independence were as follows: 'The purpose in forming a state or a government is the protection of a political society, and the development of that society in all aspects.' Atatürk believed that life, in its deepest meaning, was a continual war with nature. Separate from this was the war for civilisation being fought among the nations. In order that a nation may survive this war, 'for everything in the world, for civilisation, for life, for success, the most important factor is science.' His motto was that to seek anything other than science was to be ignorant. Undoubtedly, by this phrase, he tried to attract attention to the legality and quality of reforms:

'The aim of the reforms we have already carried out and are continuing to carry out is to form Turkish society into a modern society in every aspect. This is the basis of our reforms. Up till now, the nation has been dominated by concepts which are disabling to the functioning of the mind. If the wars which have resulted from this concept are not done away with, it will be impossible to enlighten the mind.'[16] The concepts to which Atatürk referred here were various. Basing it on his several speeches, we may classify them as follows: under-valuing human life, vagabondage, laziness, considering life a burden, elevating the moral quality of poverty, not being concerned about nature, being unable to assess the actual value of any concept, turning one's back on free thought; all these factors, which make the life of a nation meaningless, were apparent in Turkey at the beginning of the independence war. Turkey's situation at this time can again be illustrated in Atatürk's words:

'Those who have travelled in Turkey from Izmir to Erzurum, who have seen the Black Sea coast and the plains of Syria, can easily learn that our country is completely in ruins. We have not one city left that people can live in. The villages are places made of straw or little better. It is impossible for human beings to live there. We have no roads. I repeat, we have no place we may call a city. Furthermore, our people are ignorant, poor and miserable.'[17]

The Turkish revolution was launched to change this state of affairs — to provide for the forgotten rights of people, to develop the country in keeping with the present age, to find qualities in Turkey which had previously been considered non-existent, and to add new contributions to those it had once made to civilisation. The Turkish Revolution thus earned a place among the great revolutions of history. From it, as we indicated at the beginning, emerged the principles of Kemalism: republicanism, nationalism, populism, secularism, etatism and revolutionism.

Republicanism is the fundamental principle of the new Turkish state, and took its place in the Constitution when the Republic was proclaimed on 29, October 1923. Its pre-eminence *vis-à-vis* the other five principles is noted as follows: 'The first statement of this law cannot, by whatever means, be replaced or diverted — the form of government of the Turkish state is republican.'

The quoted article of the Constitution was kept unchanged, and the pre-eminence of the principle of republicanism continued.

(*a*) Republicanism was a turning-point in the political philosophy of the Turks. The new Turkish republic was a state founded by the Turkish nation, on its own account, on its own land. Throughout history, both before and after the coming of Islam, all Turkish states had been dynastic. Their names, institutions, and internal and foreign policies could only be evaluated according to the characters of their founders.

(*b*) Republicanism came into being without going through a phase of ideological preparation. From *Tanzimat* to the collapse of the Ottoman empire, most Turkish authors, reflecting various aspects of Western political ideas, showed strong opposition to the idea of founding a republic in Turkey. During the second constitutional period, none of the political parties appeared to favour a republic.

(*c*) Republicanism introduced the modern concept of national sovereignty. This principle was embodied in two clear statements in the founding of the Grand National Assembly, without the word 'republic' being used:

'No power is superior to the Grand National Assembly.'

'The Grand National Assembly has the power to make and to implement laws.'

This position, later expressed as 'Sovereignty belongs to the nation', was not to be found in the Ottoman constitution programme of the Union and Progress Party, granted by the Sultan-Caliph, which contained these words: 'The legislative power in the constitutional period of the Ottoman states, as previously, belongs to the senior member of the Ottoman family. This is the legitimate possession of the Ottoman family, the founders of the state. The Ottoman sultans are the noble caliphs of the Muslims. Therefore, the religion of the Ottoman state is Islam'.

When this statement is compared with that, previously quoted, of the Turkish Grand National Assembly, it is easy to understand that republicanism arose as a reaction to the Sultanate and Caliphate.

Nationalism. Like republicanism, nationalism is also a principle in the political, social and cultural life of the new Turkey. What we know of the nationalism of the Turks before their acceptance of Islam indicates that with that acceptance it diminished, leading to religious internationalism. As the Ottoman empire expanded, so did the Turks become a minority within it. It is not possible to prove any Turkish settlement areas in the empire other than Anatolia and Thrace. Even the Turks of these areas called themselves 'Ottomans' and 'Mohammedans' and the name 'Turk' meant nothing to them. The policy of the state towards the Turks indicated no solicitude or emotional quality, such as would have been necessary for the nurture of a nation.

Nationalism in the Ottoman empire first occurred among the non-Muslim communities, in the years following the French Revolution. The Ottomanism which the state attempted to pursue, to achieve legal and political equality and form a homogeneous Ottoman society, was unable to prevent the Christian states hiving off from the empire; nor could the Pan-Islamist movement prevent the spreading of these ideas among the non-Muslims. The Turanian movement initiated by not more than a few of the enlightened men of the second constitutional period could never reach a stage beyond that of being an ideal, the main reason being that the concept of a 'homeland' for the nationalist movement was not clearly defined.

Since the beginning of modern times, a 'homeland' in Western nations has been defined as being within the national boundaries; this has been strongly supported in art and literature. In Ottoman society, however, the homeland was defined as being within the boundaries reached during the empire's period of expansion. Pan-Islamists, on the other hand, regarded the entire territory on which the Muslims lived as homeland, while Pan-Turanians considered as homeland every inch of soil inhabited by Turks. During the reign of Abdülaziz, the expenditure section of the state budget for 1863−4, reserved 8.5 million francs for the Muslim holy land while only 1 million francs were reserved to education and cultivation, and 4.5 million for commerce, including agriculture; this shows how religion benefited to the detriment of the state. During the Balkan war, the neglect of the nation was summed up in the following saying:

'Poor Turk, will you forever be offended? What is the fate of the poor Turks in this country? To be insulted by the nations she once fed and protected? In this country other nations are highly praised — this we are willing to tolerate. But is it necessary to insult the Turk while trying to praise others?'

Thus, over the course of time, the originally Turkish Ottoman empire lost the national character which was hers by nature and became a religious body. The Turkish population were in no way distinguished from other Muslims. The Caliph of the world boasted of being the leader of all Muslims.

The state and its geography, population, language, history and laws did not possess the name 'Turk'. The Turkisation movement which Ziya Gökalp started close to the end of the second constitutional era presented two homelands: one that of all Muslims, and the other the territory (*Turan*) inhabited by all Turks. The Ottoman's homeland was an independent one consisting of both Turan and the land of the Arabs, and as the result of this concept, the state was to be called the 'Turkish-Arab state'. Undoubtedly, the pursuit of such an object could not be tolerated. Actual Turkisation began with nationalism after the collapse of the empire, and the first big step in that direction was taken with the acceptance of national boundaries at the Erzurum Congress. The independence war which followed, the foundation of Turkish Grand National Assembly and the replacement of Ottoman institutions by modern and national ones were all part and parcel of this nationalisation movement.

The process of becoming a nation set off by the Turkish reform differed clearly from the similar phenomenon taking place in other nations at the same time. These differences are apparent in history, culture and humanism. There are cultural/historical conceptions concerning the origin of Turkish nationalism. Atatürk's own definition was: 'The Turkish people forming the Turkish Republic are called the Turkish nation.'[18] The establishment of the Republic is an historical event, but Turkey is a geographical concept: the Turkish people are those who inhabit Anatolia and Thrace. This definition by Atatürk reflects a nineteenth-century view of nationhood, and pre-empts any intention of dividing Turkey into religious, sectarian or regional societies.

The second aspect of Turkish nationalism is the cultural one. In other words it has no relation with race. In a racial framework an individual is not free to feel nationality, but Turkish nationality is for people who speak Turkish, who are brought up with Turkish culture, share Turkish ideals and who live on Turkish soil; these people are Turks, regardless of race or religion.

The third aspect of Turkish nationalism is humanism. 'The Turkish nation regards itself as a prized and honourable member of the human family. Turks love all humans and have no feelings of hostility unless the country's national pride or interests are violated.'[19] Acting upon this concept, Turkish nationalism became a symbol of peace at a time when extreme racism was identified with imperialism. This love of peace found its clearest definition by Atatürk's words 'Peace in the nation, peace in the world.'

This was a time when many nations even regarded war as essential for humanity. The foreign policy of the Turkish Republic was stately different, as fundamentally based on ideas the following statement of Atatürk shows: 'Today most nations of the world have become or are becoming relatives. Therefore one has to consider the life and welfare of other nations as well as one's own and hope for the peace and prosperity of others and try to serve their welfare, as if it were one's own.'[20] Thanks to this peaceful concept of nationalism, Turkey was able to exclude herself from the Second World War.

Populism. This is the basic principle of Turkish democracy, if one interprets it as meaning the governance 'of the people, with the people, for the people'. 'People' in the Ottoman empire had no political value. Therefore, the term '*reaya*' was first used to define the majority of the Ottomans, earning their living from farming. As time passed on, this word started to be used only to describe non-Muslims. During the *Tanzimat* the word '*halk*' (people) started to be meaningful besides the word *ahali* (gathering or crowd). In the last few decades of the Ottoman empire, the 'nationality' section of birth certificates was used to denote a person's religion or sect'.

It was with the Turkish revolution that the word 'people' gained a political meaning. Atatürk used the word '*halk*' rather than *millet*, to indicate that no trace of a religious connotation remained. In a speech he made before the abolition of the Caliphate, he began: 'This parliament is the parliament of the Turkish people. Its position and authority can only be effective if based on the faith of the Turkish people and on Turkish land.' Because '*halk*' was used to supply the meaning of '*millet*', it acquired at the same time a democratic significance — to the extent that the Anatolian Agency soon issued a declaration that efforts were being made to change the Constitution. The name of the state was considered to be the 'Turkish People's Republic'.

The principle of populism conveyed by this use of the word 'people' became a source of democratic rights. Because the new Turkish state was a state of the people, and accepted as such, equality before the law had been achieved, permitting no exceptions to any families, classes or communities. Hence all the social reform movements that were developing in various directions under Atatürk's leadership were for the people.

Étatism. This principle is of Western origin. It means the participation of the state in economic affairs. Some philosophers claim étatism to have originated at the time of Plato's *Republic.* In political literature, it started to gain importance from the Renaissance onwards, as a reaction to the inequalities caused by the accumulation of wealth. Modern étatism started to develop in the nineteenth century, as a reaction against liberalism. The development of large industries, the organisation of the working class, uprisings in the colonies, particularly the failure of state power controlled by capitalists to find a solution to economic crisis, led to the concept of étatism being activated.

Étatism as established in Turkey differed from the Western understanding of that concept. The first difference lies in the phases of the Ottoman economy which, until *Tanzimat,* was closely attached to the agricultural economy. From *Tanzimat* to the First World War, it was in a phase of open market policy, surpassing liberal economics. Foreign products and capital took over. While the large states of the West exploited their colonies for the sake of the homeland, the homeland of the Turks, particularly Anatolia and Thrace, was exploited on behalf of foreign states. This lack of ability to understand economics forced the Sultan to live on loans. The result was that the lower class of the state was composed of Turks, and the upper class consisted of foreign investors and their partners — among the other minorities. The deadly result of the wars being waged from 1911 onwards, as well as the conservative and mystical propaganda directed at the Turkish people, have to be added to these factors which led to the collapse of the national economy. This propaganda was designed to make the Turks believe that poverty was a virtue, and it was to be rewarded by unimaginable benefits in the next world.

In short, Turkey had been abused for centuries. People were not equipped with the knowledge necessary to participate in a modern economy; they possessed no capital, and no precautions were taken to protect the economy. In the West, large states considered étatism as a means of developing their prosperous but unstable economies, but in Turkey the basis for a modern economy had not yet been formed. The economy had to be re-established, and it was nothing but a dream to expect the private sector to perform this; thus only the state could take on the task, basing itself on the principle of étatism.

The fundamentals of étatism, in the above context, were as follows. Étatism is a principle which has to be implemented to provide the stable continuation of relations between individuals and the state. 'To secure their survival, both state and individuals are entitled to display passions. The passions of individuals reflect private needs, while those of the state have a public motive. Individuals do not consider the public welfare at first hand.' How far can individuals transcend their personal concerns? It is a fact that economically the personal welfare of individuals is secured by competition. It is also natural that individuals do not undertake tasks from which they will not derive benefits. Under such conditions, it is essential for the state to enter the picture to provide economic stability, just as it does in political and cultural affairs.

The most important aspect of étatism is the separation of the areas of profits earned respectively by the state and by individuals. The liberal and democratic character of the Turkish republic might have been damaged had the state equipped the individual with only a narrow scope for his activity. Therefore, in 1931 étatism was promulgated, defining the areas of work as follows.

In general, the state was to take up specialised economic tasks, requiring local concentration or special time-scales; these would require continuous administration and would be in danger of becoming monopolies if left in private hands. Or the state might take up tasks answering a general demand. The control of mines, forests, canals, railroads, transportation firms, banks and utilities — these chores were to be performed by the state or by regional administrations.

The response given to the persisting private sector in trying to determine clearly where state economic activity began and ended was that although the state appeared to owe much of its character to having been founded by individuals, it could not settle the question of what precisely were the individual's rights and duties: hence the state was not in equilibrium with the private sector. The state could expand the area of its economic activity, when conditions in the nation so required.

The étatism accepted in Turkey, as explained above, is not restricted to the economy alone. It is at once 'social, ethical and national' at the same time. That workers should have justice and greater prosperity, through equitable distribution of income, was an essential factor for the safeguarding of national unity — a point which the state, as the representative of national unity, must keep in mind. In sum it is appropriate, in the conditions of our time, for the administrators of the Turkish republic to pursue a mild étatism without abandoning democratic principles. The étatism we regard as

suitable is not a system resembling communism or collectivism, both
of which completely prevent investment and economic enterprise by
individuals.

Secularism. This principle, like the others, is of Western origin. For
centuries, the term has been used in various senses, but it finally
acquired an ideological meaning in the nineteenth century, as the
differentiation of state and religion, following the state's initiative.
As to the freedom of the individual *vis-à-vis* the state, it became a
political term signifying freedom of conscience.

The principle of secularism as developed by the Turkish revolution is more extensive than its Western counterpart. Aside from the
liberation of legislative, executive and judiciary powers from religious influence, it expels entire traditions in the life of a nation tend-
ing to restrict social, individual or family activities in the name of
religion.

There are many clear historical examples of this. Although Islam
was introduced as a religion of the mind, excluding everything that
came between God and the believer. However, in the course of time,
the Ottoman empire turned into a religious state, and a pious institution, *ülema*, was allowed to enter between God and individuals.
Everything under the sun was made, by illogical assumptions, to be
dependent upon religion, and religion and state became inseparable.
Thus, the Ottoman state was separated from the eternal by a wall of
religion, and its society took on a mystical character. Thus the
Turkish revolution brought freedom of mind as well as separation of
religion from the state.

Secularisation in Turkey started with the Turkish war of independence. While a *fetva* religious opinion was required for all major acts
of state in the Ottoman empire, this was not the case in such events of
major importance as the definition of the new State's national
boundaries, the formation of the Turkish Grand National Assembly, and the abolition of the Caliphate. Atatürk, with courage as well
as his knowledge of modern political philosophy, attempted to teach
the meaning of secularisation, without using the word. He spoke as
follows to those who tried to make a fundamental link between parliament and religion: 'The government of the Turkish National
Assembly is national and it is materialistic : it worships reality. It is
not a government willing to commit murder or drag the nation into
the swamps in search of useless ideologies.'[21]

Atatürk placed freedom of conscience among the most natural
and crucial rights of the individual, requiring the utmost protection.
'Each person has liberty to think and believe freely, to possess a
political view of his own fulfilment, and to act in any way to suit

himself as far as the regulations of any religion are concerned.' After this statement, Atatürk also indicated that no individual's conscience could be guided by another.

Secularism in Turkey also covered social liberty. Atatürk believed that political freedom, freedom of conscience and all other freedoms are a mere dream unless the realisation of social freedom is the aim. It is a fact that all the torments Turkey has passed through were due to religious traditions standing in the way of social liberties. Namık Kemal wrote that these traditions were worse than death: 'Death passes over us in a minute, but traditions are eternal. They aim at the way one sits, walks, reads, cuts one's beard. . . . The traditions have reached such a point that a man cannot be in command of his own beard, let alone his family.' The development of social ethics and justice, in accordance with the development of social freedom, is another fact of Atatürk's revolution.

Revolutionism. This principle is the philosophy, guarantee and source of future hope of the five principles outlined above. It flourished first with the development of these principles. Revolutionism takes into consideration the undoubted fact that every revolution is followed by a counter-revolution, and so it is persistent in holding on to the targets reached by the revolution. In other words, it stands firmly against religion.

Atatürk's indication of the vitality of the principles is as follows: 'The source of prosperity and superiority for the nation today, just as it was yesterday and will be tomorrow, is the *reform of principles*.'[22] Thus, according to Atatürk's revolutionary concept, principles are not frozen. He defined the Turkish Revolution thus: 'It is a natural and eternal result of the revolutionary principles that life is considered to be based on the requirements of the world and on that alone.'[23]

He indicated that science leads the way towards crucial changes. 'The true enlightenment in life is science.' Here he wanted the word 'science' to cover not the feelings and mysticism but positive sciences, which are the same in all places and at all times. There is no doubt that when Atatürk recommended science as a remedy for the problems of life, he meant that it should be so in this world; positive sciences never become part of mysticism or dogma. Therefore, Atatürk's principles can continue forever to renew themselves and preserve their vitality. A new source of inspiration was obtained by the acceptance of positive sciences as a guide. Atatürk's explanation of both follows:

'We obtain inspirations not from the skies, but directly from life. What draws us along our path is the country we live in, the Turkish nation from which we originated, and the conclusions we have reached from the history of nations, filled as it is with disasters and sorrow.'

The main features of Kemalism

The existence of a relationship between the events which shape the revolution and the revolution itself is natural. Therefore the ideological phase of a revolution may be accepted as having a similar relationship to its principles. The humanism of the Renaissance and the reform movements of the eighteenth century may be regarded as the ideological phases of the French Revolution. It is a fact that no authors of the eighteenth century put forward a revolutionary theory. The so-called ideological movements could not go beyond being the preparatory phase of breaking the limitations of a conservative regime. The French Revolution started as a passage from speculation to action, within this environment.

The Ottoman empire only followed these actions which formed modern Europe after much difficulty and delay despite the fact that it was in a sense a European empire, possessing a vast extent of territory in Europe. It was also not a totally oriental empire, in that its political, diplomatic and economic relations were to an extent European. But inspite of these factors, its society was closed to Europe and to the European concept of civilisation. This was most striking in intellectual life. Teaching of the existing religions of Europe, contact with Europeans, and learning about European ways of life were all forbidden, for Turks, being considered sinful. The result was the ignorance of Turks regarding these aspects of life, and the general backwardness of the empire.

The backwardness started to be realised in the second half of the eighteenth century. This was the start of the extensive preparatory phase of the Turkish revolution, with attempts being made at an opening towards European civilisation. Gradually, these attempts succeeded: very modestly, some implementations of the European military system, art and sciences were realised, and in the nineteenth century were fully adopted. European legal institutions and education system were taken up at the same time. Early in the second half of the nineteenth century, uprisings against the authority of the Sultan started as a result of the influence of Western philosophy reaching Turkey. There had in fact been uprisings among the Christian subjects of the empire at the beginning of the century; some Christian provinces began to separate from the empire, announcing their independence or autonomy. The Young Ottomans were full of inspiration and hope that they would prevent the collapse of the empire by forming an 'Ottoman nation', based on the human rights principles of the West. These attempts were not in vain. Abdülhamid II (1876–1909) accepted the formation of an Ottoman parliament in the first years of his reign. However, this system lasted only two years, giving way to absolutism.

Nationalism, liberalism, socialism, marxism, imperialism and the anarchist movements of the nineteenth century left no appreciable mark upon the Ottoman intellectuals; just as fascism and 'national socialism' did not when they appeared in the 1920s and '30s. The reason for this was that even among the enlightened men of the Ottoman empire there were not yet many intellectuals. During the absolutism of Abdülhamid II, even the mention of these concepts in dictionaries was forbidden. On the other hand, none of these ideologies could have been implemented in an entity like the Ottoman empire, which still bore traces of its medieval character. The only concept of importance for Ottoman intellectuals up till the second constitutional era was freedom. Abdülhamid, forbidding this also, caused young men who sought liberation to make for Europe; otherwise, he would send them into exile. A very small number of the young, who had knowledge of foreign languages, remained in Istanbul, formed secret organisations and tried to develop European ideas.

During the period when industry was developing in Europe, resulting in the rise of capitalism and imperialism, the only problem for the Turks was to keep the empire from collapsing. To this end, the chief requirement was the reinforcement of economy, but although the intellectuals realised this fact, there was nothing they could do other than complain. An Istanbul newspaper of Abdülhamid II's reign wrote: 'Those who know about Europe are not strangers to the fact that the wealth of a small village in Europe is greater than that of a large Ottoman city. What is the reason for this? It is that [Europeans] work day and night? We only seem to want to turn our day into night and sleep all through. We are lazy. We seem to approve of "*armut piş, ağzima düş*" [a Turkish proverb meaning that we expect everything to be ready and prepared for us]'.[24]

Ahmet Mithat Efendi, after reviewing the situation of the country, made the following proposal: 'Peter the Great and his followers taught the Russians economics by whipping, not with the pen. I think and think, but can find no other solutions for us than this. We require a similar way of education also. We can only be turned into artists, farmers and tradesmen by whipping'.[25] The owner of the periodical *Serveti Fünun*, Ahmet Ihsan, who was later assigned to the Commercial High School as a professor, wrote in his memoirs: 'We have no books on economic geography. Practically nothing has been taught on the economic life of the country in schools up to date.

No one even knew about the existence of economics before. . . .'[26]

Turkish intellectuals, unfamiliar with even the most simple concepts of economics, believed that the welfare of the empire could be achieved through politics, and pursued their work in that area. Even so, they came across three alternative paths: Ottomanism, Pan-Islamism and Pan-Turkism. The first was inclined to gather together all the Turks of the world regardless of race, religion or sect, into a nation with a parliamentary system. This ideology weakened following the unhappy results of the Russo-Turkish war and the closing of the parliament. The conservative intellectuals, supported by Abdülhamid, then started the Pan-Islamist movement, which was of a more political than ideological character. Its inclination was to use the moral effect of the Sultan-Caliph on the Muslims of the world, and form a Muslim unity under the Caliph's leadership. This proved to be no more than a dream during a time when non-Turkish Muslim provinces were opposing the Caliph, and furthermore lived under the sovereignty of great powers. Some intellectuals, realising this, started the Pan-Turk movement, again during Abdülhamid's reign. However, this current did not enter an ideologic phase. It remained only in the realm of scientific research into the ethnic origin and language of the Turks. It became a Turkish union through the efforts of Yusuf Akçura towards the end of Abdülhamid's absolutism. Finally by the end of the Balkan wars, during the second constitutional era, it had become an extensive ideology.

Intellectuals such as Mehmet Fuad Köprülü, Ömer Seyfeddin, Ahmet Ağaoğlu , Hüseyin Zade Ali and Halide Edip (Adıvar) began working towards the systemising of Pan-Turkism during the First World War. For Köprülü and Seyfeddin, this was a national concept. Ahmet Ağaoğlu believed Pan-Turkism to be mutuality in race, language, religion and traditions. For Hüseyin Zade Ali, the chief factors were religion and language; race followed. Ziya Gökalp and Yusuf Akçura, meanwhile, expanded Turkism as far as Pan-Turanism. This was not a clear movement. The Union and Progress Party, of which Gökalp was a member, regarded the Turks in Russia as being within the limits of Pan-Turanism. Gökalp himself regarded it as a mutual cultural unity covering all Turks; he, at that time, was the country's only sociologist. He believed in saving the Ottoman empire from collapse by calling in aid the pre-Islamic Turkish civilisation and the ideas of Emile Durkheim. After extensive research, he based this liberation on the formulae of 'Turkisation, Islamisation and Westernisation'.

Turkisation freed Turks from mixed cultures and traditions. Thus, the word '*hars*' was utilised to define 'culture', a concept for which there is no term in Turkish. 'Islamisation' meant a religious reform, and Gökalp further believed that, just as in the Protestant religion, that of the Muslims had to be nationalised as far as language was concerned. The Koran was to be translated into Turkish, in which Ezan and prayers would be recited. The most interesting reform regulation of Gökalp was 'westernisation'. He completely separated culture from civilisation and regarded the latter as a materialistic concept. He believed that, whatever happened, Turks were to be westernised, or in other words, were to fit into Western culture. With this fundamental reform, a new concept was to take shape for Turks, enabling every one of them to pronounce 'I am of Turkish race, Islamic religion and western civilisation.'

Besides this, political writing started a new, 'national' development in literature. Namık Kemal introduced the concepts of homeland and liberty, following an attempt of the founder of the first journal of this character, Şinasi. Abdulhak Hamit, Sami Paşazade Sezai and Halit Ziya started a new phase in the national literature by writing novels and poetry in a Western spirit. Among this generation, Tevfik Fikret was fore-eminent in criticising old literary conventions, which reflected men as in practice hostile to nature, humanity and society. He added humanity to the concept of homeland, by expressing the complaints of society, and expounding the causes of backwardness in a new language. He worked towards familiarising a new generation with such fresh concepts as 'rights', 'civilisation', 'women's liberation' and 'the secular mind'. These may be regarded as a two-century preparatory phase leading towards Kemalist principles.

Atatürk's principles are of Western origin, having been produced at various dates in the West's great revolutions. However, in the West they have not appeared all together. In some of the revolutions, their implementation needed time. The principles which formed the Turkish revolution were actually given birth during that revolution. On the whole, they affected social life and the institutions of the state, and no doubt their uniqueness lies in their translation into action.

Atatürk's principles also differed from Western ones simply as concepts. As is well known, the great revolutions of the West have been fundamentally humanist, and were based on international declarations (yet not one was implemented in the context of a broad understanding of internationalism). Freedom and equality in the United States remained the prerogative of white men for a long time. France was a significant example of imperialism, with the conquest of Egypt by Napoleon Bonaparte, a son of the French Revolution; and she was soon imitated by other European states. As for Russia, by appealing to the working class to unite and stand up against economic powers, she soon fell away from the principle of peace.

The Turkish revolution did not start with an international declaration. The *Misak-ı Milli* (National Pact) containing the aims of the war of independence is strictly a national declaration, and its spirit is the protection of national rights. The remaining phases of the war of independence introduced humanitarian and peaceful elements; pursuant to the principles of Kemalism, this was a far cry from national selfishness. Therefore, although these principles do in a sense become an international concept, there is no reason why they should not be considered unique.

Another unique feature of Kemalist principles lies in the Turkish republic founded and developed by the Turkish revolution: each of the five principles indicates an area of that revolution. The sixth, 'revolutionism', explains the new understanding of Turkey. The accumulated effect of the principles combined together is to supply a social value to the whole.

The triad 'republicanism, nationalism and secularism' symbolises the rejection by the Turkish revolution of the Ottoman dynasty, the Caliphate and *ümmet* ideology. On the other hand, its style is the same as the classical democracy of the Western world. The triad 'republicanism, populism, and étatism' presents the social ideal of the Turkish state. 'Republicanism and revolutionism', particularly 'revolutionism', frees Kemalist principles from becoming static. If the determination of Atatürk to preserve science as the only guide in life is considered in conjunction with the principle of revolutionism, the dynamic force and influence of Atatürk's principles become more apparent.

The fact that Western authors referred to these principles as 'Kemalism', thus conferring on them the sense of an ideology, is worth mentioning at this point. Many Turkish intellectuals translated 'Kemalism' into Turkish as *Atatürkçülük*; however, most of them did not want to accept it as a political doctrine. During the development phase of Kemalism, Fascism and Hitlerism were taking their place alongside the ideologies of liberal democracy and Communism. Kemalist principles, not resembling any of these ideologies, were naturally given a distinctive name by Westerners.

The Kemalist principles discussed above retain their vitality as a concept, in action and in their influence. The institutions which they embrace in Turkey still preserve their strength, in spite of attacks upon them. Outside Turkey, they are topics for research, and furthermore are a touchstone to some other states which are seeking to discover their own styles of society and life. The principles and influence of fascism, greatly in evidence at the time when Kemalist principles first appeared, have practically disappeared today. Furthermore, it could be claimed that the extreme right and left systems of government of that time have shown signs of inclining towards Atatürk's principles. The causes of this continuing vitality may be summed up under three main headings, in relation to modern Turkish history: 'homeland' ideology, western civilisation and Turkey's international relations of Turkey.

Homeland ideology. The meaning of Atatürk's principles as a whole is most of all clear in the homeland ideology. This consists of enlivening the Turkish nation and making it happy — in sum, loving the nation. Until this ideology took shape, Turks followed various ideologies. Within the limits of general Turkish history of pre-Islam, Turks lived by a concept of world sovereignty, suitable to the conditions of that time. After their conversion to Islam, they began to implement the policy of expanding religious boundaries and achieving an extensive international empire. In the last phase of the Ottoman empire, — as we have seen — they went through an undecided phase of three ideologies: Pan-Ottomanism, Pan-Islamism and Pan-Turkism. But in none of these ideologies was any national concept of a modern homeland visible. This did great damage to the Turks. Many Turks were slain in the name of ideologies and ideals considered sacred, and many homelands were destroyed.

After the collapse of the Ottoman empire, when the boundaries of the new Turkish nation were being formed, a new ideology started to appear — that of homeland. Its spirit first appeared in a feeling of pity towards the Turkish homeland: Atatürk made this feeling clear to the nation. He in fact was the first to use the term 'homeland' in this context. It was in the first days of the independence war that Atatürk sought to turn the attention of Turkish intellectuals to the concept of homeland ideology. His response to the enlightened men who came to Ankara following the conquest of Istanbul by foreign powers, and who claimed that Ankara presented the appearance of a desert, was:

'It appears so, and we are pleased that it is so. A life has to be created from these ruins. What seems so vacant is actually full. There is a strong life in this area which is assumed to be a desert, and that is the nation, the Turkish nation.'[27] Atatürk accused the old mystical and selfish administrators who had caused the country to appear like a desert: 'The exponents of [the old] philosophy have done nothing more than cause our beloved country to appear like a dungeon. This land is worthy to become a paradise for our children and generations to follow. An economic regime to enable us to live our national life like human beings is the chief requirement.'

The old ideology had to be destroyed and the new closely examined in order to attain this end. The traces of Pan-Islamism and Pan-Turanism which still caused eyes to be turned towards lands far from the homeland had not yet completely disappeared. Atatürk stated that the political policy of the Turkish Grand National Assembly was to provide for the security and welfare of the Turkish nation:

'We are not imposters who run after great dreams and appear to perform things they cannot realise. We have already attracted many enemies due to this pretence. We did not pursue Pan-Islamism. Perhaps we said "We are practising it, we shall practise it", and the enemy said "Let us kill them before they start". The same with Pan-Turkism. And this is the entire problem. We have to know where we stand.'[28]

In many of Atatürk's subsequent speeches, the poverty and disastrous conditions of the country were taken up. He spoke of the necessity to cheer the nation. Undoubtedly, his speech on the tenth anniversary of the proclamation of the Republic was the one with the most feeling in it: 'We will make our country one of the world's most prosperous and civilised nations. We will enable our nation to enjoy the greatest resources, and bring our culture above the highest level now existing.'[29]

Western Civilisation. This phrase, as used by Atatürk, shows the precise relationship of the national ideology to civilisation. The concept he often referred to as Western civilisation was not meaningful in near-Turkish history. For a long time it was assumed to have a religious meaning, and it was therefore accepted that it could not combine with eastern civilisation, which itself had a religious character. Nevertheless, the 'civilised' Westerner, possessing his own thoughts concerning his own life and being, had not always existed. Although defined geographically, he did not emerge at a particular time in a particular country. He was formed by elements contributed by different civilisations at different times. The chief factor in this idea of civilisation was its fundamental logic.

When the Ottoman empire started to decline quickly after the eighteenth century, some Ottoman statesmen found westernisation essential. The Ottoman empire was not a completely oriental state, like China, Japan or India; its territories and its people spanned both Asia and Europe. There was, more or less, an exchange of culture between the subjects living in the West and the ethnic Turks. Also, the frequent economic and diplomatic relations should not be over looked. But despite these materialistic relations, the Ottoman state was a stranger to the civilising discoveries and movements of the West — and this was due to religion. Even the learning of Western languages was forbidden to Muslims. Until the end of the eighteenth century, there were no embassies in Western countries. The Ottomans deliberately refrained from purchasing some of the new tools and instruments manufactured in the west, claiming that they were the discoveries of infidels. Yet under the continuous 'assault' of Western nations, the Ottoman empire had no choice, if it wished to survive, but to adopt westernisation. However Islam was a form of state, a social set-up in the largest sense. Therefore, only the material aspects of Western civilisation were adopted.

Because in the nineteeth century some reform movements and ideological arguments took place, in the first two decades of the twentieth century, the influences of Western civilisation spread at least among the intellectuals. But this time, a *hars* (culture) conception spread simultaneously. Those favouring religious civilisation took advantage of this and tried to construct certain religious institutions and regulations as if they possessed a national character. But no points of mutual contact were established until the independence war.

Atatürk's view of civilisation, became one of the fundamental causes of the independence war, because the Allies did not hesitate to use civilisation themselves as a propaganda instrument to divide Turkey. They claimed that the Turks in history had never been the creators of any masterpieces of civilisation. Furthermore, they claimed that the Turks had always been strangers to Western civilisation and had even attempted to destroy it. This propaganda resulted in the claim that Turks did not deserve to survive as an independent nation.

When the Independence War resulted in a Turkish victory, the arguments over oriental and Western civilisation started again. There were three visible claims. The first was that civilisation was formed of two elements, one spiritual and the other materialistic. Because of this, we could not take up Western civilisation as a whole without our national personality disappearing. We had to be satisfied with taking up only the material institutions, instruments and manners of Western civilisation. The second was that by adopting the appropriate aspects of Western civilisation, a mixed and special civilisation would be created. The third encouraged the complete adoption of Western civilisation. The advocates of the third claim urged that Westernisation means freedom from the medieval concepts of life, and from all sorts of intellectual and ideological slavery. There were some who suggested adopting Western civilisation after eliminating some elements. But these people could not comprehend the total meaning of civilisation. A civilisation is inseparable; its superiority is in its unity, not in its sections. Western civilisation did not achieve its superiority by means of science alone, but as a whole with all its concepts.

From the beginning of the Independence War, Atatürk was the leader of those who advanced the third claim. Each and every phase of the Turkish revolution was in connection with civilisation. Let us look at some sayings of Atatürk: 'Our largest claim is to continue our nation as the most civilised and prosperous of nations. This is the dynamic ideal of the Turkish nation, which has performed a true revolution not only in its institutions, but also in its thought.' Thus when Atatürk spoke of civilisation, he clearly did not mean only moral or only material advancement. Also, he did not separate culture from civilisation: 'When we say culture, we understand all that a society can perform in the political life, in thought and in its economy as well. This is nothing more than civilisation.' Civilisation, according to Atatürk, was the total achievement of mankind as a result of his efforts in those areas of activity: political, economic and intellectual. A civilised man was one who acted logically; his mind was full of honesty and virtue. This apprehension is clear in his saying 'The truest enlightment in life is science.' Some have classified this phrase as meaningless; but Atatürk merely tried to show that the truest factor, particularly among those claiming religion and art to be the enlightening factor, was science. For he believed that science was the only true knowledge, free and international.

From his understanding of Turkish history, Atatürk believed that Turks possessed qualities of civilisation. Their ancestors had founded high civilisations at various times and in various places. But to be proud of those civilisations was not enough. Each generation of Turks had to develop the qualities of civilisation to make them creative and prove them worthy of their ancestors. Atatürk believed that what they had to do was to be attached to the Western civilisation from which Turks had stood apart for so long. Turks continued to make contributions to this civilisation; they had a share in it; and therefore, each one of the Kemalist principles reflected a concept of modern civilisation.

The relationship between the principles and international contacts. None of the principles seems to be directly concerned with international relations. Still, the independence war and the Turkish revolution was very closely related to this area.

The first significant point in the foreign policy of the Ottoman empire was no different from that observed in all other empires, namely the policy of continuous expansion of the imperial lands. This took the Ottoman empire, in the west, as far as Vienna. The decline which immediately followed that climax lasted until the First

World War. Besides the loss of the non-Turkish territories of the empire by the end of the war, the Turkish homeland was also partly occupied by the enemy. This spelt a disastrous *spiritual* loss, leaving aside the loss of land. In the eyes of the world, Turks were without honour, value or rights. In such circumstances, over-sensitivity and dreams had to be abandoned, and a new Turkish state, founded on science, logic and reality, had to be established. This was closely connected to the international principles of the new Turkey. These could be gathered around three points: (*a*) the priority of rights over power, (*b*) national rights and politics, and (*c*) the need to join with all civilised nations in pursuit of world peace and friendship.

(*a*) By the end of the First World War, Turkey had abandoned the tradition of being an empire. However, the victorious powers had not done so; on the contrary, they were attempting to expand their territories, and forgetting about the principles of great revolutions, 'respecting the rights of nations'. Trusting in their power, they believed that they could shape the world to their own liking. Turkey, by opposing the plans to dismember her, took over the principle of protecting her national rights. Atatürk showed the essential Turkish national attitude on this matter as follows: 'There has to be justice in the world, and it should be superior to force. It is to the extent that the conditions of the nation are well understood and inspire confidence that every sacrifice can be made for its protection.'

This link which Atatürk forged between justice and force was one of the fundamentals of the Turkish Independence War, and was a principal factor leading to the introduction of nations' rights in the world and their right to exist.

(*b*) What was the policy of the Turkish state, basing itself on national rights? Atatürk's response to this removed all doubt: 'To be sovereign in our land, by our own power, and to work for the welfare of our nation. . . . To expect the friendship of the civilised world and not run after unrealisable dreams. . . .' The few ideas expressed here originated from the experience of the previous centuries, which had seen the collapse of the empire. The modern frontiers of the Ottoman empire were, in a national sense, irrelevant. The state had tried to survive by granting concessions to some of the great powers and so acquiring friendships rather than ensuring its survival. The welfare of the nation was sacrificed for dreams that could not be fulfilled. No stable alliances could be achieved in such circumstances. The concept Atatürk accepted for international relations, therefore, was far from ideologies and sentimentalities damaging to the nation. On the contrary, it was highly realistic.

(*c*) *Alliances with civilised nations.* Atatürk directed the international relations of Turkey towards forming relations based on honesty and sincerity, regulated by political realities, and parallel to the acceptance of Turkish national rights by the nations of the world. His starting point to achieve this aim was: 'Turks are friends of all civilised nations.' — 'Our rules are the same for Asia and Europe — to have friends.' — 'I deeply appreciate the feeling of alliances with nations which are beneficial to our nation.'

Atatürk's thoughts on international relations were humanitarian. As is well known, the concept of humanitarianism was formulated by religious institutions abroad as well as in Turkey, a state considered as representating the orient. It was further exploited by diplomats and politicians. Turks and Christián Europeans had long regarded each other as infidels, which resulted in the limitation of humanitarianism to religious feeling and theology. The separation of religion and the state, and the organisation of the state away from religion, was unable to remove these limitations, and was only able to loosen them somewhat. In Ottoman Turkey the state and religion had been one, and thus religion did not possess any basic institutions.

This resulted in religion being a stronger weapon, and making it impossible for a national ideal to form. Atatürk not only believed in humanitarianism, but he struggled to spread it. He accepted a close relationship between national and international welfare, which he expressed as follows: 'Today, all nations of the world are practically relatives . . . and so, while one thinks of the welfare of one's own nation, one also has to consider that of other nations as well. We must work as hard as we can to achieve this.'[30]

Atatürk said this in 1937, on the verge of the Second World War. Western nations were engaged in a deep struggle. The fascist regimes were preparing for war against states with liberal systems. Atatürk knew the nature of war better than many contemporary leaders; he was a soldier and had spent much of his life at war. Still, he courageously proclaimed that wars waged according to capitalist and imperialist concepts were not to the benefit of humanity. 'To make people kill each other by means of inspiration promising happiness is an absurd and inhuman method. The only way to make people happy is to bring them closer together, make them like each other, and provide energy in subjective and religious matters to give them dynamism. The true happiness of humanity can only be achieved by multiplication of this system.'[31]

It is clear from these last words that Atatürk saw the achievement of world happiness in the achievement — and protection — of world peace. Atatürk's calls were to the whole of humanity: 'If lasting peace is sought, international precautions have to be taken to provide for the welfare of nations. All the human beings in the world have to be educated in such a way that they will abandon hatred.'

NOTES

1. Tarih IV, *Türkiye Cumhuriyeti*, Maarif Vekaleti, Istanbul, 1931, 187.
2. Reşat Kaynar, 'Atatürk Ideolojisi Nedir?', *Milliyet*, 10 Nov. 1974.
3. Falih Rıfkı Atay, *Çankaya*, Istanbul, 1969, 393.
4. Yakub Kadri Karaosmanoğlu, 'Atatürk'ün Ilkeleri Yok, Ilkesi Vardır', *Ulus*, 1 July 1971.
5. Rom Landau, article in *The Spectator*, 27 Aug. 1957.
6. Muzaffer Gökmen, *Milli Eğitim Bakanlığı Atatürk ve Devrimleri Bibliografyası*, Istanbul, 1963.
7. Istanbul Iktisadi Ticari İlimler Akademisinin Cumhuriyete 50. Yil Armağani, *Atatürkçülüğün Ekonomik ve Sosyal Yönü, Istanbul*, 11–12 Oct. 1973.
8. Afet Inan, *Türk Tarih Kurumu Atatürk Konferansları*, III, Ankara, 1970, 24.
9. Ismet Bozdoğan, article in *Milliyet*, 13 Nov. 1974.
10. Enver Ziya Karal, *Atatürk'ten Düşünceler*, Ankara, 1956, 165.
11. *Atatürk'ün Söylev ve Demeçleri*, Ankara, 1952, II, 277.
12. Karal, *op. cit.*, 133.
13. Iş Bankası, *Atatürk'ün Askerliğe Dair Eserleri*, Ankara, 1959, 14.
14. Uluğ Iğdemir, *Atatürk'ün Yaşamı*, Ankara, 1980, 32.
15. Afet Inan, *Medeni Bilgiler ve M. Kemal Atatürk'ün El Yazıları*, Ankara, 1969, 362.
16. Karal, *op. cit.*, 41.
17. *Atatürk'ün Söylev ve Demeçleri*, II, 122.
18. Inan, *op. cit.*, 351.
19. Karal, *op. cit.*, II, 124.
20. *Atatürk'ün Söylev ve Demeçleri*, II, 278.
21. *ibid.*, 57.
22. Tarih IV, *Türkiye Cumhuriyeti*, Maarif Vekaleti, 180.
23. *Atatürk'ün Söylev ve Demeçleri*, II, 240.
24. *Basiret*, 5.
25. *Türk Ziraat Tarihine Bakışlar*, 239.
26. Ahmet Ihsan, *Matbuat Hatıralarım*, Istanbul 1931, 87–8.
27. Yunus Nadi Abalioğlu, *Ankara'nın Ilk Günleri*, Istanbul, 1955, 97.
28. *Atatürk'ün Söylev ve Demeçleri*, I, 195–6.
29. *ibid.*, II, 271–2.
30. *ibid*, II, 278.
31. *ibid*, II, 269.

The Ottoman-Turkish state and Kemalism

ALI KAZANCIGIL

Introduction

A widespread view of Kemalism holds that it constitutes a radical break from the past, which transformed Turkey from a theocratic empire into a modern nation-state in which the secular-nationalist doctrine replaced Islam as the cultural foundation and overall ideology of the country's polity. Another opinion, also based on the opposition between nationalism-secularism and Islam, is that the Kemalist modernisation consisted mainly of importing from the West a number of alien values and institutions into an Islamic society with its own sophisticated cultural traditions. The situation in Iran following the overthrow of the Shah, rightly interpreted as a social revolution totally rejecting the Western civilisational model, is seen as marking the 'end of Kemalism'.[1]

To a considerable extent, the Kemalist republic was indeed radically different from the Ottoman empire, even after the latter had gone through the *Tanzimat* reforms (1839–76) and the Young Turk nationalism (1908–18). It is also true that Kemalism, which has been nurtured by concepts and doctrines such as progress, laicism, nationalism, Comteian positivism and solidarism *à la* Léon Bourgeois, owes a lot to the Englightenment, the French Revolution and nineteenth-century scientism.

In fact, Mustafa Kemal and his associates did not 'import' such ideas directly from the West, but in many instances inherited them from the intellectual wealth accumulated by several generations of Ottoman-Turkish reformers and nationalists. Kemalism built on those reform movements which started at the beginning of the nineteenth century and led them to their ultimate consequence: the creation of a modern Turkish state. The Kemalist movement had its roots deep in the past, in a process that lasted for centuries and resulted from a number of external and domestic stimuli. In this sense, the claim that Kemalism was a purely 'imported' model does not correspond to historical evidence. The emergence of the modern Turkish state and Kemalism cannot be properly analysed and explained without duly taking into account these elements of continuity.

There is a close relationship between Kemalism and the characteristics of the Ottoman-Turkish state, which can be formulated as follows: at the origins of the Turkish reform movement there was the reaction of the state élites to the crisis of the Ottoman social forma-tion. The nature of this reaction was to a great extent determined by the patrimonial patterns that survived within the late Ottoman state. As the process of incorporation of the Ottoman world-empire into the capitalist world-economy developed, and the autonomous for-mation became a peripheral one, the state élites were convinced that the only way to save the empire was to adopt 'Western ways'. As early as 1830, nine years before the proclamation of the first *Tanzimat* reform, the *Hatt-ı-Hümayun* of Gülhane, the Grand Admiral of the Empire, Halil Paşa declared: 'I am back from a visit to Russia. On my return, I became more than ever convinced that, if we are further delayed from imitating Europe, we shall be left with no alternative to the obligation of going back to Asia.'[2] This view was re-stated time and again throughout the nineteenth century.

In its ultimate stage, this consciousness was to produce the Kema-list movement which saw that unless a modern state based on the principles of citizenship, nationalism and secularism were created, it would be impossible to preserve the independence of Turkey, which would fall into the status of a colonised territory. Indeed, under the conditions prevailing in the capitalist world-economy and the inter-state system of the late nineteenth century and the first quarter of the twentieth, the alternative for Turkey was between the creation of a modern state and the loss of political independence. In an empire where the patrimonial characteristics were still strong, the élites perceived that the way to achieve this was not a social revolution but a revolution from above.

Kemalism should therefore be considered as the last and most suc-cessful response of a portion of Ottoman-Turkish élites to the age-old question: how can this state be saved? This question consistently preoccupied the Ottomans, from the *Risale* (treatise), which Mustafa Koçu Bey, a high palace official, presented to Sultan Murat IV in 1631, to the Young Turks.[3] The distinction of Kemalism is to have been able to formulate the appropriate answers and follow the right policies to achieve the goal of renovating the state and thus securing its continued independence.

Endogenous and exogenous determinations of the state

In the current literature on the state, which considerably increased after a period of relative neglect in the 1950s and 1960s,[4] two major paradigms emerge. They cut across various broad theoretical schools such as the Marxian, Weberian or structural-functionalist.

One of these paradigms puts the emphasis on the endogenous

determinations of the state. Analytically, it considers the state as an independent variable, in its relations with social classes, ideologies and the world-system.[5] In other words, the state is given as a primordial structure. The second paradigm maintains that the state is by no means a primordial structure but, in Immanuel Wallerstein's terms, a part of the 'institutional vortex' of the modern world-system, along with other institutions such as classes, ethnic/national groups and households.[6]

Besides the domestic *versus* external determinations debate, a related issue in the analysis of the state is the primacy of economic *versus* political factors. The Wallersteinian paradigm assumes the economic to be the independent variable, relegating the political to the status of the intervening variable.[7] It maintains that relatively amorphous entities have been transformed into modern states operating as part of the interstate system, within the framework and as products of the capitalist world-economy.

In one respect, however, Wallerstein is not far from those who consider the political parameters as the independent variable; he maintains that 'the state is the most convenient institutional intermediary in the establishment of market constraints (quasi-monopolies in the broadest sense of the term) in favour of particular groups.'[8] This stance, which illustrates the Marxian-Weberian character of Wallerstein's work,[9] comes close to the argument that the determinative factors in the emergence of the modern state are the processes that are political and ideological, link cultural codes, institutionalisation and social change, or are situated at the interface of the domestic and external spheres of society.

According to those who hold the latter view, i.e. the state as the independent, and economic factors as the intervening variable, the approach which overemphasises the exogenous determinations suffers from a basic weakness: it does not account for the *differentia specifica* of the states, whether at the core or at the periphery. Thus the distinctive relations between the states and the social classes, and ideologies, remain uncovered.[10]

In any case, an approach which puts too exclusive an emphasis on either the exogenous or endogenous, or the economic or political stimuli, to the exclusion of the others would not be satisfactory in elucidating the role of Kemalism and the emergence of a modern state in Turkey.

A more balanced approach is found both in Marx and Weber, to refer to these two classics. Marx generally agreed that the state structures were the instrument of the ruling class, but allowed for a relative autonomy and domination over the civil society of the state in certain historical instances.[11] And Weber, who is better known for his emphasis on world religions and the psychological impetus of the Protestant ethic for rationality and modernity, has in fact developed an institutional theory of capitalism. This involves a causal chain, starting with such 'material' components of capitalism as technology, labour force, markets etc., and in which the modern state is one of the crucial determinants of the market economy or capitalism, but still an intermediate one, the other intermediate factor being a particular economic ethic.[12]

Whether the state or the capitalist world-economy is the primordial structure remains an open debate, which possibly has to be settled concretely for each case. In the case of Turkey, the correlation between the state and, on the one hand, social classes and ideology and, on the other, the capitalist world-economy and the interstate system should be taken into account. The modern Turkish state emerged as a result of a long and gradual process. The transformation of a world-empire into a modern state was closely tied to the transformation of its autonomous economic system into a dependent formation, situated at the periphery of the European capitalist world-economy.[13] But the transformation of the state was not only a function of the impact of the European world-economy upon the Ottoman world-empire. It was also the consequence of the fundamental traits of the Ottoman polity. The *differentia specifica* of the modern Turkish state which later emerged were determined not only by the incorporation of the Ottoman formation into the European world-economy, but also by the particulars of the Ottoman history, social classes and ideologies.

A distinction is, however, to be made concerning the historical evolution of the modern state at the core and the periphery of the capitalist world-economy. In the *General Economic History*, his last work, Weber argued that the modern state, with a formal law and the principle of citizenship, was uniquely favourable to large-scale, organised capitalism. It was the bureaucratic-legal state that broke down feudalism, freed land and labour for the capitalist markets, pacified large territories, suppressed internal barriers to commercial exchanges, standardised taxation and currencies and provided the basis for a reliable system of banking, investment, property and contracts.[14]

This correlation between the state and the market economy developed, in the West, as an autonomous process, but the situation outside the core countries was entirely different. Previously autonomous formations were incorporated into the periphery of the capitalist world economy, their political structures were destabilised, paralysed and partially destroyed in the process. Not only did the modern state arise in Turkey after the social formation became peripheral, unlike in the West where the modern state and the capitalist world-economy emerged simultaneously, but the factors which shaped the Ottoman world-empire before its incorporation into the European world-economy were also very different from the factors which contributed to the emergence of the state in the West.[15]

This double determination, of timing (peripheralisation preceeding the emergence of the modern state) and of the local specificities — is crucial in the analysis of the Turkish state.

The impact of incorporation

The incorporation of the Ottoman world-empire into the capitalist world-economy lasted for several centuries. Islamoğlu and Keyder consider that after a transitional phase which covers the end of the sixteenth and the whole of the seventeenth century, the incorporation took place through a differential process, the economically more advanced regions being articulated first: the Balkans at the beginning of the eighteenth century, Egypt and the Levant in the first quarter of the nineteenth century, and finally the least developed region, Anatolia, after 1830.[16] Wallerstein and Kasaba date the actual incorporation between 1750 and 1839.[17]

The length and gradual character of this process can be explained by two factors. One was the fabulous dimensions of the Ottoman economic space, as well as its internal coherence, which were the basis of its autonomy. The second was the strength and the nature of the Ottoman state. As long as the state was able to maintain its orderly functioning, the pace of incorporation could be limited. At the same time, however, the very nature of the state did not allow the autonomous Ottoman formation either to defend itself against, or adapt to the incorporation into, the capitalist world-economy. The Ottoman system, involving the domination of the political structures over the market, and a redistributive mode of production, could not resist the expanding capitalism.

The incorporation thus entailed 'the relative diminution of the control of the Ottoman state-machinery over the productive process, circulation of commodities and capital and means of violence, and the effective harnessing of the Ottoman state to the constraints of the interstate system'.[18] The developments which took place in these various spheres have been described by the historians of the Ottoman empire, although serious disagreements exist as to their causes and periodisation: they are the dissolution of the *tımar* system, its replacement by *iltizam* (tax-farming) as the political mode of appropriation of the economic surplus by the ruling strata, and the gradual degeneration of the patrimonial slave bureaucracy (*kapıkulu*, including the *yeniçeri*). These, together with other factors such as the population explosion in the empire, a strong price inflation, and shortages in basic commodities, in the second half of the sixteenth century, led to a series of major and protracted social upheavals known as the *Celâli* revolts (1590–1610) which totally disrupted the Anatolian cities and countryside. The urban mercantile and manufacturing activities declined through the disorganisation of state-controlled guilds and *hisbe* regulations.

The breakdown of the *tımar* system and the *kapıkulu* bureaucracy resulted in the drastic limitation of Ottoman state's capacity to secure law and order, as well as to maintain its highly efficient methods of administration. Also, a major difficulty, which was to persist until the very end of the empire, now appeared: the financial crisis of the state, aggravated by the halting of territorial expansion at the end of the sixteenth century. The search for adequate financial resources was to be the principal concern of the Ottoman bureaucracy between the seventeenth and twentieth centuries.

The *mültezim* (holders of *iltizam*, or tax farmers) gradually came to control the principal sources of revenue. The *çiftlik* (large commercial farms, which were private holdings or *vakıf* lands) started to develop, and the *mâlikâne* (life-long tax-farms) spread at the expense of *miri* (state-owned) lands, which corresponded in 1528 to 87 per cent of all the Ottoman lands.[19] From our point of view, the most important aspect of the *iltizam* is that it allowed the concentration of land into private ownership, and the restructuring of agricultural production in relation to world markets.[20] The developments of *çiftlik* corresponds to the commercialisation of Ottoman agriculture, e.g. the beginning of the process of the incorporation into the capitalist world-economy, through a link between the *çiftlik* owner and the European economy *via* the merchant class (Europeans, and later the minorities in the empire enjoying extraterritorial privileges).

These developments were to be characteristic of the Ottoman transition from an autonomous world-empire into a peripheral entity, during the seventeenth and eighteenth centuries: the politically-determined division of labour of this redistributive empire *versus* the commercialisation of agriculture, involving major shifts in the relations of production and the existence of merchant capital, flourishing due to the special privileges enjoyed by the European merchants. This was the 'contradiction between the existence of commodity production and the political rationality of the Ottoman social formation',[21] which the Ottoman state was never able to overcome.

The closely correlated processes whereby the Ottoman state started gradually to loosen its grip over the productive, distributive and administrative mechanisms, and Ottoman agriculture became commercialised and linked to the capitalist world-economy, were instrumental in the complete peripheralisation of the social formation by 1840.

Tax-farming (*iltizam*) and the extension of commercial farms (*çiftlik*) provided the local notables with substantial economic and social power. These notables, called *âyan*, acquired, in collusion with the provincial governors and judges (*kadı*), a considerable political power and autonomy at the expense of the crippled central government. The most powerful *âyan*, known as *derebey*, had their private armies and controlled Ottoman provinces, to the extent that, by the beginning of the nineteenth century, the central authority was able to keep direct administrative control only over a few provinces of the empire, mainly in southern and south-western Anatolia.

As already noted, the *çiftlik* entailed new forms of relations of production and labour control. The communal agricultural production, based on isolated household units, under the administrative control of the state through the *tımar* system, was replaced by production through large estates. The commercialised agriculture brought into the empire a sort of 'second serfdom', which had appeared in Prussia and Poland from the seventeenth century on.

The rather distant administrative control of the state over the production process was replaced by the much tighter economic and social control of the *âyan* over the peasants. This had the major consequence of providing the *âyan* in the Balkans with a popular base in their nineteenth century nationalist struggles against the central Ottoman power. In Anatolia this new type of social control strengthened the antagonism in the relationship between the state élites and those of the periphery, which was to mark the Ottoman-Turkish state, up to the mid-twentieth century.[22]

In the process of incorporation-peripheralisation, the Ottoman state was increasingly subject to the requirements of the nineteenth-century interstate system, through political processes, wars and various disadvantageous political and commercial treaties (the most important of the latter being the 1838 Anglo-Ottoman commercial treaty, giving England advantages through the promotion of *laissez-faire* policy and the elimination of Ottoman state monopolies, and followed by similar treaties signed with all the Western powers). Once the process matured by the 1840s, the impact of the capitalist world-economy quickly destroyed the Ottoman manufactures and led to the control of the Ottoman economy by the Western powers, in particular through the Ottoman Public Debt Administration, created in 1881.

The corollary of this process in the political-legal sphere was of course the *Tanzimat* reforms, starting with the Gülhane Rescript of 1839.

The transformation of Ottoman-Turkish herrschaft

The mode of distintegration of the Ottoman empire can be characterised as prebendalisation (Max Weber applied this concept to the Chinese empire in *The Religion of China*). This has important implications for the direction in which the modern state was to emerge.[23] We cannot go here into a detailed discussion of this point, but should merely underline its consequences: prebendalism contributed to the maintenance of the patrimonial structure of the Ottoman empire, whereas feudalism in the West destroyed the Carolingian empire, which was also of a patrimonial nature.

It has often been argued that the Ottoman social formation was a static one, that it lacked the structural features which would have led to endogenous change.[24] This argument, partly based on the concepts of the Asiatic mode of production and oriental despotism,[25] overlooks the potential for change that existed in the Ottoman empire. What happened was that the endogenous change was hampered by the 'controlling mechanism' constituted by the Sultan, the patrimonial bureaucracy and the ideological state apparatus (*ülema*).

The very process through which European merchants were transformed into a social class deriving its strength from the market could not apply to the Ottoman merchant capital. The impossibility of effecting, in the Ottoman society, the revolutionary conversion of economic resources into political power for the benefit of the bourgeoisie, which took place in the West, was as much due to this control mechanism as to the restricted and subordinate character of private property as compared to state ownership of land. The latter is considered by many scholars as the basis of the Ottoman social formation.[26] The development of *çiftlik* and *mâlikâne* in the early seventeenth century, the increasing commercialisation of the Ottoman agriculture and the rise of *âyan* would tend to relativise the weight of the argument which holds that the Ottoman social formation is primarily characterised by the predominance of the *mirî* over private lands. It is true that the Western concept of private property defined by Roman law was introduced in Turkey in 1926, through the adoption of a Swiss-inspired civil code. In the meantime, the *Tanzimat* reforms and the Young Turk regime enhanced the status of private property. It should also be noted that the Sultan's right of confiscation of private property (with the exception of *vakıf* lands) remained in force till as late as 1826. By the end of the eighteenth century, the *âyan* were in almost total control of the provinces of the empire, but they were excluded from the centre of the state. The reason was that the ruling coalition already referred to (the Sultan, the patrimonial bureaucracy and the religious-ideological apparatus) had always been able to prevent the market mechanisms from prevailing over the political ones, as the basis of resource allocation, although it was forced to accept the generalisation of tax-farming throughout the empire and the subsequent rise of the local *âyan*. The ruling coalition had a firm hold over the state for as long as it presided over the allocation of social positions and power, and the competition for the latter went through the state and not through the market. This prebendal pattern was instrumental in extending to economically active groups, such as *âyan*, the culture and value systems of the patrimonial bureaucracy, more oriented toward consumption than capitalist accumulation. Obliged to compete for resource allocation through the patrimonial state apparatus, the *âyan*, who continued to produce commercially for the world-market, failed to develop beyond the local sphere a broader power base, autonomous from the state and the ruling élite. In other words, no autonomously functioning civil society, based on market forces and private ownership, existed in the Ottoman empire.[27] Structural features of such a civil society which Durkheim called 'secondary structures', like autonomous towns and guilds, were missing. There was also a conspicuous lack of 'calculable law'. The diffuse character of law and the absence of legitimate corporate bodies reflect the unwillingness of the Ottoman state to permit the development of structures which would escape its control.

In this context, the transformation of the Ottoman state in the nineteenth century could hardly result from the impulses coming from the civil society. There were no Ottoman 'estates', no hereditary nobility, no autonomous clergy, no bourgeoisie. The 1808 *Sened-i-Ittifak* (Document of Agreement), between the central authority and the *âyan*, granting the latter a number of privileges, was not at all the Ottoman *Magna Carta*.[28] Mahmoud II recuperated within a few years whatever the state conceded in this document, and moved swiftly to destroy the local power of the *âyan*, and re-establish the authority of the centre over the periphery.

The modernisation of the state machinery started under Mahmoud II (1808–39) in a polity where a status and not a class order prevailed. We find here, once again, the contradiction which crippled the Ottoman world-empire: the incorporation of the socio-economic formation into the capitalist world-economy was completed, during the first four decades of the nineteenth century; the patrimonial bureaucracy, which depended for its subsistence on the revenues obtained from social groups (merchants, *mültezim*) that were linked to the world market, was able to prevent the access to political power of these groups, thereby blocking a rapid evolution toward a modern state. The *Tanzimat* reforms led principally to the modernisation of the bureaucracy — the modern state was to emerge later. These reforms were accomplished as the necessary adaptation of the 'superstructure' of the peripheral Ottoman formation to the requirements of the capitalist world-economy, and were in response to the interstate system, on the one hand, and part of the political centre's moves to regain control over the provinces, and its efforts to improve the ever-shrinking financial resources of the empire, on the other. In the course of these reforms, the patrimonial bureaucracy showed a striking success in perpetuating the status order, i.e. the predominence, over the market forces, of the political-administrative determination of the stratification in the Ottoman society. The élite groups which played the leading role in the emergence of the modern Ottoman-Turkish state came from within this patrimonial bureaucracy. They were aiming at the furthering of the status order, and at maintaining the mediating role of the bureaucracy in the allocation of social positions and power.

This process from above — be it in the form of the *Tanzimat* reforms, the Young Ottomans of the 1860s and 1870s, the Young Turks of 1908, or Kemalism — was the hallmark of political change in Turkey. And the value systems and ideologies which accompanied the political change were determined by the specific nature of the Ottoman-Turkish state.

The 'inconvertibility' of the economic positions into political power was the basis of the institutionalisation of the Ottoman state. Therefore the strategy, as well as the ideological stances, of every élite group contending for power had to concentrate on the state, neglecting the economy and market forces, which in any case went under almost complete foreign control by the end of the nineteenth century.

What Weber called the 'traditional status-oriented attitude of the bureaucracy towards rational economic profit'[29] was reflected in the modernising *Tanzimat* élites' lack of interest in economic matters, which they only considered in connection with the improvement of the finances of the state. Although some interest was shown in manufacturing under Sultan Abdülmecid (1839–61), the Ottoman ruling élites as well as the intelligentsia concentrated their attention on the fields in which they made their careers — problems of state and religion — ignoring the economic sphere and those active in it, such as merchants, craftsmen and peasants. 'The rather crude mercantilism of the statesmen of the *Tanzimat* was in any case hopelessly irrelevant, both to the bustling nineteenth century and to the fatalistic Turkish population.'[30]

However, the nineteenth-century developments gradually modified various aspects of Ottoman *herrschaft*.[31] *Tanzimat* started the evolution towards a 'calculable' legal system. The provincial town notables found a limited opportunity for political participation, first through local administrative bodies which were established in the provinces and later in the very short-lived first Ottoman parliament of 1877. All this was limited in scope, but it opened new opportunities for the periphery of the Ottoman society to make its voice heard at the centre.

Besides these first strides of political participation of the peripheral élites which can be interpreted as preliminary breaches in the rule of the non-convertibility of socio-economic forces into political power, significant changes took place amongst the ruling élites, during the nineteenth century. These changes had a crucial bearing on the emergence of the modern Turkish state, for 'in a sense the Kemalist Republic was the culmination of a long process, whereby the Turkish governing élite transformed itself, the state, and finally the country'.[32]

The introduction of Westernised higher education institutions as of 1820s and 1830s, and the establishment of a secular public instruction, as of 1850s, not only led to new and more numerous generations of modernising state élites, but also strongly contributed both to the broadening of their social basis and the differentiation of professional roles.

Young Ottomans, who achieved the first Ottoman constitutionalisation, were mostly members of the small circle of ruling élites, with similar social backgrounds. The new generation of élites, trained in the military academy, the school of medicine, the school of administration (*Mülkiye*) and the secular law school, were not exclusively the offspring of the ruling élite. They increasingly came from provincial towns and more modest circles. To the old élite professions of officers and civil servants were now added lawyers and judges, applying secular laws, and journalists, a profession which developed along with the tripling of the rate of literacy in the last quarter of the nineteenth century.[33] Such new professional groups became dissatisfied with the inner circles of power, mostly staffed with traditional Ottoman state élites. The Young Turks, who took up the opposition against the Abdülhamid regime (1876–1909) after the short-lived first Ottoman constitutional experiment of 1877–8, were recruited among these new élite groups. Later, most of the Kemalist revolutionaries, including Mustafa Kemal himself, belonged to this category of somewhat marginal state élites.

The Young Turks and Kemalists, although very different from the traditional Ottoman bureaucrats, since they were trained in secular schools to become adepts of Western ideas and European-style patriotism, were the heirs to the old patrimonial tradition which assumed the dominance of the state over civil society and reserved the monopoly of legitimacy and authority to state élites, at the expense of social and economic élites. Despite their modern education they still somehow related to what Weber qualified as 'the legend of patrimonialism, deriving . . . from the authoritarian relationship of father and children. The 'father of the people' (*landesvater*) is the ideal of the patrimonial states.'[34]

The civil and military bureaucracy, together with the *ülema*, were the pillars of the empire. The Young Turks and Kemalists considered themselves as such, and indeed played the first roles in the creation of the Republic. The occupational characteristics of the Turkish deputies at the first session of the Grand National Assembly, in 1920, show that civil and military bureaucrats provided 38 per cent of the total. If one adds the religious officials (17 per cent) and the educators (5 per cent), the proportion of the bureaucratic élites in this Assembly was 60 per cent, as against 18 per cent for the professions (law, medicine, journalism), 13 per cent for banking and trade and 6 per cent for landowners.[35] And 93 per cent of the empire's staff officers and 85 per cent of its civil servants retained their positions in the republic.[36] These figures show the extent of the 'bureaucratic continuity' between the old and the new regimes.

Élite alliance as the pillar of the modern Turkish state

The new bureaucratic élites went through what was aptly called a 'paradigmatic revolution',[37] which was to distinguish Young Turks and Kemalists from the previous traditional Ottoman élites. The Kemalist movement, following the Young Turk regime, brought drastic changes into the Turkish polity. But it was definitely not a social revolution, and there were no insurrections in the cities or rural areas. This 'revolution from above' did not need mass mobilisation. Commoners participated in the Kemalist movement as soldiers and not as revolutionaries.[38]

Kemalism constituted a continuum with the *Tanzimat*, Young Ottomans and Young Turks, insofar as its major concern was the state, considered as the unique mediating mechanism and source of legitimacy in the society, prevailing over market relations. It also had to rely on the officials, legitimating symbols and certain traditional values of the former regime, until it could impose a newly-defined legitimacy. However, the Kemalists were successful in one strategic aspect of state-building, which the Ottoman reformers failed even to perceive: the capacity to narrow the gap between the political centre and the periphery and to mobilise societal resources, in building the modern state.

The structure, ideology and symbolic code of the Ottoman empire prevented such alliances between status élites and economically active social groups. The Young Turks started such an alliance, and Kemalists pushed it farther. Bernard Lewis quotes a traditional Ottoman official, *Sadrıazam* Ahmet Izzet Paşa, as having written in 1920 of the Kemalists in Anatolia; 'this group consists in the main of military commanders and their staffs, of country notables and land-owners, and intellectuals.'[39] This accurate description illustrates the above-mentioned alliance, which precisely allowed the Kemalists to create a modern state capable of maintaining, unlike the Ottoman empire, the political independence of the peripheral Turkish forma-tion within the twentieth-century interstate system.

As noted earlier, several factors were at play, by the end of the nineteenth century, which contributed to the weakening of the patri-monial patterns of the state, leading gradually to the closing of the gap between the bureaucratic and civil élites. The Young Ottomans in the 1870s and the Young Turks later developed a concern with the welfare of the masses and paid attention to the grievances of provin-cial notables. Even if this concern with the periphery was a theoreti-cal one, it constituted a novelty, as compared to the attitude of earlier *Tanzimat* élites, who did not try to compensate through modern social measures for the dissolution of *hisbe*, the traditional Ottoman welfare system. Another factor was the provincial and modest backgrounds of the younger generations of modernising élites, who became acquainted, through the secular educational system, with Western ideas of patriotism and the welfare of the nation. Contrary to *Tanzimat* élites, who were accused of ignoring the people, they associated the ideal of saving the state with the nation, i.e. the people.

Young Turks were not ideologically monolithic. The dominant group was that of westernisers, but there was also among them a pro-Islamic group. The westernising Young Turks believed, according to the formulation of one of their thinkers Abdullah Cevdet, that 'there is no second civilisation; civilisation means European civilisation.'[40] They also 'singled out positivism — and later a solidarism inspired by it — as their favourite ideology. Educated in state schools estab-lished to modernise bureaucracy, but brought up also with the ideal of preserving the state, these young men found in the social engineer-ing aspects of Comte the legitimation of their élitist outlook. Science was the rock on which they leaned.'[41] Young Turk ideologues dreamed of several of the socio-cultural reforms Mustafa Kemal was later able to implement: abolition of polygamy, replacement of the *fez* by European headgear, new rights for women, complete secularisation of the educational and legal systems, and purification of the Ottoman language. The major ideologue of the Young Turks, Ziya Gökalp, advocated the separation of religion and the state. And the Union and Progress government, before and during the First World War, did take steps to secularise the law, grant improved rights to women and reform the laws governing the land tenure. Local and general elections enlarged political participation. Provincial branches of the Union and Progress party provided an institutional base in Anatolia which the Kemalist movement was to use in 1919–20 to organise the national resistance.

Even more important for the future Kemalist state was the economic thinking of Young Turks. Their concrete achievements in economics were limited, although innovative, such as the creation of the first private enterprises with Turkish capital and the first Turkish bank. But the idea which inspired these achievements was significant: economic nationalism, implemented through a national economic policy, which was later to constitute one of the pillars of the modern Turkish state. Feroz Ahmad has shown both the success of their policy in laying the foundations of a national capitalist economy, and in defining the contours of an étatism or state capitalism, which would ensure both the leading role of the state bureaucracy in economic development and the creation of a national bourgeoisie, nurtured by the state.[42] The political economy of the Young Turk regime was the forerunner of that of the Kemalist republic, which regarded economic sovereignty as the basis of political independence. The étatism, officially adopted in 1931, gave the state the role of pioneer in industrialisation, without excluding private business. It seemed natural to the state élites that they should also serve as guides to the nation in economics as they did in other fields.

This conception, which confirmed the preponderant role of the state élites over civil élites, but which in the long run led to the creation of a strengthened bourgeois class, was to characterise the history of the Kemalist state until 1946. At that date, the transition from the single-party to the multi-party system occurred, marking the political independence of the civil élites and the definitive shift from a stratification determined at least partly through the state and prebends to a class order involving a social stratification based on market forces. The very rapid rhythm of the state-directed industrialisation between 1927 and 1939 — only the Soviet Union and Japan fared better during this period[43] — opened up new opportunities to Turkish business and managerial groups and contributed to their growth.

Ideologically, Mustafa Kemal held a position close to westernising and positivist Young Turks. He firmly believed in progress and science, and was an heir to nationalist, secular and populist trends. But his conception of Turkish nationalism differed from the racial-cultural pan-Turkism of the Young Turks. First, he never adhered to the ultra-chauvinism of Young Turk leaders. Secondly, while Ziya Gökalp defined the nation as people with the same education, language and religion — but non-territorial, insofar as the Turks were part of Islam; Kemalist nationalism was above all territorial. This was expressed in the National Pact of 1919–20, the political programme of the Turkish resistance movement. The 1935 programme of the Republican People's Party, which declared that 'the Fatherland is the sacred country within our present boundaries, where the Turkish nation lives' reflects the same view.[44] This aspect is one of Mustafa Kemal's major contributions towards the creation of the modern Turkish state.

Another ideological tenet of Kemalism was populism. Contrary to the rather limited interest in it shown by the Young Turk regime, Mustafa Kemal used populism as a major ideological instrument in forging the alliance of the state élites and the civil élites. According to changing political circumstances, he gave this doctrine various contents: in his populist programme of 13 September 1920, he presented populism as a way of overcoming the gap between bureaucracy and people, since in Turkey the dominant class was not the capitalist but the bureaucratic one. In September 1921, his populism manifested a certain socialist inspiration; he defined his Government as the 'people's government'. The national struggle was against imperialism and capitalism, which sought to destroy the Turkish nation. In February 1923, his populism was of a solidarist kind, maintaining that in a classless society such as Turkey social development should be through a solidary division of labour which would benefit everyone. Finally, the populism of 1931, as defined in the Republican People's Party programme, reflects an élitist, 'for the people, with or without the people' kind of populism.

The Kemalist state could be characterised as Jacobin. No wonder that Young Turk and Kemalist élites, with their positivist, secular and nationalist ideology, did not adhere to the ideas of Prince Sabahattin (1877–1948), the Turkish proponent of a doctrine of individual initiative and decentralisation, influenced by Le Play and Edmond Demolins. The later ideology of the *Kadro* movement (1932), created around a periodical of that name by a rather marginal group of radical Kemalists who dreamed of providing a socio-political philosophy for the Kemalist regime's new étatist economic policy, was typically élitist.[45]

Legal issues played a role in the creation of the modern Turkish state that was perhaps more important than elsewhere. Due to the patrimonial background of the state élites, there existed a tendency to see socio-political issues as legal problems. In this sense, Kemalism could be qualified as a revolution through law. In a speech at the opening of the new law school in Ankara in 1925, Atatürk declared that 'the greatest . . . enemies of the revolutionaries are rotten laws and their decrepit upholders'.[46] To the Kemalists, the vehicles of the revolution were the state and the legal order; the nation was to be created through these instruments, and the initial stimuli for economic development and the strengthening of the civil society were to come from the state.

The Kemalists' nationalist, populist, secularist and positivist options could obviously not be accommodated under the old Ottoman empire. They required a different legitimacy, with a new content. The provisional constitution which the Grand National Assembly adopted on 20 January 1921 under the title 'Law of Fundamental Organisations' defined the new legitimacy by stating that 'sovereignty belongs without reservation and conditions to the nation; the system of administration rests on the principle that the people personally and effectively directs its own destinies.'[47]

The new state and its élites remained the repositories of the new legitimacy. But the latter is now different: an ethnically and territorially defined nationalism replaces the universal non-territoriality of Islam. The modern state, as in the Ottoman empire, retains the monopoly of legitimacy, which it is reluctant to share with the periphery and socio-economic groups. However, its origins are no longer in the person of the Sultan-Caliph but in popular sovereignty; and its goal is no longer the conservation of the traditional status order but the creation of a nation and economic development. Through the abolition of the Caliphate on 3 March 1924, Mustafa Kemal eliminated any possible reference to the former legitimacy in the republican state created on 29 October 1923. The abolition of *Şeriat* courts on 8 April 1924 and the adoption of the Swiss Civil Code, as adapted to Turkey, on 17 February 1926 completed and extended secularisation to family and personal matters. Thus the modern Turkish state, based on civil rights, came into existence. Individualistic values and capitalist accumulation were encouraged, which, together with the economic policies of the state, led within three decades to the growth and political emancipation of the bourgeoisie.

The renaissance of the Turkish state was made possible through an alliance directed by bureaucratic élites and involving the Turkish merchant class, provincial notables and landowners. The Young

Turks initiated this alliance; the Kemalists perfected it. The alliance did not altogether eliminate the gap between the political centre and the societal periphery, grant legitimacy to an autonomous civil society, or modify the reluctant attitude of the bureaucratic élites *vis-à-vis* the political participation of the masses;[48] but the momentum was set in that direction. In August 1917, one of the leading ideologues of pan-Turkism, Yusuf Akçura, warned: 'If the Turks fail to produce among themselves a bourgeois class by profiting from European capitalism, the chances of survival of a Turkish society composed only of peasants and officials will be very slim.'[49] Akçura's warning concerned the consequences of the peripheralisation of the Ottoman socio-economic formation, submitted to the economic pressures of the capitalist world-economy, and the political pressures of the interstate systems. If a modern Turkish state were not created, eliminating the remnants of the redistributive Ottoman world-empire, and favouring the emergence of a civil society based on market relations, Turkey could not preserve its independence.

The Kemalist movement transformed the state, adapting the peripheral Ottoman formation to the requirements of the capitalist world-economy. The forms, direction, rhythm and outcomes of this transformation were conditioned by the specific features of the Ottoman-Turkish polity — which were very different from those of the Western societies in which the modern state first emerged.

In 1919–20 the odds were heavily against the Kemalists, and in favour of Turkey becoming a colony or a British or American mandate territory rather than an independent modern state. Quite a number of the leading associates of Mustafa Kemal did in fact advocate the mandate solution as a lesser evil. This, with many other examples, shows the extraordinary achievement of Mustafa Kemal in creating the modern Turkish state. Also remarkable was how, during those two fateful decades of Turkish history between the world wars, he routinised his charisma and institutionalised the state, which later facilitated a rather smooth passage to a multi-party regime, and allowed a broadened political participation. Considering the history of the Ottoman-Turkish state, these were remarkable developments. But Turkey still had a long way to go until, to paraphrase Gramsci, the 'primitive and gelatinous' civil society became a 'sturdy structure', with 'hegemony' replacing coercion, and 'the state which is everything' becoming the 'moat' surrounding the fortress of civil society.[50] A considerable distance has been covered since Atatürk's time, although the road, with such landmarks as 1950, 1960, 1971 and 1980, still has many miles ahead. That, however, is another story.

NOTES

1. Paul-Marc Henry, 'La fin du Kémalisme', *Le Monde*, 11 Dec. 1979.

2. Quoted by Hasan-Âli Yücel in his Introduction to the abridged Turkish edition of Stanley Lane-Poole's *Life of Lord Stratford de Redcliffe*, London, 1888 (*Lord Stratford'un Türkiye Hâtiralari* (S.L. Poole' den kisaltarak çeviren Can Yücel), Ankara, T. Iş Bankasi Kültür Yayinlari, 1959, x).

3. Bernard Lewis, *The Emergence of Modern Turkey*, London, Oxford University Press, 1961, 208.

4. J.-P. Nettl, 'The State as a conceptual variable', *World Politics*, vol. XX, July 1968, 559–92, Nettl noted that, at the time he was writing his article, the state was not a very fashionable research topic in the social sciences. See also my editorial in the issue 'On the State', *International Social Science Journal*, vol. XXXII, no. 4, 1980, 585–99.

5. See, for example, Bertrand Badie and Pierre Birnbaum, *Sociologie de l'Etat*, Paris, Grasset, 1979; Theda Skocpol, *States and Social Revolutions: a Comparative Analysis of France, Russia and China*, Cambridge University Press, 1979.

6. Immanuel Wallerstein, 'The States in the Institutional Vortex of the Capitalist World-Economy', *International Social Sciences Journal*, vol. XXXII, no. 4, 1980, 743–51.

7. Immanuel Wallerstein, *The Capitalist World-Economy*, Cambridge University Press, 1979, 293.

8. Immanuel Wallerstein, 'The States . . .', *loc. cit.*, 745.

9. Randall Collins, 'Weber's Last Theory of Capitalism: a Systematisation', *American Sociological Review*, vol. 45, no. 6, Dec. 1980, 925–42.

10. Pierre Birnbaum, 'States, Ideologies and Collective Action in Western Europe', *International Social Sciences Journal*, vol. XXXII, No. 4, 1980, 671–868.

11. Karl Marx, 'Eighteenth Brumaire of Louis Bonaparte', in Lewis Feuer (ed.), *Marx and Engels: Basic Writings on Politics and Philosophy*, New York, Doubleday, 1959.

12. Randall Collins, *loc. cit.*, 931. It should be remembered that while for Marx the emergence of the state is basically linked to the transition from classless to class societies, for Weber the modern rational/legal state, based on citizenship, was produced through a certain combination of military and religious factors.

13. Fernand Braudel maintains that the Ottoman empire in its classical age was a world-economy. See *Civilisation matérielle, économie et capitalisme, XVe — XVIIIe siècle*, vol. 3: *Le temps du monde*, Paris, Armand Colin, 1979, 402–19. Immanuel Wallerstein argues that it never was one; see *The Modern World-System: Capitalist Agriculture and the Origin of the European World-Economy in the Sixteenth Century*, New York, Academic Press, 1974, 57. But he agrees to the autonomy of the Ottoman world-empire *vis-à-vis* the European world-economy in the sixteenth century, *ibid.*, 68.

14. Randall Collins, *loc. cit.*, 932.

15. Şerif Mardin, 'Center-Periphery Relations: a key to Turkish poli-

tics?', *Daedalus*, Winter 1973, 170.

16. Huri Islamoğlu and Çağlar Keyder, 'Agenda for Ottoman History', *Review*, I, 1 (Summer 1977), 53.

17. Immanuel Wallerstein and Reşat Kasaba, 'Incorporation into the World-Economy: Change in the Structure of the Ottoman Empire, 1750–1839', mimeo., Fernand Braudel Center for the Study of Economies, Historical Systems and Civilisations, State University of New York at Binghampton, 1980, 2. See also Immanuel Wallerstein, 'The Ottoman Empire and the Capitalist World-Economy: Some Questions for Research', pp. 117–22, in Okyar, Osman and Inalcık, Halil (eds.), *Social and Economic History of Turkey (1071–1920)*, Ankara, Meteksan, 1980.

18. Immanuel Wallerstein and Resat Kasaba, *loc. cit.*, 2.

19. Halil Inalcık, *The Ottoman Empire: the Classical Age, 1300–1600*, New York, Praeger, 1973, 110. On *çiftlik* see Fernand Braudel, *La Méditerranée et le monde méditerranéen à l'époque de Philippe II*, vol. 2, 4th ed., 1979, 67–8. On *mâlikâne-divânî* see Ömer Lütfi Barkan, 'Mâlikâne-divânî sistemi', *Türk Hukuk ve Iktisat Mecmuası*, no. 2, 1939, 119–84.

20. Immanuel Wallerstein and Reşat Kasaba, *loc. cit.*, 10.

21. Huri, Islamoğlu and Çağlar, Keyder, *loc. cit.*, 47.

22. On centre-periphery relations in the Ottoman empire see Şerif Mardin, *loc. cit.*, and Metin Heper, 'Center and Periphery in the Ottoman Empire: with Special Reference to the Nineteenth Century', *International Political Science Review*, vol. 1, no. 1, 1980, 81–105.

23. See the discussion on these points in Immanuel Wallerstein, *The Modern World-System . . .*, *op. cit.*, 57–63; also Max Weber, *The Religion of China*, transl. and ed. H. H. Gerth, New York, Free Press, 1951 and 1964.

24. Ilkay Sunar, 'Anthropologie politique et économique: l'Empire Ottoman et sa transformation', *Annales: Economies, Sociétés, Civilisations*, 35, nos. 3–4, May–Aug. 1980, 551.

25. See Perry Anderson, *Lineages of the Absolutist State*, London, NLB, 1974, 462–549, for an excellent critical analysis of these concepts.

26. Perry Anderson, considers, following Marx that 'the economic bedrock of the Osmanli despotism was the virtually complete absence of private property in land' (*ibid.*, 365).

27. Şerif Mardin, 'Power, Civil Society and Culture in the Ottoman Empire', *Comparative Studies in Society and History*, vol. 11, no. 3, June 1969, 274 ff.

28. Stanford J. Shaw, and Ezel Kural Shaw, *History of the Ottoman Empire and Modern Turkey*, vol. II, Cambridge University Press, 1977, 3.

29. Max Weber, *Economy and Society*, ed. Guenther Roth and Claus Wittich, Berkeley, University of California Press, 1968, vol. II, 1109.

30. Bernard Lewis, *op. cit.*, 451.

31. Şerif Mardin, 'Power, Civil Society . . .', *loc. cit.*, 269.

32. Bernard Lewis, *op. cit.*, 478.

33. *ibid.*, 455.

34. Max Weber, *op. cit.*, 1107.

35. Frederick W. Frey, *The Turkish Political Elite*, Cambridge, Mass., M.I.T. Press, 1965, 181.

36. Dankwart A. Rustow, 'The Military: Turkey', in Robert E. Ward and Dankwart A. Rustow, (eds.), *Political Modernisation in Japan and Turkey*, Princeton, Princeton University Press, 1964, 388.

37. Ilkay Sunar, *loc. cit.*, 571.

38. Ellen Kay Trimberger, *Revolution from Above: Military Bureaucrats and Development in Japan, Turkey, Egypt and Peru*, New Brunswick, N.J., Transaction Books, 1978, 17.

39. Bernard Lewis, *op. cit.*, 458.

40. *ibid.*, 231.

41. Şerif Mardin, 'Power, civil society . . ., *loc. cit.*, 277.

42. See Feroz Ahmad, 'Vanguard of a Nascent Bourgeoisie: the Social and Economic Policy of the Young Turks, 1908–1918', in *Social and Economic History of Turkey (1071–1920)*, *op. cit.*, pp. 329–50.

43. Bernard Lewis, *op. cit.*, 465.

44. *ibid.*, p. 317.

45. Dankwart A. Rustow, 'Atatürk as Founder of a State', in *Prof. Dr. Yavuz Abadan'a Armağan*, Ankara, Siyasal Bilgiler Fakültesi Yayınları, 1969, 534.

46. Bernard Lewis, *op. cit.*, 268.

47. ibid., 251.

48. Ali Kazancıgil, 'La participation et les élites dans un système politique en crise: le cas de la Turquie', *Revue française de science politique*, vol. XXIII, no. 1, February 1973, 5–32.

49. Feroz Ahmad, *loc. cit.*, 345, quoted from Niyazi Berkes. *The Development of Secularism in Turkey*, Montreal, McGill-University Press, 1964, 426.

50. Pierre Birnbaum, loc. cit., 673.

Atatürk as an institution-builder

DANKWART A. RUSTOW

Kemal Atatürk combined, in a single act of historic creation, a number of distinct achievements: the transformation of a decadent empire into a vigorous nation-state, a victorious war to assert the new nation's independence, and an educational program that merged earlier social and cultural divisions in a common commitment to secular progress. Above all, Atatürk created a set of institutions that built organically upon the legacies of the past, responded effectively to the contingencies of the present, and equipped his people for the challenges of an uncertain future.

The transition from empire to republic meant an end to the dreams of glory that had held so many Ottoman-Turkish leaders spellbound during the preceding decades: dreams associated with an Ottoman and Islamic imperial past and dreams seeking the basis for a future empire in linguistic affinities with Turkish populations as far north as the Urals and as far east as Sinkiang. Kemal and his followers, instead of indulging in such nostalgist or escapist fantasies, accepted the severely reduced boundaries resulting from centuries of military defeat. Specifically, the National Pact — Kemal's original political program of 1919 — defined the regions within the lines drawn by the peace treaty of 1913 at the end of the Balkan wars, and by the armistice of 1918 at the end of the First World War, as the nation's irreducible territory. The Ottoman empire had only once in its 600-year history experienced a period of peace as long as twenty-nine years; by contrast, the Turkish Republic, within those reduced boundaries, has lived at peace with its neighbors for more than half a century since its proclamation. This renunciation of imperialist ambitions and of a near-permanent state of war was one of the most difficult, and surely the most creditable, of Atatürk's many achievements.

Before inaugurating that half-century of peace, Kemal mobilised his countrymen to one supreme and final military effort — this time for the defence of their Anatolian 'mother-country'. The military antagonists were many: Armenians eager to establish their own nation-state in the east; French forces advancing northward from Syria; British military units which occupied the Sultan's capital of Istanbul and other coastal positions, but which Mustafa Kemal was careful not to engage in direct combat; and the Sultan's own forces dispatched against the Anatolian 'rebels'. The most serious threat came from the full onslaught of the armies of Greece, pursuing an imperialist, pan-Hellenic dream of their own, advancing eastward from the Aegean coast in the summers of 1919, 1920 and 1921, and by August 1921 reaching the very outskirts of Kemal's temporary capital of Ankara. Yet the Greek armies were halted in 1921 and routed in 1922, and by the autumn of that year all foreign troops had departed from the area claimed as Turkish in Kemal's National Pact.

This successful defence against partition into foreign colonies, mandates, or protectorates was the Kemalist movement's most urgent and notable achievement. For three centuries after the voyages of Vasco da Gama and Columbus, European imperialism had relentlessly expanded around the globe. As the imperialist advance continued, it was running into resistance from its own colonists in North America in 1776–83, in Latin America in 1810–25, and in South Africa in 1899–1902. The Japanese, in the war against Russia in 1904–5, became the first non-European people to win a decisive victory against such imperialist expansion. Meanwhile, the European imperialist advance, in its final phase from about 1880 to 1920, concentrated on the Islamic Middle East. And here it was that the Kemalist movement, in defeating Greece and its Allied backers in 1919–22, were in effect saying to European imperialism: Thus far and no farther. The Ottoman empire had been militarily the weakest of the Central powers in the First World War. But as Germany was forced to sign the vindictive peace of Versailles, and as the treaties of St.German and Trianon were carving up the defunct Austro-Hungarian empire, it was the Ottoman Turks under Kemal who rallied to a further effort that in due course earned them a negotiated, rather than an imposed, peace. The Greek-Turkish war of 1919–22 is known to Turks as their War of Independence. Unlike the wars fought by the Swiss and the Dutch in the thirteenth and sixteenth centuries, or the American wars under Washington and Bolivar, it was a war to preserve independence, not to establish it anew. Nonetheless, when Kemal's Turkey is compared to the approximately one hundred 'new nations' proclaimed after 1918 and 1945, it stands out as one of the very few — and among those few as the first — to have earned its independence in a war of national liberation.

Victory in the Turkish War of Independence and recognition of the newly-proclaimed Republic by the powers enabled Kemal and his followers after 1923 to turn to internal tasks of peaceful reconstruction. In the defunct Ottoman empire, a small, specially-trained ruling élite had governed a miscellany of culturally diverse subject classes — merchants, craftsmen, farmers; Muslims, Christians, Jews, Turks, Greeks, Arabs, Armenians, Serbs, Bulgarians, Kurds, and many others. The new Turkish republic, in contrast to most 'new nations', was ethnically homogeneous: over 90 per cent of its population spoke Turkish as their mother-tongue, and over 98 per cent professed Islam as their religion. Meanwhile, the nationalist consciousness fostered by Kemal Atatürk and his associates served to bridge the wide gap that had earlier separated the Ottoman governmental élite from the Anatolian peasant majority; it thus provided one of the essential pre-requisites for later efforts at economic development and democratisation.

In the centuries of Ottoman defeat, attitudes towards Europe had been ambivalent: there had been admiration for its military strength, its administrative and economic efficiency, even its individualism and romantic poetry, but there had also been profound revulsion against the threat that European imperialism and its infidel armies posed for all that was most cherished in the Islamic and Ottoman traditions. Abdullah Cevdet, one of the cofounders of the 'Young Turk' Society of Union and Progress, had expressed the positive aspect of that ambivalence in an essay of 1913: 'There is no second civilisation; civilisation means European civilisation, and it must be imported with both its roses and its thorns.'

Eight years later, in the decisive phase of the War of Independence, the pious Muslim poet Mehmed Âkif, in a hymn full of nationalist fervour dedicated to 'Our Heroic Army', was to express the negative aspect of that same ambivalence:

'Fear not, how can that monster called Civilisation

Choke, with the last tooth in its jaw, the faith of an entire nation?'[1]

Ottoman reformers for the past century and a half had developed their own formula for accepting and rejecting parts of the European impact. The administrative and military reforms of Selim III (1789–1807) and the *Tanzimat* period (1839–56), and the railroad and telegraph concessions awarded by Abdülhamid II (1876–1909), were introduced from a sense of compelling necessity: reorganisation along European lines was required to ward off Europe's military might. But there was to be no acceptance of European ideology; nationalism, in particular, was dreaded as a subversive emotion that might incite the empire's Christian subjects to secession and its Muslim subjects to conspiracy.

By 1918, nevertheless, the previous half-measures of westernisation had been found to be wanting, and in the War of Independence Mustafa Kemal had saved what remained of the empire precisely on the basis of a new, Turkish nationalism. He had 'foiled the foreigner's shameless hand' in the 'monstrous' design that Akif had decried. And in so doing he had equipped his countrymen psycho-

logically to espouse Cevdet's uncompromising program of Westernisation, without any feeling of duress but rather with a sense of
free choice.

Within that Kemalist programme of westernisation, some changes
were symbolic and highly visible: Roman instead of Arabic letters;
the counting of years from 'the birth' (of Jesus) rather than 'the
flight' (of Muhammad); Sunday rather than Friday as the weekly day
of rest; the wearing of Western-style dress, including the brimmed
hat instead of the turban or fez; and the adoption of hereditary
family names. Other measures, such as the enactment of European
law codes, were essential parts of the incipient social and economic
revolution.

The major effort, however, went into education. One of the more
amusing acts of Kemalist legislation was a decree of 1928, proclaim-
ing 'every Turkish citizen, man and woman', to be a member of a
'National School', and designating as its 'headmaster . . . the President of the Republic, His Excellency *Gazi* Mustafa Kemal Paşa'.[2]
Soon the *Gazi* himself could be seen, chalk in hand before a black-
board in a public park, instructing his citizen-pupils in the use of the
newly-adopted Roman alphabet. Meanwhile, the Republic's ordi-
nary program of education did away with the two separate, narrow
curricula available in Ottoman days — one in Turkish and French
for military and civil servants at their specialised training schools,
and the other in Arabic for Muslim clergy in their traditional semi-
naries (or *medreses*). Instead there was now a single comprehensive
system of schooling, with dramatically increasing attendance. And
training at the newly-founded universities and technical schools
became the major avenue of upward social mobility. A motto of
Atatürk's inscribed over the main portal of Ankara University pro-
claims 'In life, the truest guide is science.'

Kemal Atatürk's record as an institution-builder includes the con-
vening of the Grand National Assembly at Ankara on 23 April 1920,
the founding of the People's Party (later Republican People's Party
or RPP) in August 1923, the proclamation of the Republic of Turkey
on 29 October 1923, the enactment of the Law on the Unification of
Instruction (*Tevhid-ı Tedrisat Kanunu*) in March 1924, and the
adoption of European law codes in 1926. Although Turkey since
Atatürk's time has undergone both a major transition from a single-
party dictatorship to a democratic multiparty system and three different episodes of military intervention in the political process, all of
the five institutions just listed have survived intact and none of them,
indeed, has ever been seriously questioned.

This durability is closely connected with another striking characteristic of Kemal's performance: the gradualism of major institutions established one at a time over a six-year period. The dates just listed, indeed, understate this gradualism; for those formal ceremonies and official enactments may be considered the third of four phases of Kemal's record as an institution-builder. These, I would suggest, overlapped considerably and included: (1) a preparatory phase (*ca.* 1915–May 1919); (2) an experimental phase (November 1918–March 1924); (3) a decisional or institutional phase (September 1919–26); and (4) a consolidation phase (1923–38).

These four phases coincided approximately with major stages in Mustafa Kemal's own public career. During the *preparatory phase* he held some of the highest commands in the Ottoman military service. In 1915 he was a divisional commander in the crucial defence of the Gallipoli peninsula against the British and Allied invasion.[3] Later he stabilised the front in the south-eastern section, served as aide-de-camp to the crown prince (later Sultan Mehmed VI Vahideddin), and converted the rout on the Syrian front into an orderly retreat.

During the second, or *experimental phase*, he made his transition from soldiering to politics. He began in the winter of 1918–19 by spinning out as many connections as possible in the imperial capital — with court officials, staff officers at general headquarters, journalists, and civilian politicians. He was disappointed in his hope of obtaining the ministry of war; indeed he could find no one in any responsible position in Istanbul ready to take the lead in organising the country for national defence against enemy occupation.

Instead he obtained, in the spring of 1919, an assignment as inspector of the Ottoman military forces to be demobilised in the interior of Anatolia. From this vantage-point, he established close contact with resistance groups that had formed under military or civilian aegis here and there in Eastern and Central Anatolia. Deprived of his military position, he resigned from the Sultan's army, and instead acted as the head of a 'representative committee' appointed by two successive nationalist congresses, and later as President of the Grand National Assembly which he himself convened at Ankara.

During the third, or *decisional phase*, he briefly resumed his military function, as supreme commander against the Greek forces in the final campaign of the summer of 1922, and was given the title of *Gazi* (or 'Victor'). He assumed the leadership of the newly-formed People's Party, and in October 1923 was elected to the first of his four successive terms as President of the new Republic of Turkey.

During the final, or *consolidation phase*, he was proclaimed, as we noted, to be 'headmaster' of the 'national school'. In later years, his favourite leisure-time activity as a gentleman farmer symbolised his personal concern with the country's economic development. In 1934, in consonance with the new requirement of family names for all Turkish citizens, he was given the surname Atatürk (or 'Father Turk'). Thus for the final four years of his life, His Excellency *Gazi* Mustafa Kemal Paşa became, officially and more succinctly, Kemal Atatürk. It is a tribute to the solidity of Kemalist institutions that Turkey in 1938 achieved that rarest of feats for a one-party personalist system — a smooth and undisputed succession on the founder's death.

What distinguishes the four phases, above all, are the essential political expectations held by Mustafa Kemal, and the functions performed by himself and the organisations or institutions that he headed.

During the *preparatory phase*, he was able to observe at first hand the fatal weaknesses of the Ottoman empire, its reliance on German military advice and subservience to German military aims, and the ineptitude and irresponsibility of the empire's own political and military leaders. The Ottoman government had lightly committed itself to enter into the war at a time when the failure of the German offensive on the Marne already foreshadowed the ultimate defeat of the Central powers. As Ottoman armies were fighting an uneven battle against British forces moving northward from Syria and Iraq, the Ottoman high command allowed one army corps to be cut off in the Hijaz (in the Muslim holy city of Medina, where it surrendered three months after the October 1918 armistice); another army corps to serve as an auxiliary to German and Austrian forces in Poland (to maintain the fiction of the Ottoman empire as a full-fledged ally); and a large 'army of Islam' to be dispatched toward the Caucasus (with its Turkish-speaking population in Russian Azerbaijan). Evidently pride and pan-Islamic and pan-Turkish dreams prevailed over strategic calculations for defence of the homeland. And three days after the armistice, the Union and Progress party leaders, Enver, Talat and Cemal Paşas, who had been most responsible for the empire's involvement and defeat in the World War, secretly fled abroad — putting their personal safety above any concern for their country's fate.[4]

It was during those years of the World War that Mustafa Kemal's disaffection from the Ottoman political establishment became complete. He learned to despise the adventurist and opportunist figures, such as Talat Paşa and Enver Paşa, whom plot and intrigue had raised to political power and military command. He refused a number of military assignments late in the World War, and instead went for a health cure to Karlsbad, and to accompany the crown prince on a foreign trip. Back in command on the southern front at the time of the armistice, he vainly sought to persuade the compliant Istanbul government to resist encroachments beyond the original cease-fire lines by which the British occupied the strategic port of Iskenderun (Alexandretta).

Some of the later principles of Kemal's political action began to emerge in this preparatory phase. Military planning ought to serve Turkish, not German purposes. In war, political and propaganda aims such as pan-Islam and pan-Turkism must yield to sober military calculation. And one of the most compelling of such calculations dictates that armies under overwhelming attack should retreat to a compact defensive position. Nonetheless, positions such as Iskenderun and Mosul, that rightfully belong to Turkey under an international agreement such as the armistice of Mudros, should be defended by all available means. The greatest valour shown by field commanders and their troops will be of no avail if their political superiors in the capital are fearful, unrealistic or weak. National defence in times of defeat requires not only tenacious and steadfast political leaders and wide popular support, but also an effective network of organisation to connect the two.

Reflections such as these — grim, sober and defiant — must have prompted Kemal to launch into the second, or *experimental* phase of his career. The aim was constant: to organise the nation in such a way as to assert its full independence despite the empire's collapse, and to preserve that independence for future generations. Or, as he himself was to put it in retrospect, the goal was 'that the Turkish nation should live in dignity and honor. This goal could be achieved only by the possession of complete independence.'[5] The experiment consisted in finding the appropriate means.

Mustafa Kemal personally had to choose between a military or a political role, or some combination of the two. But the major choice, for him and others concerned about the country's future, was between a strategy based on Istanbul or on Anatolia. An Istanbul strategy meant operating within the established framework of Ottoman institutions; it was a loyalist and politically conservative program and it implied trying to salvage the country's independence, or some semblance of it, mainly by diplomatic manoeuvring. Thus a number of Ottoman diplomats hoped to exploit latent differences among the major Allied powers as the peace negotiations proceeded; politicians such as Damad Ferid Paşa were cultivating close relations with the British and their representatives in Istanbul; others were hoping to establish closer relations with France. A sizeable group of nationalist intellectuals thought that the country's integrity might be preserved under a United States mandate. An Anatolian strategy, on the contrary, meant building up solid popular and local support for the effort at national resistance; it implied a populist and radical program, and an effort to assert national independence by military force. An Istanbul strategy would avoid, in the face of overwhelming foreign pressure, any divisive internal issues; but how would it overcome the fatal weaknesses that had plunged the empire into defeat and collapse, and opened its capital to enemy occupation? An Anatolian strategy would build up resistance at a safe distance from Allied forces in Istanbul and along the coasts, but it would be internally divisive. And how could armed forces that had collapsed after four years of fighting at the front hope to prevail in yet another military encounter against the same antagonists?

The alternative strategies had contrasting implications, not only in the immediate struggle for national survival but also for the more distant political future. An Istanbul strategy meant preservation of the existing political framework; it would not have been followed by any third, institution-building phase. A combined Istanbul and Anatolian strategy was likely to result in a revived, popular sultanate. An exclusively Anatolian strategy, on the other hand, would have revolutionary implications — with a further phase of the experiment required to determine whether this was to be an Islamic or a Westernising revolution.

As the experiment proceeded, Mustafa Kemal may be said to have begun with a pure Istanbul strategy, shifted to a combined strategy with the emphasis first on Istanbul and then on Anatolia, and at last to a pure Anatolian strategy. In the short run, an Istanbul strategy supplemented with efforts in Anatolia seemed the most promising. If the machinery of the war ministry and the imperial general staff could be enlisted for the nationalist cause, then the scattered efforts at resistance could be effectively, and if necessary secretly, coordinated. If the Sultan or the imperial cabinet were to encourage such efforts, or at least to condone them, they would be given an invaluable sanction of legitimacy. If a nationalist parliament could express itself strongly, it might prompt the Sultan to appoint a more activist cabinet; at the very least, it would allow the activist-nationalist elements in the military establishment to claim that they were implementing the wishes of the constitutionally elected representatives of the people.

All such hopes came to naught. Kemal's contacts at the imperial palace can have given him scant encouragement. A press campaign glorifying his earlier military role in defending the Dardanelles in 1915 did not earn him the war ministry or any other high office in the capital. The Union and Progress Party, after the flight of its three leaders, was in disarray. The parliament, instead of facing the perils of the future, sought to apportion blame for the past by an elaborate inquiry into the political machinations by which the empire had entered the World War. In December 1918, the Sultan dissolved the solidly Unionist House of Representatives, and there were no plans for new elections. Mustafa Kemal seems to have toyed briefly with plans for a military coup in the capital — but wisely decided against it.[6] In view of the growing presence of Allied troops, a military coup that defied both the Sultan and the occupation forces would have been a foolhardy undertaking.

Some of Kemal's more activist military friends had already concluded that effective resistance could be organised only from the eastern provinces, safely beyond the reach of Allied forces; they had, in sum, decided on an Anatolian tactic. Thus Kazım Karabekir Paşa in mid-March of 1919, had gone to Erzurum as commander of the 15th army corps. The appointment in early March of a collaborationist cabinet under Damad Ferid Paşa, and the beginning of a campaign by the British to arrest and deport to Malta prominent Unionist or nationalist political and military figures, indicated that little could be done from Istanbul, and indeed that Mustafa Kemal's personal safety might be in danger.

Reluctantly Mustafa Kemal decided to move his own activities to Anatolia — with all the risks of political division or even civil war that an Anatolian strategy implied. Using his connections within the military establishment and giving assurances of his loyalty to the regime that satisfied Damad Ferid, he obtained a crucial military assignment in the north-east of the country. As inspector of the 9th army (later renumbered 3rd army) based on Erzurum, Sivas and Samsun, he was to ensure that units under his command would be smoothly demobilised. Yet at such a distance from both the Sultan and British occupation units, demobilisation could be easily delayed or even converted into remobilisation; and civilian committees encouraged rather than disbanded. Kemal saw to it that his official instructions included wide authority to communicate, without reference to Istanbul, with neighboring military commands, and also with civil authorities both in his own military region and in immediately adjacent districts. When an old military friend at a farewell dinner inquired: 'Are you going to do something, Kemal?', he quietly replied: 'Yes, I am going to do something.'[7]

Mustafa Kemal embarked for Anatolia on 16 May 1919. Only the day before, the first Greek military units had landed in the western port of Izmir (or Smyrna). During the following week, a Paris newspaper published the text of the secret treaty of 1915 in which the Allies envisaged the partition of the Ottoman empire. There were

nationalist meetings in Istanbul, and intense organisational and protest activity in the provinces, under the slogans of 'defence of rights'
and 'rejection of annexation' (*müdafaa-i hukuk, redd-i ilhak*).
Mustafa Kemal attended a regional congress of these Defence of
Rights groups at Erzurum (23 July–7 August 1919), and himself
called a nationwide Defence of Rights congress to Sivas (4–11
September).

Yet even while these Anatolian activities were in full bloom,
Mustafa Kemal was careful not to cut his movement off from the
capital, and to keep open the possibility of a resumed Istanbul
strategy. When his friends in the war office tipped him off that, in
view of his unauthorised political activities, he was about to be
recalled to Istanbul, he resigned from the military service before the
official order could reach him. The most immediate political
demand of the Erzurum and Sivas Congresses was for early elections
for a new House of Representatives, and by October 1919 the
Anatolian nationalists seemed to have won a full political victory.
The Sultan dismissed the anglophile Damad Ferid Paşa, the new
grand vezir called for elections, Unionist and nationalist candidates
won an overwhelming election victory, and on 28 January 1920 the
new House unanimously endorsed the National Pact.

The domestic political victory precipitated a renewed foreign crisis.
In early March, the Supreme Allied Council decided on full-scale
military occupation of Istanbul. On March 15 and 16, the occupation forces began their round-up of nationalist leaders, five of them
being arrested in the very building of the House of Representatives.
Mustafa Kemal's response was to call to Ankara an 'Assembly with
extraordinary powers', or (as he later called it) Grand National
Assembly. It opened on 23 April 1920, including some 200 deputies
from those parts of Anatolia under Kemalist control, and some ninety
members of the Istanbul House who had made their way past the
Allied occupation forces in the capital.

The break between Istanbul and Ankara became complete as
Damad Ferid was reappointed to the office of grand vezir. In a series
of *fetvas* issued in April 1920, the highest religious dignitary in the
Sultan's government, the *Şeyhülislam*, declared the Anatolian
movement to be in open rebellion against the Sultan, and its
members to be outlaws whom every devout Muslim ought to kill. But
even then Kemal proved solicitous to maintain the thread of
Ottoman-Muslim legitimacy as far as possible. A set of counter-
fetvas, signed by the Müftü of Ankara, and endorsed by 152 other
Anatolian *müftüs* declared null and void the pronouncements of a
government and monarch who, by virtue of enemy occupation of
the capital, had become prisoners of the infidel enemy. And indeed

it is clear, from documents published since, that the *fetva* by Şeyhülislam Dürrizade Abdullah was issued at the request of Allied occupation authorities.

Soon Sultan Mehmed VI Vahideddin was dispatching military units — known as the Disciplinary Forces or the Army of the Caliphate — against the Kemalist 'rebels'. Loyalist uprisings in various locations of Central Anatolia in the spring of 1920 added to the danger. Yet by the summer of 1920, the Kemalist forces and the Ankara Assembly had established their authority throughout Central and Eastern Anatolia — and thus prevailed in the gravest and most direct confrontation with Istanbul.

The stage thus was set for the more important external aspect of the experiment: whether the military and popular resistance organised in Anatolia could assert itself against the foreign invading forces; or whether the Sultan's policy of co-operation with the victorious Allied powers — leading ultimately to the humiliating peace treaty of Sèvres — was the only feasible course. Where the Sultan's forces had failed to quell the Kemalist 'rebellion', Greek armies now undertook to 'pacify' the Turkish hinterland. In July 1920, they occupied the ancient Ottoman capitals of Bursa and Edirne. The offensive of the summer of 1921 carried them to within 30 miles of Ankara — where the government was making preparations to move to Kayseri.

But such a move turned out to be unnecessary. Under Mustafa Kemal's personal command, the Turkish nationalist forces defeated the Greeks in the decisive battle on the Sakarya in September 1921. The following summer's campaign was a further series of Kemalist victories. In September 1922 the Greek troops evacuated Anatolia, and the following month the British and French units evacuated Istanbul. Turkish national independence had been asserted by military force within the 1918 armistice lines: the goal of Kemal's 'National Pact' was attained.

Diplomatic successes kept pace with the military advances. In August 1920, the Ankara Assembly sent its first foreign mission to Russia, where the Soviet government was waging a similar nationalist and revolutionary struggle against forces dispatched or supported by the Allies. In March 1920, Moscow and Ankara signed a formal friendship treaty. The punitive peace treaty of Sèvres in the meantime had been recognised by the Allies to be a dead letter. When the British government in February 1921 invited both an Istanbul and an Ankara delegation to renewed peace talks in London, the Istanbul spokesman decided to yield the floor to the delegate from Ankara. In August 1921, even before the decisive battle on the Sakarya, the Supreme Allied Council in Paris decided to remain neutral in the war between Greeks and Kemalists. In March 1921, the French government became the first of the major Allies to conclude a diplomatic agreement with Ankara. Following the Kemalist military victory of 1922, the Allies made a last divisive attempt by inviting delegations from both Istanbul and Ankara to a renewed peace conference; but in view of the Ankara Assembly's decision to abolish the Sultanate, and the Sultan's flight abroad, it soon became clear that only the Ankara government would negotiate for Turkey. After months of tenacious bargaining, Ismet Inönü — the nationalist field commander turned diplomat — signed the peace treaty of Lausanne on 24 July 1923; this constituted a full vindication of the Kemalist position.

The remainder of the experiment was internal. The abolition of the Sultanate (1 November 1922) left the form of government ambiguous. The Ankara Assembly had for some time exercised the attributes of sovereignty. The choice of the traditional birthday of the Prophet Muhammad as 'National Sovereignty Day' and the election of the Ottoman crown prince Abdülmecid to the office of 'Caliph of Muslims' (*Halife-i Muslimin*) fitted in with the widespread desire for an Islamic-populist state. Mustafa Kemal's own position of unquestioned authority within the Assembly and the nation might have pointed in the direction of a secular monarchy. Mustafa Kemal made it clear that the question would have to wait until after the peace treaty. It was finally resolved by the proclamation of the republic (30 October 1923), the election of Mustafa Kemal as its President, and by the abolition four months later of the Caliphate (3 March 1924).

The process of *institution-building* began as the experimental phase was proceeding — indeed soon after Mustafa Kemal arrived in Anatolia. At the end of the Erzurum Congress (7 August 1919) the assembled delegates formed a Society for the Defence of Rights of the Eastern Provinces, and a few days later Mustafa Kemal registered with the *vilayet* of Erzurum the formation of a representative committee (*hey'et-i temsiliye*) for that Association. At the Sivas Congress the movement was enlarged into a Society for the Defence of Rights of Anatolia and Rumelia (that is, Asiatic and European Turkey, listed in that order); the Representative Committee continued its intensive activity, and on 13 September Mustafa Kemal declared it to be the 'nation's agency for communication' (*milletin merci-i muhaberatı*).

One immediate purpose of this organisational activity was to substitute for the loss of Mustafa Kemal's official assignment from Istanbul: the very day that he was elected chairman of the Representative Committee, the Istanbul government expelled him from the military forces, cashiered his rank, and withdrew his military decorations. But 'agency for communication' also indicated the main activity in which Mustafa Kemal had been engaging since his arrival in Anatolia three months earlier. As he explained later,

I was faced with the necessity of piecing together with the greatest care and sensitivity all the private and public opinions and sentiments, to gauge the real trend and to arrive at a feasible decision . . . So as to secure the application of a decision it was also very important to ascertain the point of view of the army.[8]

His contacts with the army continued unimpaired regardless of the Istanbul government's measures against him: General Karabekir, after learning of the Istanbul government's recall order, saluted him ceremoniously and made it clear that he would continue to consider him his superior. The same *de facto* co-operation continued with his close friend Ali Fuat (Cebesoy), commander of the 20th army corps at Ankara, which officially had never been included in Kemal's army inspectorate.

The major purpose of the network of communication which Kemal was busy setting up in the summer and autumn of 1919 was to organise the necessary civilian support to enable those military units to undertake the task of national resistance. But beyond that, the communications system could also be used for political pressure toward the outside. To convince his adversaries in Istanbul and in London that the nationalist movement could not be quelled, he set out 'to make the world hear the nation's voice in robust tones'. A secret circular from Ankara in the spring of 1920, for example, unloosed a 'whirlwind of telegrams' so as to forestall an unfavourable cabinet change in Istanbul. In only three days, as many as 217 of these were received by the House of Representatives alone, which duly reprinted them in its minutes. Others went to the Sultan's palace and various ministries. How many the British Embassy in Istanbul may have received over the months, we do not know, since its chief political officer, the Dragoman, stuffed them uncounted, and perhaps unread, into what he aptly called the '*vox populi* sack'. Once, when the Istanbul war minister inquired about the origin of such floods of messages, Kemal replied with an air of great innocence that these were 'entirely an expression of the grief and concern emanating from the bosom of the nation'.[9]

An American newspaper correspondent who visited Kemal's headquarters at Sivas in September was full of admiration: 'I have never heard of more efficient communications. [. . .] Within half an hour, Erzurum, Erzinjan, [. . .] Diyarbekir, Samsun, Trebizond,

Angora, Malatya, Kharput, Konya, and Brusa were all in communication.' Later, when a Turkish journalist asked Mustafa Kemal how he had won the war of independence, he replied smilingly: 'With the telegraph wires.'[10]

Telegraphic communication, of course, was a technique that Kemal carried over directly from his military to his civilian activity. Before leaving Istanbul for his Anatolian assignment, he had arranged for a personal cipher to be used only between himself and the war ministry, and we already noted that he specifically secured authority to communicate directly with a wide range of military and civilian officials within and beyond his own army inspectorate. One of his rare public outbursts of anger recorded in this period occurred when a hostile minister in Istanbul undertook to cut off the telegraphic link between Kemal's Ankara headquarters and the Sultan's palace: 'Cowards, criminals', he fulminated; 'You are preventing the nation from making submissions to its monarch . . . Get some sense into your heads . . . As you sell your consciences to foreigners, . . . keep in mind the responsibility which the nation will be exacting from you.'[11] Yet the network of communications in Anatolia itself was extensive and secure enough to provide the basis for a political system that would have no need to appeal to a timid monarch closeted in his palace. The daily newspaper which the Kemalist movement began to issue at the time of the Sivas Congress was called 'National Will' (*Irade-i Milliye*); as the movement transferred its headquarters to Ankara, and the National Assembly began its operations, the title became 'National Sovereignty' (*Hakimiyet-i Milliye*).

Kemal's concern, throughout his early Anatolian years, was to find a secure popular basis for the movement of national resistance, while avoiding a break with Istanbul for as long as possible. His technique of disguising the novelty of the institutions he was creating served both to maximise support in Anatolia and to postpone the showdown with Istanbul. Thus, as already noted, he spoke of a 'representative committee' to be 'the nation's agency for communication', not of a provisional government; he called for an 'assembly with extraordinary powers', not for a constituent assembly; and even after he changed its name to 'Grand National Assembly' he left it open whether it was a Turkish or an Ottoman nation in whose name the delegates were assembled.

How essential such caution was to his effective leadership in those early days was illustrated by an incident in that Assembly in May 1920. One of the members of the *de facto* cabinet, the commissioner of health, had emphatically referred to the Anatolian movement as a Turkish movement, and this drew a strong protest from a delegate of Circassian background. Mustafa Kemal, as the presiding officer, intervened to say: 'Gentlemen, with the request that this matter should not come up again, let me point out that what is intended here . . . are not only Turks, not only Kurds, not only Lazes, but the Muslim elements comprising all of these, a sincere community'.[12]

The converse of such cautious delaying tactics was the announcement of major innovations as *faits accomplis*. When the Ankara Assembly on 1 November 1922 abolished the monarchy, it did so upon a motion that declared that the Sultanate had ceased to exist on 16 March 1920, the day of the reinforced British occupation of Istanbul (even though, at that time, the Kemalists had loudly proclaimed their loyalty to their Sultan who, unfortunately, had been captured by the enemy). In proposing the proclamation of a 'Republic of Turkey' a year later, the Kemalists emphasised that the essential decision had been taken two or three years earlier. ' "Sovereignty belongs unconditionally to the nation". Once you have said that, ask whomever you like, and they will tell you that it means a republic. That is the name of the newborn child.'[13] The Sultanate was not declared abolished until after the nationalist military victory had been confirmed by the armistice of Mudanya on 11 October 1922. Similarly, the most drastic measures breaking with the past — the proclamation of the Republic (29 October 1923) and the abolition of the Caliphate (3 March 1924) — were delayed until well after the signing of the peace treaty of Lausanne (24 July 1923).

Camouflage first, and rapid surprise moves later: this adaptation of military tactics to the political arena testified to Kemal's keen power instincts. In a setting where organised opposition could readily have overwhelmed his radical program, his public statements suggested first that opposition was unnecessary and later that it would be hopeless. Thus at all times he kept in full control of both the direction and the pace of events.

The proclamation of the Republic, the abolition of the Caliphate and the adoption of European law codes in 1926 completed Mustafa Kemal's major institutional innovations. His achievement was revolutionary in that it enforced a drastic change of direction from the Ottoman and Islamic past, and implemented a program of nationalism and integral westernisation that, only a decade or two before, would have seemed visionary and unrealistic. (When the poet Mehmed Emin in 1896 boasted 'I am a Turk . . .', this was shrugged off in polite Ottoman society as the rantings of an autodidact who had begun his life as a fisherman; and as late as 1913, Abdullah Cevdet, presented his programme of radical westernisation as a utopian dream.[14]) But the Turkish transformation never generated any uncontrolled, accelerating momentum such as was characteristic of the English, French and Russian (or more recently the Iranian) revolutions. The threads of legitimacy were severely strained, but there was never any break in institutional continuity, never any organisational vacuum. The new institutions proved durable in part because they had been prepared and tested, both for their support at home and their recognition abroad, before they were irrevocably announced. There followed those dramatic changes of external symbolism — dress, alphabet, calendar, family names — and the intensive educational effort that were noted earlier, and which, taken together, may be considered the fourth, or *consolidation* phase of Atatürk's achievement.

The substitution of national for dynastic sovereignty implied a momentous change; yet in at least two basic respects, Atatürk's political achievement was true to the Ottoman tradition. The Ottoman empire had started as a military organisation that expanded into an administrative establishment that came to rule, with remarkable efficiency and tolerance, over populations on parts of three continents. Yet the military establishment and the military effort had always remained at the core of the Ottoman political system. The unending string of military defeats since 1774 resulting in enemy occupation of the Sultan's very capital, therefore implied an irreparable loss of legitimacy. By contrast, Mustafa Kemal had asserted the new principle of national sovereignty in a series of military victories — won, as it happens, on the same Bithynian battlefields which had first launched the Ottoman armies on their own series of victories. And Atatürk's shift, following those victories, to a major educational effort was equally true to the original Ottoman spirit: the palace school in which the sultans trained their military officers and civil servants had been among the most characteristic Ottoman institutions from the earliest days.

These elements of continuity, along with Kemal's cautious technique of implementation, all lent durability to his radical programme of innovation. A further source of strength was the combination of élitism and democracy characteristic of Kemal's political ethos — a combination that allowed the Kemalist movement to play a pivotal role in the course of Turkish social history.

The Ottoman policy of westernisation, through which the empire defended itself against the overwhelming European threat, had resulted, by the late nineteenth century, in the emergence of a new ruling class. The major training centres for this westernised Ottoman élite were the *Harbiye*, or military school, founded in 1834, the *Mülkiye*, or civil service school, dating from 1859; other schools were devoted to the training of schoolteachers. Although many of the pupils of those schools were themselves the sons of officers or civil servants in Istanbul, a growing proportion were recruited from the Muslim population of large and small towns throughout the empire. Muslims from the European provinces — Turks, Albanians, Bosniaks — were over-represented; Arabs from the Asian and African provinces were under-represented; and non-Muslims, such as Greeks, Slavs, Armenians, Maronites and Jews, were under-represented at the *Mülkiye* and excluded from the *Harbiye*. This rather skewed recruitment to some extent foreshadowed the gradual transformation of the multinational Ottoman empire into a Turkish nation-state; yet it is noteworthy that the Society of Union and Progress of 1889, which represented the first spontaneous and durable political organisation within this new élite, was founded in 1889 by five students at the military medical college in Istanbul, of whom one was Albanian, two were Kurds and two (a Circassian and an Azeri) from the Caucasus — none of whom, that is to say, was an Ottoman Turk.[15]

On completion of their training, the members of this Ottoman political élite were assigned to posts throughout the empire — the civil servants to large and small towns as provincial or district administrators, the military officers to troublesome frontier districts such as Macedonia or the Arab provinces, the teachers to secondary schools in the major cities. Frequent rotation of assignments tended to reinforce the homogeneous character of this bureaucratic élite and to provide a minimum of cohesion for the far-flung Ottoman state.

With the empire's disintegration, some members of this Ottoman élite continued their careers in successor-states such as Albania, Syria or Iraq. Thus the group of young Arab nationalists who rallied around Sharif Faisal in the Arab revolt of 1916, in the short-lived Syrian kingdom of 1920, and in the kingdom of Iraq after 1921 were mostly graduates of the Ottoman military school of Iraqi background. Yet the vast majority of the late Ottoman imperial élite remained in what became the Turkish Republic — the proportion among *Mülkiye* graduates being 85 per cent and among the graduates of the general staff course of the *Harbiye* as high as 93 per cent.[16] Although this élite had been unable to keep together and defend the overextended Ottoman empire, it furnished the essential trained cadres who, under Mustafa Kemal's circumspect and energetic leadership, instituted the more compact Republic of Turkey.

Mustafa Kemal himself was trained as a member of this late Ottoman élite. But his search for effective means of saving the Turkish-populated remnant of the defeated empire led him far beyond the empire's élitist tradition. In his first speech on arriving in the town of Ankara in December 1919 (which comes closest to outlining his entire political creed in a single document), he acknowledged that 'at the beginning of any enterprise there is need . . . to go from above downward'. Therefore 'certain initiators are providing guidance in giving to nations the directions they need to be given. In this way organisation can be built from above downward'.[17]

Yet he was keenly aware that the enterprise could not succeed unless there was a strong response from below:

Today the nations of the whole world recognise only one sovereignty: national sovereignty. . . . we begin our work from the village and the neighborhood and from the people of the neighborhood, that is, from the individual. [. . .] A structure that in this way rises from below to the top, from the foundation to the roof, will surely be sturdy.[18]

His appeals to national sovereignty, his proclamation of the Republic, his abolition of the monarchical institutions of Sultanate and Caliphate, his replacement of traditional Islamic with modern Western symbols all served the same overall purpose — of winning for his nation a condition of independence that would be so securely rooted in the sentiments and devotion of every Turkish citizen as to force its acceptance and recognition by 'the nations of the whole world'.

Kemal Atatürk thus was an élitist by training, and often by bearing, but he was a populist by political necessity and by ideological conviction. The political institutions he created for his Republic were democratic: universal suffrage, exercise of all the attributes of sovereignty by an elected assembly, election of the president of the Republic by that same assembly for a period co-extensive with its own term. For several decades, these democratic institutions were in practice attenuated by the monarchical and aristocratic elements implicit in a one-party regime with strong personalist leadership. The experiments with the Republican Progressive Party of 1924–5 and with the Free Republican Party of 1930 showed that neither Atatürk personally nor the Turkish political élite collectively were ready to proceed to a full-fledged multi-party democracy. Yet when Atatürk's successor Ismet Inönü in 1945 judged the time ripe to proceed in that direction, there was no need for substantial revisions in the Constitution, laws, or symbols left behind from the Atatürk period. Indeed the simple announcement by Inönü that the time had come to take more seriously the democratic professions of Turkey's constitution and his own party's program was enough to launch the democratisation process in its next phase.[19]

The Atatürk revolution has thus been followed by a further social transformation — including the transition from a personalist one-party regime to a competitive multi-party system, rapid development in agriculture and industry, and an explosion of rising expectations and social conflicts. In this more recent revolution the going has not all been smooth. Repeated military interventions in the democratic process (1960/1, 1971/3, 1980/?); periodic severe economic slumps and foreign payments difficulties; and the mounting wave of terrorism of the 1970s have been among the more obvious symptoms of the difficulties.

Yet it is notable that, despite the widening scope and intensity of political controversy, Atatürk's major institutions remain unquestioned. There has never been any movement for restoration of the Sultanate or Caliphate. While literacy based on the Latin alphabet is steadily increasing, only a small minority of Turks know the Arabic script. (The spoken and written language itself has changed so rapidly — in line with Atatürk's own attempts at purification of Turkish from Arabic and Persian elements — that his own *Great Speech* of 1926 is now commonly printed in an adapted semi-translated version). Women are far closer to full social equality than in Atatürk's own day. The massive movement of 'guest workers' to factories in West Germany and elsewhere in Europe — and back to Turkey — is spreading to the lower classes the westernising revolution that started with Vezirs and Paşas in Ottoman days, and progressed to lieutenants and schoolteachers during the Kemalist period. Whatever the difficulties of Turkey's current democratic revolution, whatever the political and ideological controversies, and whatever the mounting social tensions, Atatürk's legacy is securely embodied in the political institutions of the Turkish nation-state.

NOTES

1. Cevdet's article 'A Very Wakeful Sleep' was published in the journal *Içtinad*, no. 89 (Istanbul 1913); quoted here from Bernard Lewis, *The Emergence of Modern Turkey* (2nd edn., London: Oxford University Press, 1968), 236. Âkif's hymn, first published in the Kemalist movement's official newspaper *Hakimiyet-i Milliye* on 17 February 1921, was designated by the Ankara Assembly (12 March) as the 'Independence March'; the first eight lines are the national anthem of the Turkish Republic. The quotation (my translation) is from lines 15–16. The following reference to Akif alludes to lines 17–18:

Comrade, don't let the dastards enter in your land.
Make your breast a shield and foil their shameless hand.

2. Decree of 11 November 1928.
3. The protracted battle, named after Gallipoli in British and after Çanakkale in Turkish military annals, was decisive: had it been lost by the

Ottomans, the Allied navies would have had clear sailing through the Dardanelles in 1915, or this would have led to the occupation of Istanbul, ended the Ottoman war effort, and allowed the Western allies to reinforce the Russian front well before the collapse and revolution of 1917.

4. The flight of the three leaders, presumably, was prompted by fear of political trials or courts martial that would have awaited them in Istanbul. Ironically, none of the three escaped a violent death — Talat (Berlin, 15 March 1921) and Cemal (Tbilisi, 21 July 1922) at the hands of Armenian assassins of the radical nationalist Dashnak party; Enver in a local skirmish of Uzbek nationalist forces against superior Bolshevik units (Dushanbe, 4 August 1922). On the latter two, see my articles 'Djemal Pasha', and 'Enwer Pasha', *Encyclopaedia of Islam*, 2nd edn; Leiden, E.J. Brill, 1959, vol. II, 531–2 and 698–702.

5. *Nutuk: Gazi Mustafa Kemal Tarafından*, Ankara, 1934, vol. I, 194.

6. See Mustafa Kemal's memoirs of the 1916–19 period, published in part in 1926, and more extensively by Falih Rıfkı Atay, (ed.), *Atatürk'ün Bana Anlattıkları*, Ankara, 1955, 94ff.

7. *ibid.*, 124.Cf. the article 'Atatürk', *Türk Islam Ansiklopedisi*, I, 733.

8. *Nutuk, op. cit.*, I, 194.

9. *ibid.*, I, 286 and passim; Sir Andrew Ryan, *The Last of the Dragomans* (London, 1951). The above passage is adapted from my essay 'Atatürk as Founder of a State' in D.A. Rustow (ed.), *Philosophers and Kings: Studies in Leadership*, New York, Braziller, 1970, 217 (previously published in *Daedalus*, vol. 97 [1968], no. 3).

10. Louis Browne of the Chicago *Daily News*, quoted by Patrick Balfour [Lord Kinross], *Atatürk: The Rebirth of a Nation* (London, 1964), 193; Enver Behnan Şapolyo, *Kemal Atatürk ve Millî Mücadele Tarihi* (3rd edn, Istanbul 1958), 349. See also the lavish public praise which Kemal bestowed on the telegraph operators in the *Great Speech* (*Nutuk, op. cit.*, I, 139).

11. *ibid.*, I, 94.

12. See the proceedings of the Assembly, 1 May 1920 (*T.B.M.M. Zabit Ceridesi*, Devre I, Ictima 1, vol. 1, 3rd edn, Ankara 1959, 165; the 'T' in the title for Türkiye, is an inadvertent anachronism of the editors.

13. *Nutuk, op. cit.*, II, 274, quoting the historian Abdurrahman Şeref.

14. See Cevdet's title, above, note 1. The 'Young Turks', who received that appellation by their European hosts in their political exiles, back home called themselves 'New Ottomans', or the 'Ottoman Society for Union and Progress'. Until the turn of the century, the adjective Turk was used mainly as a designation for the illiterate peasantry of Anatolia. Mehmed Emin (Yurdakul) in the years of the Republic was celebrated as a leading nationalist poet.

15. The first three were non-Turkish Ottomans, the fourth neither Ottoman nor Turkish by background, and the fifth a Turk from outside the empire. (There is, however, some dispute whether this fifth was included among the actual founders. See Lewis, *op. cit.*, 197.)

16. See my article, 'The Military: Turkey', in R.E. Ward and D.A. Rustow (eds.), *Political Modernisation in Japan and Turkey*, Princeton, 1964, 388. The tabulation is based on biographical directories published in

Turkey, and includes only graduates for whom information on later careers is in those sources; the small proportion of 'unknowns' may bias the count slightly in favour of those remaining in Turkey.

17. See the speech of 28 December 1919, reprinted in *Nutuk*, *op. cit.*, III, 259; and *Söylev*, *op. cit.*, II, 12. The latter source gives the date erroneously as 28 December 1920, the other gives no date.

18. *Nutuk*, III, 259; *Söylev*, II, 11.

19. President Inönü's speech was given on 19 May 1945, the twenty-sixth anniversary of Mustafa Kemal Paşa's arrival in Anatolia.

The nature of the Kemalist political regime

ERGUN ÖZBUDUN

Introduction

Much has been written on various aspects of the Kemalist experiment in Turkey, including its political aspects. A large part of this writing, however, remains descriptive rather than analytical, concentrating on the unique aspects of the Kemalist regime. The aim of the present essay is to provide a more theoretical and comparative perspective on the nature of the Kemalist political regime. We hope that such an attempt may also contribute to the recently growing body of theoretical writings on regime changes and transitions, as well as on authoritarian regimes.

One reason for the considerable interest the Kemalist regime should present for the comparative political analyst is that it is one of the very few cases of a peaceful transition from an authoritarian to a democratic polity. Sartori, for example, has forcefully argued that competitive and non-competitive party systems cannot be placed along a single conceptual continuum. In other words, one type of system does not spontaneously change into another, such system change can only occur discontinuously, i.e., 'via system breakdown': In his view, 'along the continuum of party politics there is a point at which we are definitely confronted, as a rule, with a break, and thereby with a boundary. While the one party can be easily transformed into a hegemonic party, the step that follows is a most difficult one. The loosening of a monocentric system occurs either in the form of a lessening of coercive control, or by switching from the single party to the hegemonic party arrangement, but the evidence largely confirms that neither is a takeoff position in the direction of pluralism . . . [A] free polity requires the establishment of a different system, of a system based on entirely different principles and mechanisms.'[1] Linz observes similarly, but somewhat less categorically, that 'if we were to accept the interpretation that such [authoritarian] regimes lie on a continuum between democracy and totalitarianism, we should find many examples of transitions from authoritarianism to one or the other without serious crises or revolutionary changes. This however does not seem to be the case; even when the transition to some kind of democracy has been done with little bloodshed, the democracy has often been unstable. Evolutionary cases are rare.'[2]

The exceptional character of this transition in Turkey can be explained, at least partly, by the nature of the Kemalist political regime itself. Although it was an authoritarian regime, many of its characteristics made it a logical candidate for potential democratisation. We will discuss the historical origins, social basis, ideology, and organisation of the Kemalist single-party, the Republican People's Party (RPP), since each of these variables had, in our opinion, an impact on the eventual democratisation in the mid-1940s. In discussing each variable, an effort will be made to evaluate it in the light of recent theories on authoritarianism. Finally, we will try to place the RPP rule in Turkey in the current typologies of authoritarian regimes. The actual process of transition to a multi-party system will not be dealt with here, since we would like to focus on the nature of the political regime as it evolved in Kemal Atatürk's lifetime.

The origins of the RPP

The RPP was officially founded on 9 September 1923. Its origins, however, go back to the years of the Turkish War of National Independence (1919–22). In fact, the RPP was based on the former Defence of Rights societies created to resist the Greek and Allied invasion of parts of Turkish homeland after the end of the First World War. At first, these societies were only local resistance groups with no national co-ordination and unity. One of Mustafa Kemal's great acts of leadership was to forge a unified nationalist movement out of a myriad of such groups. With this purpose in mind, he first organised a regional congress in Erzurum (23 July 1919) sponsored by the Society for the Defence of Rights of Eastern Anatolia, and then a nation-wide congress in Sivas (9 September 1919) at which all Defence of Rights societies were united into a single organisation, thenceforth called the Society for the Defense of Rights of Anatolia and Rumelia. The culmination of these efforts was the opening of the Turkish Grand National Assembly in Ankara on 23 April 1920, following the reinforced occupation of Istanbul by the Allied forces and the dissolution of the last Ottoman parliament.

The First Grand National Assembly (1920–3) functioned as a constituent assembly in all but name, and was an extremely important instrument in providing a legal basis and popular legitimacy for the nationalist movement. Although all its members were united in the goal of securing the country's independence and territorial integrity, they were deeply divided on almost every other issue. There were radical reformers and political conservatives, secular minded intel-

lectuals and men of religion, even a few members of communist lean-
ings. Many were former members of the now defunct Union and
Progress Party of the second consitutionalist period (1908–18).[3]
While no formal political parties existed in the First Assembly, many
small groups or factions emerged almost from the beginning. To
impose some semblance of order on the Assembly proceedings,
Mustafa Kemal formed his own supporters into a group called the
'Defence of Rights Group of Anatolia and Rumelia,' more commonly known as the First Group (10 May 1921). This move
prompted the conservative opponents of Kemal to form their own
group, called the Second Group. While the First Group usually commanded a majority in the Assembly, the demarcation line between
the two was not clear and members switched easily from one side to
the other. Consequently, the Second Group was able to carry the day
on some important votes.[4]

In the months following the victorious termination of the War of
Independence, Kemal disclosed to some journalists his intention to
establish a political party based on populist principles. It was to be
called the People's Party. The party was officially established about
a year later, in September 1923. In the mean time, the Grand
National Assembly decided to hold new elections, and in the elections of August 1923, no member of the opposition Second Group
could get re-elected. But there soon developed another opposition to
Kemal in the newly elected second term of the Assembly. This opposition was led by some generals closely associated with Kemal during
the years of the War of Independence, and soon organised itself into
a political party, the Progressive Republican Party, on 17 November
1924. However, the Sheikh Said revolt that broke out in the Eastern
provinces in February 1925 brought this multi-party experiment to
an abrupt end. The 'Law for the Maintenance of Order', passed on
4 March 1925, gave the government wide extraordinary powers.
Martial law was declared, and the Independence Tribunals (revolutionary courts created in 1920 to deal with treasonable activities)
were reactivated. The Progressive Republican Party was closed on
3 June 1925, by a decision of the Council of Ministers which implicated it with the revolt although no concrete proof of such a connection was established. Thus the Republican People's Party (RPP)
ruled Turkey from 1925 to 1945 without the presence of an opposition party, except for the brief Free Party interlude in 1930 to be discussed below.

Several points seem worth emphasising in connection with the formative years of the RPP. First, it took several years for Mustafa
Kemal and the RPP to consolidate their monopolistic position. Both
in the First and Second Assemblies, the RPP and its predecessor the

First Group encountered serious organised opposition. Rustow distinguishes three periods in the development of the Kemalist regime: the War of Independence, when Kemal broadly rallied all available forces; a second period (1923 – 7), when he forcibly consolidated his authority; and a third, when he exercised it with leniency.[5] A second characteristic of great importance is that the RPP was not created top-down as an effectively centralised instrument after the consolidation of power by Kemal. On the contrary, it was based on the amalgamation of various pre-existing local resistance groups. Such local Defence of Rights societies naturally included people from different social backgrounds and with different political values. No matter how much unity and centralisation was imposed upon the nationalist movement in later years, the RPP still retained some of the pluralistic characteristics associated with its origins. This may have contributed to the smoothness of the transition to a competitive system in the 1940s.

The social basis of the RPP

Such pluralistic features can perhaps best be seen in the social composition of the RPP. The party has generally been described as having been born out of an alliance between the central military-bureaucratic-intellectual élite and local notables. The local Defence of Rights societies were often led by military officers and government officials, many of whom had previous connections with the Union and Progress Party.[6] But in an extremely war-weary country, these officials needed the support of local notables in order to mobilise human and material resources for their war efforts, particularly since they did not have the backing of the official government in Istanbul. Such support was not always forthcoming. Local notables, most of them landlords and merchants, did not display a consistent pattern of behaviour in this regard at least in the early stages of the nationalist struggle. Many took an active part in organising or supporting the local Defence of Rights societies, but many others balked; some supported the Sultan's efforts to suppress the nationalist movement, and some even chose to reach an accomodation with the enemy. Local participation in the resistance movement was greatest in those regions that were likely to be permanently annexed by the invading foreign forces, namely the Aegean provinces and Eastern Thrace on the one hand and the Eastern provinces on the other threatened respectively by the Greeks and by the Armenians.[7] In contrast, most of the anti-nationalist revolts instigated by the Istanbul government took place in central Anatolia, which was not immediately threatened by enemy occupation: Bolu, Konya, Ilgin, Yozgat, and so on.

In addition to local notables, religious leaders, namely scholars of Islam (*ülema*) and the heads of Islamic brotherhoods (*şeyh*), constituted the only other force capable of mobilising local popular support for resistance. As with the notables, not all religious leaders supported the nationalists. Some openly sided with the Sultan and his government in Istanbul, which in turn collaborated with the invaders. But many others gave their wholehearted support to the nationalist cause. For example, when the *Şeyhülislam* (the head of the official religious hierarchy) of the Istanbul government issued a *fetva* (religious opinion) declaring that the killing of the rebels (i.e. the nationalists) was a religious duty, 153 Anatolian *müftüs* countered with an opposite *fetva* declaring that a *fetva* issued under foreign duress was invalid and that to resist foreign occupation was a paramount religious duty.[8]

The composition of the Defense of Rights Congresses and of the First Grand National Assembly shows the heterogeneous nature of the nationalist movement. For example, out of the fifty-four delegates to the Erzurum Congress, seventeen were local notables (landlords and merchants), six were religious leaders, and the rest came from official and professional backgrounds.[9] The First Grand National Assembly (1920–3) included, in addition to a large number of officials (43 per cent), a substantial element engaged in trade (12 per cent) and agriculture (6 per cent), and many members in religious occupations (17 per cent).[10] Thus, although the officials (the military-bureaucratic élite) were the leading element in the nationalist movement, they had to combine their efforts with those of local notables and religious leaders.

In discussing the social basis of the RPP, it should be borne in mind that the Turkish revolution was not a social revolution; rather, it combined features of a war of national liberation and of a political revolution.[11] As such, it was not directed against a particular social class, but against foreign enemies and their Turkish collaborators. Consequently, it sought a cross-class appeal, and did not produce clearly identifiable coalitions of class interest. Thus one cannot discern clear differences between the social backgrounds of, respectively, the nationalists and those who supported the Sultan and rebelled against the nationalist government in the early years of the War of Independence. Although little systematic evidence is available on the sociological characteristics of the anti-nationalist rebels, it appears that they also brought together some government officials and many local notables and religious functionaries.[12] Regarding the 'political' nature of the Turkish revolution, it must be emphasised that its revolutionary character derived from its re-definition of the bases of political legitimation and the boundaries of the political community. It appears exaggerated, however, to argue that 'this shift was connected with an almost total displacement of the former ruling class.'[13] Again, little difference exists in the social backgrounds of the Kemalist and the Unionist political élites.

After the Greek invasion of Anatolia was decisively defeated in 1922 and the final peace treaty was signed in Lausanne in 1923, Kemal and his supporters turned their attention to secularising reforms, such as the abolition of the Caliphate and of the Ministry of Şeriat, the closing of religious schools, the abolition of the Şeriat courts, the adoption of Western codes of law, the closing of the derviş convents and the ban on the activities of Islamic brotherhoods (tarikat), the adoption of the latin alphabet and international numerals, the banning of the traditional Muslim fez headgear and so on. Such moves obviously put an end to the wartime co-operation between nationalist officials and religious elements. This can be seen in the declining number of people in religious occupations among the members of the Grand National Assembly. Their percentage fell from seventeen in 1920 to eleven in 1923, four in 1927, three in 1931, two in 1939, and one in 1943.[14]

Another wartime alliance, however, continued throughout the single-party years, namely that between the military-bureaucratic élite at the national level and small-town and rural notables at the local level. Frey has convincingly shown that the official element was dominant at the level of the national legislature during the single-party years, but that in the Assembly there was also a sizeable group of locally based deputies (Table 1). It is probable that this finding accurately reflects the relative strengths of the two elements in the RPP coalition: the military-bureaucratic élite was the major partner, but local notables also wielded considerable influence particularly at the local level.

This ruling coalition differs from the 'reactionary coalition' described by Moore[15] in that its military-bureaucratic component was the dominant element instead of being an instrument for landed and industrial interests. It has often been observed that in the Islamic Middle East, due to the absence of feudalism in the Western sense of the word, the military (and the civilian bureaucracy) did not have strong social and political links with the landed upper strata. Instead, the officers were recruited 'from various social groups including the very lowest' and they had their 'primary attachments to the government'. The interplay of social background and professional socialisation factors led to a 'statist', and in some Middle Eastern countries a more distinctly socialistic, orientation among them.[16] Thus the alliance between the Turkish military-bureaucratic élite and the landed interests was the outcome of the political

CHANGES IN THE OCCUPATIONAL COMPOSITION OF THE GRAND
NATIONAL ASSEMBLY IN ONE-PARTY YEARS (1920–46)
(percentages)

Occupation	I 1920	II 1923	III 1927	IV 1931	V 1935	VI 1939	VII 1943	VIII 1946
Official	43	54	54	45	48	47	47	36
Professional	18	20	22	22	24	27	31	35
Economic	19	14	16	22	19	19	16	24
Others	21	11	9	10	8	7	5	4

Source: Adapted from F. W. Frey, *The Turkish Political Elite*, Cambridge, Mass., M.I.T. Press, 1965, 181. The 'official' category includes government, military and education. 'Professionals' include lawyers, medical doctors, dentists, pharmacists and veterinarians. 'Economic' occupations are agriculture, trade and banking. 'Others' include religion and journalism.

exigencies of the War of Independence period, rather than the inevitable result of compelling social and economic factors. After the consolidation of the regime, such co-operation could continue, since the Kemalists' emphasis on secularising reforms did not pose a threat to the interests of local notables. If anything, their influence seems to have increased through their newly-won government and party connections.

A second major difference between the Turkish case and the reactionary coalition is the absence of business interests in the former. Turkey in the 1920s was a predominantly agrarian country with only insignificant industry. In 1922, there were a total of 75,411 industrial workers scattered among 32,721 manufacturing 'establishments', an average of 2.3 workers per establishment. Almost two-thirds of such dwarf establishments were in textiles, i.e. family looms. Another figure, based on the 1913–15 census of manufacturing industries and evidently using a somewhat more stringent criterion, put the total number of manufacturing plants at only 282, and the total number of workers at around 15,000.[17] Furthermore, most of the larger business concerns were in the hands of either foreign nationals or members of the non-Turkish, non-Muslim minorities. The absence of businessmen and merchants in the top political élite of the country is also highly significant. As can be seen in the Table above, the proportion of deputies coming from 'economic' professions (comprising trade, agriculture, and banking) remained, on average, about one-fifth of all deputies throughout the single-party years. Merchants constituted about half of this group. While the First Assembly had a sizeable representation of merchants (12 per cent), 'this delegation was reduced more than any other, save that of the clerics, in Atatürk's Second Assembly.' In the Fourth Assembly which followed the Free Party episode (see below) there seemed to be a deliberate effort by the RPP leadership to broaden the party's social base and particularly to increase its appeal to economic occupations. Thus from the Third to the Fourth (1931–5) Assembly, the proportion of those in economic occupations among the newly-elected deputies rose from 17 to 41 per cent (and merchants among them from 9 to 20 per cent), corresponding to a sharp decline of officials from 57 to 23 per cent. However, the Fourth Assembly remained a 'deviant case', and by 1935 the old pattern was re-established.[18]

Could the Turkish revolution have followed a different route in matters of social and economic policy? As Otto Kirchheimer stated in a more general context, 'did the man or the group have to act the way he, or they, did? What other options were open? To what extent do the circumstances attendant upon the rise of a new regime determine its subsequent actions?[19] One may perhaps speculate that the military-bureaucratic leadership of the RPP could have allied itself with urban, especially rural, lower classes, and have followed a more or less socialistic path. Indeed, during the early years of the nationalist regime, some members of the National Assembly seemed sympathetic toward the Soviet experiment.[20] More realistically, however, this was a very dubious option. As has been shown above, the industrial working class was too small to provide a mass basis for such a policy. Poor peasants, on the other hand, while constituting a great majority of the population, were not a politically mobilised force. Although the distribution of land ownership was highly unequal, as it still is, a substantial majority of peasants (87 per cent, according to the 1913 figures) owned some land; about 5 per cent could be termed large landowners, and only 8 per cent were landless peasants.[21] In large parts of rural Turkey, deferential and client-elistic patterns prevailed between landowning notables and poor peasants, the traces of which can still be found in the less developed regions (particularly the eastern and the south-eastern) at the present day.[22] Thus, even the lands expropriated from certain Eastern notables (as a political, rather than socio-economic measure) following the suppression of the 1925 revolt were never effectively distributed and were eventually returned to their former owners.[23] Conceivably, a bolder and more imaginative policy would have removed the worst features of feudal clientelism in the eastern region. But this is far from saying that the peasant masses were, on the whole, ready and mobilised to provide a social revolutionary impetus to the Kemalist regime, even had the regime been inclined to act in that direction.[24]

The ideology of the RPP

Linz, in his analysis of authoritarian regimes, argues that while 'totalitarian systems have ideologies . . . authoritarian regimes are based more on distinctive mentalities which are difficult to define.' In this distinction, ideologies are 'systems of thought more or less intellectually elaborated and organised, often in written form, by intellectuals, pseudo-intellectuals, or with their assistance,' whereas mentalities 'are ways of thinking and feeling, more emotional than rational, that provide non-codified ways of reacting to situations.'[25]

This description seems to fit the Kemalist doctrine. Students of the Kemalist movement often point out that its doctrine grew out of action, rather than action being based on pre-conceived ideas. Certain statements of Atatürk provide supporting evidence in this regard, for example his famous maxim. 'We resemble none but ourselves.'[26] Yakup Kadri Karaosmanoğlu, an author close to Atatürk, quotes the following exchange with him: 'My general, this party has no doctrine . . . Of course it doesn't, my child; if we had a doctrine, we would freeze the movement.'[27]

The First Grand National Assembly was an ideologically, as much as socially, heterogeneous body. Moreover, the need to maintain unity in the face of external threat precluded Atatürk from taking doctrinaire positions. The only principles that emerged in this critical period were the idea of a completely independent nation-state[28] and a rather vague notion of 'populism'. In Kemal's early statements, populism had openly anti-imperialist and anti-capitalist overtones. He said, for example, in a speech on 1 December 1921: 'When we think in terms of social doctrines, we are a working people, a poor people, striving to save our lives and independence. Let us know ourselves. We have to work to live and to achieve our liberations. Therefore, all of us have rights. [. . .] But we acquire such rights only through working. In our society there is no place or rights for a person who wants to lie down and does not want to work. [. . .] Populism is a social doctrine which aims to base its social order on work. [. . .] To protect this right and to keep our independence secure, all of us pursue a doctrine which justifies nationwide struggle against imperialism that wants to destroy us and against capitalism that wants to devour us.'[29] In later years, however, such anti-capitalist overtones were dropped, and populism came to mean only popular sovereignty and equality before the law, as well as a rejection of class conflict. Thus the RPP programme, adopted at the Fourth Party Congress in May 1935, defined populism as follows:[30]

'The source of will and sovereignty is the nation. The Party considers it an important principle that this will and sovereignty be used to regulate the proper fulfilment of the mutual duties of the citizen to the State and of the State to the citizen. We consider the individuals who accept an absolute equality before the law, and who recognise no privileges for any individual, family, class, or community to be . . . populist. It is one of our main principles to consider the people of the Turkish Republic, not as composed of different classes, but as a community divided into various professions according to the requirements of the division of labour for the individual and social life of the Turkish people. The farmers, handicraftsmen, labourers and workmen, people exercising free professions, industrialists, merchants, and public servants are the main groups of work constituting the Turkish community. The aims of our Party . . . are to secure social order and solidarity instead of class conflict, and to establish harmony of interests. The benefits are to be proportionate to the aptitude, to the amount of work.'

The other doctrinal principles that emerged in time were republicanism, nationalism, secularism, étatism and reformism. Together with populism, these principles were incorporated into the Party programme by the Third Party Congress in 1931, and were symbolised by the six arrows in the Party emblem. In the constitutional amendment of 1937, the same six principles were also incorporated into the Turkish Constitution, denoting the basic characteristics of the state. One indication of the relative insignificance of ideology in the RPP is that, since its establishment in 1923 until the Third Party Congress in 1931, the RPP did not have a party programme as distinct from the party constitution, and the constitution contained no guiding political philosophy beyond a few generalities.[31]

Among these principles even étatism, which seems to have certain concrete public policy connotations, was highly pragmatic and flexible in nature. Étatism meant an interventional economic policy involving direct economic activity by the state through its public economic enterprises. Étatist policies were evolved in the 1930s, not as a result of a clear-cut ideological choice but as a gradual and pragmatic response to the effects of the world economic crisis and as a means of industrialising the country in the absence of a sufficient accumulation of private capital. The 1930s witnessed intense debates within the RPP on the definition of étatism and on the extent of étatist policies. While the conservatives wanted to limit the scope of public economic enterprises to those areas unattractive to private investors because of the amount of capital needed or because of low profits, the more radical wing of the party called for the establishment of such enterprises wherever public interest deemed it necessary. Usually the radical wing prevailed in the 1932–9 period. New public economic enterprises played an important role in the industrialisation of the country.[32]

It may be argued, however, that étatism may not have held the same lofty place as the other principles of the RPP. Although some party spokesmen, most notably the Secretary-General Recep Peker, denounced economic liberalism on clearly doctrinal grounds, the more common outlook was that differences of opinion on economic policies should be tolerated and even legitimately discussed within the party. In this sense, étatism was not considered nearly as sacred as, for example, republicanism and secularism. It is interesting that the Free Party opposition of 1930 was created mainly with the purpose of providing *economic* alternatives and criticisms.[33] Intra-party debates on étatism continued after the dissolution of the Free Party, and, following 1939, étatist policies were gradually modified by the RPP itself. Especially after the transition to a multi-party system, the conservatives within the RPP were able to deprive étatism of much of its original meaning.

If it is true that authoritarian regimes tend to have mentalities rather than ideologies, then the mentality that fits the RPP best is a 'positivist' mentality. In fact one can discern underlying most of these doctrinal principles, a positivist spirit permeating the party's activities.[34] This spirit was forcefully expressed by Atatürk himself: 'The torch the Turkish nation holds in her hand and in her mind on her road to progress and civilisation is positive science.' 'In the world, the truest guide for everything, for civilisation, for life, for success is science. It is foolish to look for guidance outside the realm of science.'[35] Clearly this was more a matter of mentality than of ideology.

Clement Moore, who distinguishes four types of one-party ideologies (totalitarian, chiliastic, tutelary, and administrative), puts Atatürk's Turkey into the tutelary category.[36] A tutelary ideology is one which combines an instrumental function with the goal of a partial social transformation. This characterisation generally fits the Kemalist ideology. Indeed, Kemalism was oriented toward a partial, not total, transformation of Turkish society. Repeating an often-stated Kemalist maxim, it aimed at putting Turkey on a level with 'contemporary civilisation', making it a modern, strong, fully independent nation-state. It did not dream about creating a totally new society or a new type of man, as did totalitarian ideologies. Kemalism was instrumental in the sense that it was closely associated with action; as we have pointed out above, many Kemalist principles grew out of action and in response to concrete needs and situations. As Rustow has observed, Kemal 'displayed little interest in social and economic change as these terms have come to be understood since the Mexican, Russian, and anti-colonial Revolutions. For him, economic improvement and a bridging of class differences were practical requirements of national solidarity and international stature, rather than deeply felt needs of human justice and dignity.'[37]

By the same token, the RPP ideology displayed the inherent contradictions commonly found in tutelary regimes. When the limited goals of partial social transformation were largely achieved, the ideology ceased to be a source of legitimacy. Precisely because of its instrumental character, it was left vulnerable to rational criticism. Once a secular, republican nation-state seemed securely established, it became legitimate to ask whether Kemalist goals could not be better pursued under a competitive political system. The lack of a significant 'expressive' component prevented the Kemalist ideology from transforming itself into an 'administrative' single-party ideology by making the party, *qua* institution, the object of a diffuse respect and attachment, divorced from the specific content of its policies. In a real sense, therefore, the success of the Kemalist reforms undermined the long-term legitimacy of the single-party system in Turkey.

Perhaps the only expressive component of Kemalism is *devrimcilik*, which can be translated into English either as reformism or revolutionism. This principle sometimes meant a commitment to specific Kemalist reforms, and sometimes a more general commitment to permanent change and progress, as well as a rejection of gradualism and evolutionism.[38] Had the latter aspect of *devrimcilik* been systematically emphasised, the RPP ideology could conceivably have acquired more distinctly expressive characteristics. In this event, the party would perhaps have been viewed as the institutional embodiment of the Turkish Revolution and as its only true and legitimate representative, something like the Mexican PRI.[39] This was not the case, however, since reformism remained the vaguest and the least clearly articulated of the six arrows.

No component of the RPP ideology provided a permanent justification for the single-party system. As Duverger succintly states, 'the Turkish single-party system was never based upon the doctrine of a single party. It gave no official recognition to the monopoly, made no attempts to justify it by the existence of a classless society or the desire to do away with parliamentary strife and liberal democracy. It was always embarrassed and almost ashamed of the monopoly. The Turkish single party had a bad conscience.'[40] Ismet Inönü forcefully expressed this guilty conscience many years after the transition to democracy: 'When I saw the neighbouring countries holding free elections, I was so ashamed that I could not even look at the walls of my room.'[41]

Interestingly, both Atatürk and Inönü were careful in observing constitutional norms. The 1924 Constitution which was adopted by the second term of the Grand National Assembly, by that time strongly dominated by Kemalists, made the Assembly the supreme organ of the state and the repository of executive as well as legislative power. The belief in legislative supremacy was so deeply entrenched and emotionally held during the years of the First Assembly (1920–3) that, in the course of the debates on the Constitution, the Assembly rejected or modified many proposals favouring a somewhat stronger executive. For example, the draft Constitution prepared by the Constitutional Committee gave the President of the Republic, apparently with the blessings of Mustafa Kemal himself, the power to dissolve the Assembly and to veto bills. Such a veto could be overridden by a two-thirds majority. At the end, the Assembly rejected the entire article on dissolution, and the veto power was restricted in such a way that the President's objection could be overridden by a simple majority. The Assembly also rejected a seven-year term for the presidency as proposed by the Constitutional Committee; the term was made to coincide with that of the Assembly, i.e., four years. Another article of the draft Constitution which gave rise to strong objections was the one that made the President commander-in-chief of the armed forces. Most deputies considered this a direct assault on the principle of national sovereignty as represented solely by the Assembly. Finally, the article was modified so as to vest the supreme command of the armed forces in the Assembly.[42] Even in the heyday of the single-party system, all important decisions were always made by the Assembly. No doubt, ratification by the Assembly of decisions already made by the top leadership of the party was a foregone conclusion. Nevertheless, the careful observance of constitutional norms is indicative in itself; it meant that the legitimacy of governmental decisions derived from compliance with constitutional principles, rather than from the party's higher claim to permanent monopoly.

Also significant is the fact that electoral laws were constantly democratised, although admittedly in an abstract sense, under the RPP rule. Thus in 1923 the franchise was extended to all males over eighteen years of age, and the tax-paying requirement for first and second electors was lifted. In 1930, direct elections were introduced for municipal councils. In 1934, women were granted the right to vote (both as first and second electors) and made eligible to become deputies.[43] In the elections of 1931 and 1935, the RPP did not nominate a certain number (thirteen in 1931, and sixteen in 1935) of candidates for deputyships, to leave room for independents.[44] Thus, both constitutionally and electorally, a democratic façade was carefully maintained, so much so that the transition to multi-partyism in 1946 required not a single change in the Constitution and only relatively minor changes in other laws. This is not merely to say that the transition took place within the rules of the previous single-party regime (as was also the case in post-Franco Spain), but also that the 'rules of the game' did not change even after the transition was completed (unlike the Spanish case) and the RPP lost power to the opposition Democrat Party. The 1924 Constitution remained in effect, in a multi-party context, until the military intervention of 1960.

The organisation of the RPP

Organisationally, the RPP was closer to an old-fashioned cadre party than to a modern totalitarian party. Linz counts a number of indicators by which one can assess the functional importance of the party in an authoritarian regime: 'the number of high officials that were active in the party before entering the élite; the membership figures; the degree of activity indicated by the budget; agit-prop activity; the prestige or power accorded to party officials; the presence of party cells or representatives in other institutions; the importance of training centers; the attention paid to party organs and publications; the vigour of ideological polemics within the party factions.'[45] By most of these criteria, the RPP did not appear as a particularly strong single party.

There was little systematic ideological indoctrination in or by the RPP. Türker Alkan, in his analysis of political socialisation process through civics textbooks, found that there was little emphasis on the main principles of the RPP doctrine, especially during the lifetime of Atatürk, and almost no effort to build a personality cult around Atatürk himself.[46] Similarly, throughout the single-party years, few books were written to analyse and systematise the party doctrine. The only effort of some significance was made by the journal *Kadro* in the early 1930s. *Kadro*'s philosophy was 'a superficial combination of Marxism, nationalism, and corporatism,' with a strong dose of élitism. But its founders were people only marginally associated with the high levels of the RPP hierarchy. Although *Kadro* met with initial approval from some official circles, it soon died 'as a result of the suspicions of Marxism and communism which it aroused as soon as it started discussing social classes.'[47]

Nor were there any significant purges within the RPP. Considerable freedom of discussion could be observed within the Assembly and especially in the deliberations of the RPP parliamentary group. Most members of the top élite were recruited not on account of their prior party organisational work, but more often than not on the basis of either their early involvement in the nationalist movement in the War of Independence years or their successful performance in the state bureaucracy. As Frey observed, a majority of ministers did not have a long parliamentary experience at the time of their first appointment as ministers, the average period being a little over one parliamentary term, or four years.[48] This suggests that in many cases, top political élite positions were filled by people with a successful bureaucratic career but relatively little parliamentary and party experience.

Perhaps most important of all for our purposes, the RPP was not really a mass mobilisation party. This supports Linz's argument that authoritarian regimes tend to encourage apathy and depoliticisation, while totalitarian systems insist on mobilisation and participation.[49] The RPP remained largely a cadre party, an élite organisation, dominated by the official élite and local notables. The RPP leadership made no notable effort to broaden the party's popular base and to enlist the support of the peasant masses; instead, it concentrated its attention on the small westernised élite.

To be sure, there was some degree of mobilisation, especially in the early years of the Kemalist regime. But this was directed first toward securing the country's independence and territorial integrity in the face of external threat, and then toward consolidation of the party's popularity among the members of the élite, particularly among the educated youth. The RPP did not attempt and evidently felt no need to mobilise the peasant masses into some form of active political participation. As Frey rightly points out, the essence of the Turkish Revolution is that it concentrated on the extension and consolidation of the precarious beachhead won by the Westernized intellectuals, to make it secure beyond all possible challenge. 'It was not . . . a revolution "from the bottom up" — an attempt to remould the society by starting with the peasant masses.'[50]

The establishment of the People's Houses and the People's Rooms starting from 1931 can perhaps be viewed as an effort of mobilisation. In February 1949, there was a total of 478 People's Houses and 4,322 People's Rooms, the latter having been established in villages and small towns. However, the People's Houses, although associated with the RPP, were conceived as a measure of social emancipation and of raising the general cultural standards, rather than as an instrument of political mobilisation or ideological indoctrination. This can be seen in the branches of their activity: language and literature, fine arts, drama, sports, social work, adult education, libraries, village welfare, museums and cultural exhibits.[51]

This lack of interest in mass mobilisation on the part of the RPP leadership has led Huntington to describe it as an example of 'exclusionary one-party systems'. In his view, both the exclusionary and the revolutionary (totalitarian) types of single parties have their origins in a sharp social bifurcation, but they differ in the ways in which they react to the original bifurcation and to the subordinated social force. The exclusionary systems 'accept the bifurcation of the society and use the party as a means of mobilising support from their constituency while at the same time suppressing or restricting political activity by the subordinate social force.' The revolutionary single-party systems, on the other hand, 'attempt to eradicate the bifurcation of society by shrinking society to correspond to its constituency through liquidation of the subordinate social force or by expanding its constituency to correspond to society by the assimilation of the subordinate social force.' Thus he argues that during RPP rule 'political participation was effectively limited to the westernized urban classes and the mass of the traditional peasantry were excluded from power.'[52]

In our view, the distinction between the revolutionary and the

exclusionary single-party systems does not exhaust all possible sub-
types of this category. There seems to be place for a 'tutelary'
category which can be reduced into neither of the two types. A
tutelary system, like all other authoritarian regimes, limits political
participation, but does not aim at the indefinite exclusion of the subordinate group from politics. On the contrary, by emphasising the
role of an educator, it strives gradually to broaden the scope of political participation. In fact, an exclusionary single-party system is
likely to be found only in societies where the original bifurcation is
ethnic or religious, in other words of a permanent nature. Other
cleavages (e.g. economic and cultural) change in time and cannot,
therefore, serve as a basis of permanent exclusion. This is especially
so if the cleavage is, as in the Turkish case, between modernisers and
traditionalists. As modernisation proceeds and modern values are
shared by an increasingly large section of the population, this
criterion cannot be maintained as a basis of legitimacy of a single-
party system.

The RPP and limited pluralism

One of the main characteristics of authoritarian regimes, according
to Linz, is their toleration of 'limited pluralism' in contrast to totalitarian systems. To be sure, certain groups may be, and usually are,
excluded from political participation, but others, as long as they do
not threaten the basic objectives of the regime, are allowed to maintain a more or less autonomous existence without the complete
regimentation of a totalitarian system.[53]

The degree of social pluralism, in turn, seems to be associated with
the level of socio-economic modernisation. In less developed
societies, the authoritarian single party may not have to compete
with a variety of groups which themselves are the products of modernisation. Whereas in semi-developed or developed countries, an
authoritarian regime may have to come to some accommodation
with such groups unless it evolves into a totalitarian system.

One difference between the Turkish and the Spanish single-party
systems, for example, may be found in the different degrees of social
pluralism which existed when they came to power. The much higher
level of social pluralism in Spain resulted in a weak single-party
system, where the Falange was only one of the many pillars of the
regime.[54] The structure of the Ottoman state and the lower level of
socio-economic modernisation, on the other hand, did not encourage social pluralism, and concentrated political power in the hands
of state officials. The Ottoman state remained much more autonomous *vis-à-vis* the society than was the case in Europe, a situation
which can be described as absence of a 'civil society'. Consequently,

the RPP could consolidate its power with relative ease and without too strong competition from other social forces.

This also explains why the RPP did not have to resort to widespread violence and terror as a means of consolidation. Only three groups had to be forcibly suppressed, and two of them were relatively minor ones. These were some militant Islamic brotherhoods, the ex-Unionist leaders, and the Communists. The first were involved in the eastern revolt of 1925 and a number of other less serious incidents of rebellion. Interestingly, religious reaction against Kemalist reforms came from such brotherhoods much more than from the official *ülema*, since the *ülema* were part of the state apparatus, the world of officialdom in the Ottoman system. The brotherhoods, on the contrary, often had their roots in the folk culture and were not, in a cultural and institutional sense, connected with the state structure. This may also explain the different ways in which the Kemalist regime dealt with these two kinds of religious groups. While the activities of the brotherhoods were legally banned and suppressed, the official *ülema* were eventually re-incorporated into the public bureaucracy, although in a much weaker form as functionaries of the newly-created 'Directory of Religious Affairs', a seemingly paradoxical institution under the militantly secularist Kemalist Republic.[55]

The second opposition group (ex-Unionists) was seen by Kemal, perhaps rightly so, as a serious threat to his leadership. Thus a score of the former Unionist leaders were implicated in a plot to assassinate Kemal and were sentenced to death by the Independence Tribunal in 1926. The third group (the Communists) was considered dangerous since it could become an instrument of Soviet influence in Turkey and thereby threaten national independence. Consequently, some Communists were tried by the Independence Tribunal in 1925, and received relatively mild prison sentences. Commenting on the extent of violence used by the Kemalist regime, Rustow concludes that 'in modern times few political transformations of such magnitude have been accomplished at such modest cost in lives. Not only was Kemal restrained in his use of violence, but the violent interlude ended after a few years.'[56]

While Turkey did not display a high degree of *social* pluralism in the 1920s and the 1930s, some measure of *political* pluralism was tolerated within the party. This was demonstrated by the relative freedom of discussion in the Assembly and the party's parliamentary group on a variety of issues. For example, issues of étatism and of economic policy in general were freely and extensively debated in the 1930s. Perhaps a more telling fact in this regard is that, in 1930, Kemal himself encouraged the establishment of an opposition party.

At his suggestion, one of his close friends and a former prime minister, Fethi Bey (Okyar) created the Free Republican Party which favoured more liberal economic policies. This experiment in political pluralism came to a quick end after a few months when it appeared that the new party was attracting substantial popular support (in view of the RPP leadership, this included the support of 'reactionary elements'). When Kemal withdrew his moral support, the Free Party leadership decided to dissolve the party. Nevertheless, the experiment remains a highly significant one. Although Kemal may have had no more than a hegemonic arrangement, in the Sartorian sense, in his mind when he encouraged a tame opposition, this move clearly demonstrated that the RPP leadership did not regard its monopoly as ideal or permanent.[57] It signified that the RPP doctrine did not go much beyond providing a definition of the boundaries of legitimate political action. It did not claim to provide, as do totalitarian ideologies, 'some ultimate meaning, sense of historical purpose, and interpretation of social reality'.[58]

In the light of the foregoing discussions, where can we place the RPP in a typology of authoritarian regimes? Linz, using three dimensions (degree of pluralism, degree of mobilization, and degree of ideologisation) distinguishes seven types of authoritarian regimes: bureaucratic-military authoritarian regimes, organic statism, mobilisational authoritarian regimes in post-democratic societies, post-independence mobilisational authoritarian regimes, racial and ethnic 'democracies', defective and pre-totalitarian regimes, and post-totalitarian regimes.[59] The two relevant categories for our case are the military-bureaucratic type and the post-independence mobilisational type. As Linz admits, many regimes remain on the borderlines between these ideal types. 'Many of the regimes combine in a more or less planned or accidental way elements from the different types, giving more or less importance to one or another in different phases of their history. [. . .] Authoritarian regimes in reality . . . are likely to be complex systems characterised by heterogeneity of models influencing their institutionalisation, often contradictory models in uneasy co-existence.'[60] Thus the Turkish case combines elements of military-bureaucratic regimes with those of post-independence mobilisational regimes.

In this combination, we feel that the military-bureaucratic characteristics were the dominant ones. It is true that the emergence of the RPP bore certain similarities to the emergence of post-independence mobilisational single parties (such as representation of national aspirations and grievances, obliteration of class cleavages etc.) and that the RPP played a more important role in the political system than the official government-sponsored single parties in

98 *Ergun Özbudun*

purer forms of military-bureaucratic regimes. Nonetheless, in contrast to post-independence mobilisational regimes, most of which appeared in Africa, the RPP regime inherited from the Ottoman empire a well-developed civil service and a large professional army. As we have seen above, people from military and bureaucratic backgrounds occupied a predominant place in the top political élite of the country throughout the single-party years. In other words, as in other military-bureaucratic regimes, 'the main support for the regime and the recruiting ground for the élites of the system were found largely in . . . state bourgeoisie . . . in contrast to a bourgeoisie with its connotation of a stratum linked with a modern economy.' Also as in other military-bureaucratic types, the RPP regime made 'a considerable effort to operate within a legalistic framework', enacting a constitution modelled after the Western democratic type, holding on to parliamentary forms, 'demanding obedience from civil servants and officers not on the ground of an identification with policies, programs or charisma but on the basis of legal authority'.[61] Finally, as has been elaborated above, little effort was made to mobilise the masses and to indoctrinate them by means of a coherent, systematic, elaborate ideology. All these characteristics bring the RPP regime closer to the military-bureaucratic model.

NOTES

1. Giovanni Sartori, *Parties and Party Systems*, Cambridge University Press, 1976, pp. 273–82, esp. 281.
2. Juan J. Linz, 'An Authoritarian Regime: Spain' in Erik Allardt and Stein Rokkan (eds.), *Mass Politics: Studies in Political Sociology*, New York, Free Press, 1970, 280–1.
3. Sabahattin Selek, *Anadolu Ihtilâli*, vol. 2, Istanbul, Burçak Yayınevi, 1966, 200–4.
4. *ibid.*, 220–4; see also Michael M. Finefrock, 'The "Second Group" in the First Turkish Grand National Assembly', *Journal of South Asian and Middle Eastern Studies*, III, Fall 1979, 3–20; Tarık Zafer Tunaya, *Türkiye'de Siyasî Partiler*, Istanbul, Doğan Kardeş Yayınları, 1952), 533–39.
5. Dankwart A. Rustow, 'Atatürk as Founder of a State' in *Prof. Dr. Yavuz Abadan'a Armağan*, Ankara, A.Ü. Siyasal Bilgiler Fakültesi Yayını, 1969, 532.
6. Selek, *op. cit.*, vol. 1, 93, 108, 219.
7. *ibid.*, vol. I, 64, 69, 71, 93–9.

8. *ibid.*, vol. I, 73–80; Bernard Lewis, *The Emergence of Modern Turkey*, London, Oxford University Press, 1968, 252.

9. Selek, *op. cit.*, vol. 1, 270; Frederick W. Frey, *The Turkish Political Elite*, Cambridge, Mass., M.I.T. Press, 1965, 77.

10. *ibid.*, 181; see also Mahmut Goloğlu, *Üçüncü Meşrutiyet*, 321–51.

11. In fact, Sabahattin Selek (*op. cit.*, vol. I, 214–15) distinguishes two phases in the development of the nationalist movement: the first (1919–20) when the revolutionary legitimacy was established, the counter-revolution (anti-nationalist revolts) was defeated, and the irregular guerrilla forces were either eliminated or put under the control of the National Assembly government. This phase involved only minor skirmishes with the Greek and other occupying forces. The second (1921–2) is the phase of the War of Independence in the proper sense, when the regime was able to concentrate its efforts on defeating the external enemy.

12. *ibid.*, vol. 1, 350–9.

13. S.N. Eisenstadt, *Revolution and the Transformation of Societies*, New York, Free Press, 1978, 233.

14. Frey, *op. cit.*, 181.

15. Barrington Moore, Jr., *Social Origins of Dictatorship and Democracy: Lord and Peasant in the Making of the Modern World*, Boston: Beacon Press, 1966, chap. 8. Moore defines the 'reactionary coalition' as a working coalition between the landed upper classes and the emerging commercial and industrial interests. This coalition maintains its control through a powerful state apparatus, viz. the army and a rationalised, centralised civilian bureaucracy. Its historical function has been to transform an agrarian society into an industrial one through a 'capitalist and reactionary' route, namely by repressing peasants and the industrial labour force.

16. Morris Janowitz, *Military Conflict: Essays in the Institutional Analysis of War and Peace*, Beverly Hills, Sage Publications, 1975, 146–75. Janowitz further notes (161–2) that 'at the root of the military ideology of the Middle East is the theme of the acceptance, in varying degrees, of collective public enterprise as a basis for achieving social and economic change. In the Ottoman Empire the conception of statism was central and the military an integral part of this ideology.' For arguments along similar lines, see Ergun Özbudun, *The Role of the Military in Recent Turkish Politics*, Harvard University, Center for International Affairs, Occasional Papers in International Affairs, no. 14 (Nov. 1966). Andrew C. Janos observed similar phenomena in Eastern European countries between the two world wars: 'Very early in the process of political development the administrative bureaucracy, or in some cases (such as Yugoslavia and Poland) the military, had emerged as autonomous forces in the political arena. Contrary to popular belief this administrative-military complex . . . was not the handmaiden of established social classes or of the national community as a whole, but eventually became an interest group in its own right. Members of the public administration and the military had developed a particular social consciousness.' ('The One-Party State and Social Mobilization: East Europe between the Wars' in Samuel P. Huntington and Clement H. Moore, (eds.), *Authoritarian Politics in Modern Society: The Dynamics of Established*

One-Party Systems, New York, Basic Books, 1970, 205.

17. *Türkiye'de Toplumsal ve Ekonomik Gelişmenin 50 Yılı*, Ankara: Başbakanlık Devlet İstatistik Enstitüsü, 1973, pp. 37−41.

18. Frey, *op. cit.*, 183−4, 208−12; Walter F. Weiker, *Political Tutelage and Democracy in Turkey: the Free Party and its Aftermath*, Leiden, E.J. Brill, 1973, 203−4.

19. Otto Kirchheimer, 'Confining Conditions and Revolutionary Breakthroughs', *American Political Science Review*, 59, Dec. 1965, 964−74.

20. Mete Tunçay, *Türkiye'de Sol Akımlar*, Ankara, A.Ü. Siyasal Bilgiler Fakültesi Yayını 1967; Elaine D. Smith, *Turkey: Origins of the Kemalist Movement and the Government of the Grand National Assembly, 1919−1923*, Washington, D.C., Judd and Detweiler, 1959, 47−50, 64−72.

21. *Türkiye'de Toplumsal ve Ekonomik Gelişmenin 50 Yılı*, 24.

22. Ergun Özbudun, 'Political Clientelism in Turkey', in S.N. Eisenstadt and René Lemarchand (eds.), *Political Clientelism, Patronage and Development*, London, Sage Publications, 1981.

23. Şevket Süreyya Aydemir, *İkinci Adam: İsmet İnönü*, İstanbul, Remzi Kitabevi, 1966, vol. 1 308−12.

24. One may wish to add other dimensions to such speculation. Thus, an authoritarian socialist path would presumably have involved either a Soviet-type regime, or some version of Islamic socialism. The former could have compromised Turkish national independence, especially in view of the geographical proximity of the Soviet Union. The latter would have run counter to the secularist designs of the Kemalist leadership. Full national independence and secularisation being cherished goals for the regime, both courses were extremely unlikely to be adopted.

25. Linz, 'An Authoritarian Regime: Spain', 257−9; also his 'Totalitarian and Authoritarian Regimes' in Fred I. Greenstein and Nelson W. Polsby (eds.), *Handbook of Political Science*, vol. 3: *Macropolitical Theory*, Reading, Mass., Addison-Wesley, 1975, 266−9.

26. *Atatürk'ün Söylev ve Demeçleri*, 1, Ankara, Türk İnkilâp Tarihi Enstitüsü, 1961, pp. 196−7.

27. Şevket Süreyya Aydemir, *Tek Adam: Mustafa Kemal*, vol. 3, İstanbul, Remzi Kitabevi, 1966, 502, 446, 459.

28. Muammer Aksoy, 'Atatürk'ün Işığında Tam Bağımsızlık İlkesı', *Prof. Dr. Yavuz Abadan'a Armagan*, Ankara, Siyasal Bilgiler Fakültesi Yayını, 1969, 689−799.

29. *Atatürk'ün Söylev ve Demeçleri*, 1, 196.

30. Official translation quoted by Suna Kili, *Kemalism*, İstanbul, Robert College, 1969, 78; see also Aydemir, *op. cit.*, vol. 3, 449−52.

31. Kili, *op. cit.*, 35, 60−6.

32. Korkut Boratav, *100 Soruda Türkiye'de Devletçilik*, İstanbul, Gerçek Yayınevi, 1974, 133−375.

33. Weiker, *op. cit.*, 57−9, 143, 249−53.

34. Taner Timur, *Türk Devrimi: Tarihî Anlamı ve Felsefî Temeli* Ankara, Siyasal Bilgiler Fakültesi Yayını, 1968), 112−16. See also Mardin in this volume.

35. *Atatürk'ün Söylev ve Demeçleri*, II, 275; Timur, *op. cit.*, 113.

36. Clement H. Moore, 'The Single Party as Source of Legitimacy' in Samuel P. Huntington and Clement H. Moore (eds.), *op. cit.*, 48–72, 61–2.

37. Rustow, *op. cit.*, 569.

38. Weiker, *op. cit.*, 253–6.

39. For a comparison between the RPP and the Mexican PRI, see Ergun Özbudun, 'Established Revolution versus Unfinished Revolution: Contrasting Patterns of Democratization in Mexico and Turkey' in Huntington and Moore, *op. cit.*, 380–405.

40. Maurice Duverger, *Political Parties*, New York, Wiley, 1959, 277; also Frey, *op. cit.*, 337–8.

41. Metin Toker, *Tek Partiden Çok Partiye*, Istanbul: Milliyet Yayınları, 1970, 50–1.

42. Ergun Özbudun, 'Parliament in the Turkish Political System', *Journal of South Asian and Middle Eastern Studies*, 2, Fall 1978, 50–1.

43. Frey, *op. cit.*, 423–30; Servet Armağan, *Türk Esas Teşkilât Hukuku*, Istanbul, I.Ü. Hukuk Fakültesi Yayınları, 1979, 192–9.

44. Frey, *op. cit.*, 434; Weiker, *op. cit.*, 158–67.

45. Linz, 'An Authoritarian Regime: Spain', *op. cit.*, p. 264.

46. Türker Alkan, 'Turkey: Rise and Decline of Political Legitimacy in a Revolutionary Regime', *Journal of South Asian and Middle Eastern Studies*, 4, Winter 1980, 37–48.

47. Karpat, *op. cit.*, 70–2.

48. Frey, *op. cit.*, 286.

49. Linz, 'Totalitarian and Authoritarian Regimes', *op. cit.*, 268–9; also his 'An Authoritarian Regime: Spain', *op. cit.*, 259–64.

50. Frey, *op. cit.*, 40–3. Given the great gap between the élite culture and the folk culture, it is doubtful that such a mobilisational effort would have succeeded even if the RPP leadership had chosen this path. For the historical origins of this cultural gap, the deep dichotomy between the 'court' (or élite) culture and the 'little' (or folk) culture, see Şerif Mardin, *Din ve Ideoloji*, Ankara, Siyasal Bilgiler Fakültesi Yayını, 1969, 101–14.

51. Karpat, *op. cit.*, 380–1; Tunaya, *op. cit.*, 596–8; Weiker, *op. cit.*, 168–83.

52. Samuel P. Huntington, 'Social and Institutional Dynamics of One-Party Systems', in Huntington and Moore, *op. cit.*, 15–16.

53. Linz, 'Totalitarian and Authoritarian Regimes', *op. cit.*, pp. 265–6.

54. Juan Linz, 'From Falange to Movimiento Organización: the Spanish Single Party and the Franco Regime, 1936–1968' in Huntington and Moore, *op. cit.*, 128–203.

55. Bernard Lewis (*op. cit.*, 409 ff) makes a similar distinction between the position of the *ülema* and that of the brotherhoods *vis-à-vis* the Kemalist regime: 'The great secularizing reforms of 1924 were directed against the *ülema*, not the dervishes; but it soon became apparent that it was from the dervishes, not the *ülema*, that the most dangerous resistance to laicism would come. The *ülema*, long accustomed to wielding the authority of the state, were unpractised in opposing it. The dervishes were used to independence and opposition; they still enjoyed the confidence and loyalty of the common people.'

56. Rustow, *op. cit.*, 539–40.

57. Although the very short life of the Free Party does not allow us to reach definite conclusions, certain facts indicate the licensed and limited nature of the opposition as envisaged by Atatürk. Most importantly, the Free Party's continued existence was dependent upon its loyalty to Republicanism and secularism. This was made clear in Atatürk's letter to Fethi Bey giving his approval for the formation of the new party. Atatürk said: 'I am glad to observe once again that we are united on the principle of secular Republic. In fact, this is the principle which I have always sought, and will continue to seek, resolutely in political life . . . Rest assured, sir, that *within the principle of secular Republic*, any kind of political activity by your party will not be obstructed' (for the text of the letter, see Tunaya, *op. cit.*, 633, italics mine; see also, Weiker, *op. cit.*, 68–9). Furthermore, Atatürk's perception of the relations between the RPP and the Free Party, as well as his own perceived role, does not give one the impression that what was intended was a full-fledged, truly autonomous opposition party. Thus he said: 'I expect to see much struggle between the two parties and their leaders, but I welcome it with great pleasure. It will strengthen the foundations of the Republic. I can now say to you that even during your bitterest fights, I will gather you together at my table, and ask each of you 'What did you say and why did you say it?', 'What was your answer and how do you justify it?' I admit that this will be a great pleasure for me' (*Atatürk'ün Söylev ve Demeçleri*, II, 255–6; Weiker, *op. cit.*, 70).

58. For these characteristics of totalitarian ideologies, see Linz, 'Totalitarian and Authoritarian Regimes', 191, 196–8. For a similar assessment of the Free Party episode, see also Duverger, *op. cit.*, 277.

59. Linz, 'Totalitarian and Authoritarian Regimes', 277–353.

60. *ibid.*, 283.

61. *ibid.*, 287–8.

Kemalism and world peace

VLADIMIR I. DANILOV

One of the salient features of the twentieth century is the emergence of powerful national liberation movements in colonial and dependent countries. The main aim of each such movement is political independence. Any national movement logically strives to form a national state.

Once such a state is established, the newly-free nation needs to define the principles of its further development and in particular to decide how to carry out social and economic reforms, wipe out obsolete feudal relations, eliminate foreign capital domination, democratise public and political life as well as governmental institutions, revive national culture, and promote its progressive trends.

In addition to the need to tackle social, economic and political tasks at home, the young state is also faced with the problem of how to find its niche in the world economy and international relations, in other words, to outline the principles and practice of its foreign policy.

The newly-free states, on present showing, have already gained ample experience both in the internal and the external fields. This experience has revealed certain trends and laws in the development of such countries, which proceeds in the period of confrontation between the two opposite social systems. The latter factor is essential in examining any key problem, both domestic and foreign, of the liberated countries.

As far as the domestic scene is concerned, these states, for all the variety of their social, economic and political conditions, face one common task — that of achieving economic independence. But this internal objective inevitably transforms itself into its dialectical opposite — an external goal, for economic independence is acquired within international intercourse and through integration. What is more, with the present struggle going on between the two social systems, a developing country has to choose between capitalist and socialist integration.[1]

The foreign policy of any particular developing country (including its external economic policy) is closely connected with the way this choice is made. At present, in spite of the great diversity of national, regional and other factors, there are two dominant trends in Eastern countries' foreign policies — on the one hand, positive neutralism and non-alignment, and, on the other, military-political bloc alignment.

The first trend is a desire of the newly-independent countries to pursue an independent policy in the interests of their national liberation revolutions (with the two opposite world systems meanwhile locked in opposition). Countries advocating positive neutralism, unlike countries of traditional neutrality, such as Switzerland, want to co-operate actively in world affairs. A policy of non-alignment is pursued by those young states which, while remaining within the orbit of the world capitalist economy, belong neither to the imperialist states nor to the socialist countries. In other words, being economically dependent on the world capitalist system, these states refuse to enter into its military and political blocs but seek to follow an independent foreign policy in their own interests.[2]

The second trend is represented by developing countries which have lost faith in independent development and in their own just foreign policy aims and have found themselves dragged into military—political groupings and blocs whose orientation in general is contrary to their national interests.

So there is now a wealth of experience accumulated by the politically independent Asian and African nations. And no small contribution to it has come from the Turkish people, from Kemalism which we understand as a system of ideas and principles, as well as practices of the Turkish national liberation movement and of the Turkish Republic that came into being after its victory. Kemal Atatürk, who gave his name to this movement, did a lot to develop its ideology and practice. At present he is internationally known as the leader of the Turkish national liberation movement and founder of the Turkish Republic, as one of the outstanding men in the national liberation movements of the twentieth century.

Turkey's experience has a place of its own in the national liberation movements of our century, for Turkey was one of the first to embark on that path. That experience and Kemal Atatürk's activities, and their historic significance, especially as regards the organisation and triumphant victory of the national liberation movement, can be fully appreciated only bearing in mind the fact that they date back to more than fifty years ago, when just some of the links in the world colonial chain began snapping.

In looking at the experience of the Turkish national liberation movement now, it can be said that it had both general and specific features, the general ones deriving from its nature as a national liberation movement, and the specific ones from the international situation of those days and the particular historical development of the Ottoman empire. One of the specific traits was that when the

Turkish people rose in struggle for national independence, they were not a colonial people. They were only threatened with such a prospect, when, with the First World War over, the Entente powers had prepared and were implementing division plans not merely for the Ottoman empire but also for Turkey proper.

These general and specific elements in the national liberation movement in Turkey were, no doubt, projected into the Kemalists' foreign policy, its theory and practice. And much of the credit for this should go to Kemal Atatürk who was midwife to a foreign policy totally different from that of the Ottoman empire.

The distinguishing traits of that policy and its significance for world peace are worth examining in the context of two principal periods: the national liberation movement and the rise and development of the Turkish republic prior to the Second World War. That examination covers the new Turkey's foreign policy which was conducted during the lifetime and under the leadership of Atatürk, i.e. at a time when its main qualities were especially obvious.

The origins of Kemalist foreign policy principles in the period of the National Liberation Movement

As is generally known, following the Mudros armistice of 30 October 1918, which actually meant the end of the Ottoman empire, the Turkish people found their sovereign rights and independence in grave jeopardy. In his well-known speech Kemal Atatürk recalled how the nation and the army, brought to the verge of a yawning chasm, were desperately looking for a way out. Three possible alternatives were suggested: the first was to ask for Britain's protection; the second to try to get America's mandate; and the third to carry out scattered operations in different parts of the country, each having its own purpose.

'None of these solutions', said Kemal Atatürk, 'appealed as correct . . . In the situation there could be only one decision and that was to form a new Turkish state based on national sovereignty and possessing independence without any limitations and reservations.'[3]

When ways of salvation were sought, said Kemal Atatürk, many implicitly believed in two things: one, not to be hostile to the Entente powers and second, to remain devoted body and soul to the Sultan and the Caliph.[4]

And there and then Atatürk spelled out his attitude to these two things. He said: 'To ask for protection from a foreign state means showing lack of human dignity, one's impotence and helplessness. Those who have not sunk so low cannot imagine bringing themselves under foreign rule of their own free will.'[5]

Going back to his chosen decision, Atatürk stressed: 'To get our decision implemented . . . it was necessary to rise up against the Ottoman government, the Sultan and the Caliph and involve the whole nation and the army in the uprising. It was necessary for the whole people to come out arms in hand against those who wanted to encroach on the land of the Turkish people and its independence.'[6]

Kemal Atatürk pointed out that this decision was considered and adopted by himself and his associates before he left Istanbul and arrived at Samsun in May 1919.[7] Thus, such a key issue as the attitude to the imperialist powers was decided at that time. It was to be not pleading for their protection, but organising a nationwide armed struggle against them. The primary intent of that struggle was to set up a sovereign and independent national Turkish state. This idea was to form the main content of the Kemalists' foreign policy, which was further developed in the course of the national liberation movement.

The Erzurum and Sivas congresses of the Society for the Protection of Rights, held respectively in July-August 1919 and September 1919 with Atatürk's participation and under his direction, played a marked role in defining the principles and purposes of the Kemalist movement's foreign policy.

In his opening address at the Erzurum Congress, Kemal Atatürk exposed the imperialist plans for the partition of Turkey, and pointed to the Sultan government's inability to defend the interests of the country and the nation. The Turkish nation, he emphasised, would be able to overcome all the difficulties in the struggle for its liberation. He drew the delegates' attention to the fact that the peoples of Egypt, India, Afghanistan, Iraq and Syria were also waging a heroic struggle against the British and French colonialists.[8]

We consider these statements made by Atatürk in the middle of 1919 very important. In them he quite unambiguously defined his attitude to the imperialist powers, ranking the Turks among the nations fighting against the colonialists and for their liberation. At the same time he underlined the solidarity of these nations engaged in the battle against a common enemy. He said that he had told the Congress about the fight of the oppressed nations 'to boost morale'.[9]

The Erzurum Congress adopted an appeal to the people which contained a number of propositions in one way or another linked with foreign policy: within the national frontiers all districts of the country would be a single whole and could not be separated from each other; the nation would in any case fight as a single entity against foreign intervention and interference in its affairs; foreigners would not be granted rights and privileges threatening the political sovereignty and social order of the Turkish nation; neither a mandate nor protection by a foreign power could be accepted.[10]

It was stressed in the decisions of the Sivas Congress that the Representative Committee, led by Kemal Atatürk, which was set up at the Erzurum Congress, should, among its other functions, represent the national liberation movement on the international scene. The resolutions of the Sivas Congress confirmed all the Erzurum decisions in the field of foreign policy. It was stressed, in particular, that the territories within the limits determined by the Mudros armistice agreement were a single indivisible whole. The decisions also stressed the resolve to fight against any intervention and occupation of any part of Turkish territory.

In spite of the fact (as this has already been stressed above) that the idea of the United States mandate had earlier encountered a clearly negative reaction, that question again surfaced at the Congress. At that time there were many supporters of such a mandate both among political and public figures in Istanbul and among the Kemalists. Their view was to a certain extent reflected in the position of Atatürk's comrade-in-arms, Bekir Sami Bey. His position was reported to Atatürk late in July 1919 as follows: 'Independence is desirable and preferable. If, however, we decide to attain complete independence, our country will be divided into many parts . . . In view of such a situation, the mandate of a state which can keep our integrity intact, is preferable to the independence of two or three *velayets*. I believe it would be in the best interests of our country to request the establishment of America's mandate. [. . .] I talked this over with the American representative. He said that . . . it was necessary to address this request to Wilson and the United States Congress.' Then the American conditions for a positive answer to that request were laid down. They included the 'spread of the mandate to the entire territory of the Ottoman state'.[11]

By and large, the advocates of the mandate either feared a massive national movement against the occupationists or did not believe in its success. A fierce battle flared up at the Congress between the advocates and opponents of the mandate. The latter, led by Kemal Atatürk, gained the upper hand.

Kemal said during the debate at the Congress: 'The question is virtually taking on a simple form: either we work for complete independence or agree to the mandate of another state.'[12] In contrast to the supporters of the mandate who (like, for instance, Refet Bey, a delegate of the Congress) claimed that the 'mandate and independence do not contradict each other'[13] its opponents, led by Atatürk, advanced the slogans of 'national sovereignty' and 'complete independence', which were eventually supported by a majority of Congress delegates: these slogans pre-conditioned the progressive

character of the national movement and became its programme
demands.

On the basis of Atatürk's activities at the early stage of the
national liberation movement and his participation in the Erzurum
and Sivas Congresses, it is necessary to highlight a feature which was
typical of him as diplomat even at that time. He combined firmness
in questions of principled importance for the fate of the national
movement, national sovereignty and independence with high flexibility and the ability to take into account the specifics of a concrete
situation. Even on the question of the mandate, Atatürk did not
assume a tough position, realising that it was supported by influential circles in Istanbul as well as many delegates to the Sivas Congress, including a number of his close associates. Instead, as was
stressed by Blanco Villalta, a former Argentinian diplomat who
spent some years in Turkey in Atatürk's time, he set in motion all his
art of public-speaking, eloquence and wit in order to prevent the
elimination of the national movement which had been started with
such difficulties and victims by a cowardly acceptance of the mandate.[14] Simultaneously, Kemal did his best to explain to US public
opinion the true meaning of the events in Anatolia and the character
of the national liberation movement which 'emerged as a result of
the allies' expansionist activities, in particular Britain's desire to deal
with the Turkish nation in the same way as it had dealt with India and
Egypt.'[15] This explanation was given, among other things, in
Atatürk's memorandum to General Harbord, whom President
Wilson had sent to Anatolia to discuss the mandate.

It is important to stress two elements which were reflected in the
resolution of the Sivas Congress. Item 7 of that resolution read: 'Our
nation highly values the ideas of modernisation; it realises full well
our position and our needs in the technical, industrial and economic
fields. That is why on condition that the independence of our state
and our nation in domestic and foreign policy questions and the integrity of our country are preserved . . . we shall gladly accept technical, industrial and economic aid from any state which will show
respect for the ideals of nationalism and will not pursue the aim of
seizing our country.' This is a very important provision which determined in principle the future attitude of Kemalists to foreign
technico-economic and financial aid.

The same item went on: 'Our most cherished national aspiration is
an early conclusion of peace on humane and fair conditions in the
name of humanity's good and universal peace.'[16] This is how one of
the fundamental principles of the foreign policy of Kemal and the
Kemalists — the striving for the consolidation of universal peace
and international security, emerged. These and other decisions of

the Sivas Congress were of particular significance because, in contrast to the Erzurum Congress, all the regions of Anatolia and Istanbul were represented in Sivas — in other words, the whole of the Turkish nation was represented there.

The foreign policy principles of the Kemalist movement were reaffirmed in such a major document as the National Pact. It was drafted at a conference of Kemalist deputies in Ankara in December 1919 and adopted by the Fourth Chamber of Deputies in Istanbul on 26 January 1920, on the initiative of a group of Kemalists. The National Pact determined the frontiers of the Turkish state and pointed out that it constituted 'a single whole which cannot be divided either *de jure* or *de facto* for any reason whatsoever'. 'For us, like for any other state, the main condition of existence is complete independence and freedom for ensuring the possibility of our development,' it pointed out. The Pact also determined the status of Thrace, the security of the Marmara Sea and Istanbul, and the regime of the straits. In our view a very important provision was contained in the preamble to that document. It stressed that the 'principles laid down in the National Pact set the limit to the sacrifices which it is possible to make in order to achieve a fair and lasting peace.'[17] Thus, the Kemalists stressed their constructive position and their readiness to conduct peaceful negotiations and make all sorts of concessions so long as the latter did not compromise the boundaries of the state set by the National Pact and its complete independence.

Such was the main line of Atatürk himself. In his statements, written instructions, telegrams and addresses made in the course of the national liberation struggle, he stressed dozens of times that the chief aim was unconditional sovereignty and national independence. 'Like a blacksmith who strikes with his hammer in one and the same place, he, too, concentrated on one and the same aim.'[18] It is necessary to work for peace and to conduct negotiations about peace but not at the price of independence, which cannot be a bargaining counter at any negotiations. It is necessary to be flexible and to show readiness for concessions but not on the main questions of principle. This major foreign policy principle of Atatürk had a great role to play in the victory of the Turkish national liberation movement. Moreover, it is still topical and important today for any liberation movement. Peace achieved by concessions on questions of principles which concern state sovereignty and national independence can be neither genuine nor lasting. On the contrary, it is fraught with the danger of conflict and, consequently, the threat of war.

While working out the principles of their foreign policy, the Kemalists were to determine their attitude to the foreign policy principles of the Ottoman empire on the ruins of which they were going to build a new Turkey. Even at the very beginning of the national movement Kemal clearly realised that in the struggle started by people their interests should be placed above the interests of the house of Osman and the caliphate. He came out against the attempts to impose the aims of protecting the interests of the Islamic world on the Turkish national liberation movement because they were alien to it. At the same time, Atatürk more than once criticised the policy of Pan-Turanism conducted by the Young Turks. In the above-mentioned memorandum to General Harbord he stressed, among other things: 'We regard Pan-Turanism as a very harmful tendency.' He regarded the ensurance of the life and prosperity of the country and the nation as the main task of the Kemalists.[19]

Thus, Atatürk rejected the ideas and practices of the Ottoman empire, the ideology of Pan-Islamism and Pan-Turanism and the aggressive foreign policy based on this ideology. Speaking in the Grand National Assembly on 1 December 1921, he qualified Pan-Islamism and Pan-Turanism as 'illusions which are a long way from any practical value' and which 'aroused fear and anxiety in the rest of the world'. 'The Government of the Grand National Assembly has a firm policy of its own. It is aimed at ensuring the life and independence of Turkey in the framework of its set national boundaries.'[20]

A question may arise as to whether Atatürk thus rejected the idea of solidarity and Turkey's alliance with other Islamic countries. Far from rejecting this idea, he considered this necessary. In his view, however, solidarity was to be built not on the obsolete notion of the leading role of the Ottoman empire but on an equitable union and co-operation among sovereign Muslim nations in the interests of peace and economic development. Atatürk set forth, and did his best to implement, this principle of foreign policy, which we regard as one being of major importance in present-day conditions. Precisely such co-operation and solidarity of Muslim countries can today contribute to the efforts to rebuff the political and economic pressure of the imperialist powers and transnational corporations.

As the national liberation struggle mounted, the Kemalists formulated new principles of foreign policy and began to put them into practice. Turkey set out to develop relations with Soviet Russia. This was largely facilitated by the promotion by the Soviet side of the Leninist principles of foreign policy, which were basically different from the foreign-policy principles espoused by tsarist Russia. The Decree on Peace adopted by the Second Congress of the Soviets on 8 November 1917, and the call 'To All Working Muslims of Russia and the East' made on 3 December 1917, proclaimed the principles of equality, freedom and independence of all nations and condemned the imperialist policy of seizing foreign territories and enslaving other peoples.

Atatürk watched the developments in Soviet Russia closely and sympathetically. Addressing the Erzurum Congress, he said: 'The Russian people, being aware of the threat to their independence and seeing that they are threatened with foreign intervention on all sides, unanimously rose against these attempts to achieve world domination.'[21] Addressing the Grand National Assembly on 14 August 1920, he said in 'The Reply to the Question about the Situation on the Eastern Front' that the revolution in Russia was aimed at liberating the people 'from the cruel oppression and coercion by the imperialist and capitalist system.' 'In spite of the fact that the Western imperialists used all their might, all their means', he went on, 'the Russians have been successfully upholding the gains of their revolution.'[22]

All these statements serve to show that Kemal saw a great deal in common in the situation in Turkey and Soviet Russia at that time. This may explain why on 26 April 1920, two days after the opening of the Grand National Assembly, the Assembly's chairman sent an official letter to the Soviet government, in which he proposed establishing diplomatic relations and asked for financial and military aid. The letter said in part: 'We undertake to pool all our work and our military efforts with the Russian Bolsheviks with the purpose of fighting the imperialist governments and liberating from their power all the oppressed.'[23]

Some Turkish scientists doubted the existence of that letter. A.M. Shamsutdinov, a leading Soviet expert on Turkey, provides in an article mentioned below a number of convincing facts that prove the existence of the letter. Here is one of his proofs. An annual report of the People's Commissariat for Foreign Affairs to the Eighth Congress of the Soviets[24] says: 'The government of the Grand National Assembly sent a letter to the Soviet Union, which is signed by the Assembly's Chairman Mustafa Kemal Paşa, on April 26 but we did not receive the letter until early June.'[25]

On 3 June 1920, People's Commissar for Foreign Affairs G.V. Chicherin sent a letter in reply on Lenin's instruction, in which he wrote that the Soviet government had expressed its consent to establishing diplomatic and consular relations with Turkey without delay and beginning negotiations. The letter said in part: 'The Soviet government is watching with lively interest the heroic struggle waged by the Turkish people for their independence and sovereignty and at this difficult time for Turkey it would be happy to lay the firm foundations of friendship which would unite the Turkish and

Russian peoples.'[26] This meant recognition of the Grand National
Assembly government. Soviet Russia was the first country to recognise it and in the middle of 1920 established diplomatic relations.

On 4 July 1920 Bekir Sami Bey, minister of foreign affairs in the
GNAT government, replied that the response of the Soviet government was received with 'great pleasure and satisfaction'.[27] That was
the beginning of friendly relations between Soviet Russia and revolutionary Turkey.

This came as disquieting news for the West, particularly Britain
and France which did everything to prevent a rapprochement
between Turkey and Soviet Russia. In the above-mentioned address
to the Grand National Assembly on 14 August 1920, Kemal Atatürk
noted this by saying: 'The Entente powers led by Britain are doing
everything to destroy and crush us and, using their wealth and might,
are trying to prevent the Bolsheviks who seek to liberate all
oppressed mankind from holding out their hand in friendship to our
oppressed nation.' He further said: 'The Bolshevik republic,
however, has undertaken the practical initiative to safeguard its own
existence and, having set itself free from the merciless claws of the
Entente, to hold out its hand to us and conclude an alliance with our
nation.'[28]

The Entente powers failed to prevent the Soviet-Turkish
rapprochement. Diplomatic contacts and negotiations, continuing
throughout 1920 and 1921, resulted in the signing in Moscow on
16 March 1921 of a Treaty on Friendship and Fraternity. All the
clauses of that treaty were imbued with the spirit of mutual confidence and co-operation. The treaty set forth the solidarity of the two
sides in the struggle against imperialism and solved a number of
major practical problems. It substantially strengthened the
Kemalists' positions at home and abroad. The two countries also
reached agreement whereby Soviet Russia was to grant the GNAT
government financial aid to the tune of 10 million gold roubles.[29] In
the early 1920s Soviet Russia also supplied Turkey with arms,
ammunition and other military hardware.[30]

The book of memoirs by Semyon Aralov, the first Soviet ambassador in Ankara, contains some interesting facts about organisational and financial aid which Soviet Russia gave to Turkey in
arranging military training in the newly-formed Turkish army and
building a printing shop.[31] All this together constituted substantial
moral and material support for the Kemalist movement by revolutionary Russia.

Some people say that the Soviet-Turkish accommodation was an
act of expediency. True, the fact that both the Kemalist movement
and Soviet Russia had to fight for independence against the imperial-

ist powers brought them together. But this was not the decisive factor. It was the new principles of foreign policy that united the two countries. The foreign policy of the infant Soviet state was governed by the Leninist principles of support for the national liberation struggle and peaceful co-existence of states with different social systems.

The Soviet government had no illusions about the Kemalist movement. It knew only too well that it was a bourgeois nationalist movement, but it supported that movement because it was directed against imperialism and embraced the cause of national independence. In his memoirs Semyon Aralov quotes Lenin as saying: 'It's a fact that Mustafa Kemal Paşa is no socialist but . . . he is conducting a bourgeois-national revolution and he is a progressive-minded man and clever statesman. He understood the importance of our socialist revolution and he is sympathetic towards Soviet Russia. He is waging a war of liberation against the invaders. [. . .] We must help him, that is help the Turkish people.'[32]

Anatoly Glebov, a Soviet diplomat who worked in the Soviet permanent mission in Turkey in 1921–3, recorded in his memoirs the following remark made by Soviet Commissar for Foreign Affairs G.V. Chicherin in his conversation with Mikhail Frunze: 'Friendship with Kemalist Turkey is not an act of expediency for us. It is our position of principle. It is Lenin's policy. [. . .] It is resistance to imperialist coercion that unites us with all oppressed nations.'[33] So the main objective of the Soviet policy was support for the national liberation movement, not political expediency or the 'export of revolution'.

On the other hand, Kemal Atatürk's attitude to Soviet Russia was prompted by his understanding of the great importance of the friendship and support of the socialist state for the cause of the national liberation movement and the building of the republic and his appreciation and support of the principle of peaceful co-existence. Aware of the differences in ideology of the socialist revolution and the Kemalist movement, he nevertheless realised the need and mutual advantage of peaceful co-existence and wide-ranging co-operation. For him too it was a long-term policy of principle, not an act of expediency. 'The basis of our foreign policy is the strengthening of fraternal ties with the Russian Soviet republic which was the first sincerely and openly to recognise our full and genuine independence and to hold out a hand in friendship to us,' Kemal Atatürk said in his opening address to the third session of the Assembly on 1 March 1922.[34]

History owes a debt to Atatürk for his ability to understand correctly the character and role of co-operation with a socialist country.

His policy of promoting friendship and co-operation with Soviet Russia contributed to the strengthening of political stability and peace in the region. It was one of the main principles of his foreign policy and till now it has not lost its significance.

The conclusion of the Soviet-Turkish Treaty of 1921, combined with the military success of the Kemalists, enabled them to attain their foreign policy objectives in relations with the West in the course of the struggle for independence. When it began, the Sultan government in Istanbul and the Western powers did not want to attach any serious importance to the national liberation movement. In his speech, Kemal Atatürk recalled that the Sultan government's Minister of the Interior Adil Bey cabled instructions to the Elaziğ governor Galip Bey in September 1919 for 'fighting bandits', meaning the Kemalists.[35] In modern terminology, used sometimes in the West today with regard to the national liberation movements, Kemal and his associates might well have been called 'terrorists'.

However, as early as 1921, the Kemalists were recognised both in Istanbul and in the West as a real national force. That was demonstrated by the invitation of a delegation of the government of the Grand National Assembly of Turkey (GNA) to the London Conference (21 February–14 March 1921), called by the Entente to revise the fettering Treaty of Sèvres it had imposed on the Sultan government in August 1920. At the opening of the Conference, the British prime minister Lloyd George declared: 'There is an impressive force under Mustafa Kemal in Anatolia opposing the Treaty of Sèvres. That is why it is necessary now to revise that Treaty so as to establish a lasting peace over there.'[36] At the same time, the London Conference aimed to drive a wedge between Moscow and Ankara.

Neither the one nor the other aim was ever attained. The draft revision of the Treaty of Sèvres, proposed by the Entente, did not satisfy the GNA government. The Entente likewise failed to draw the Kemalists into an anti-Soviet bloc, compelling them to make peace with the Sultan government. The 'peace' proposed by Lloyd George did not correspond to the peace as seen by the Kemalists. Atatürk issued strict instructions for his delegation not to depart under any circumstances from the principles of the National Pact. On the other hand, the leader of the Ankara delegation, Bekir Sami Bey, Foreign Minister in the GNA government, entered into separate negotiations with representatives of Britain, France and Italy in London, without Atatürk's sanction, and reached agreement with them at the cost of unprincipled concessions and actual betrayal of the interests of the national liberation movement. Bekir Sami Bey's action was severely criticised in the GNA, and he resigned from his post at Kemal Atatürk's request.[37]

The London Conference showed that the Entente was not giving up its imperialist aims in Anatolia, that the peace negotiations had failed so far to ensure national independence, and that it would still have to be fought for. In the middle of 1921, the armed forces of the Kemalists won a series of impressive military victories over the Western allies, on the one hand, which brought contradictions within their camp to a head, and, on the other, reinforced the GNA government's international position. One upshot was that by early July Italy had pulled her troops out of Anatolia. At about the same time, France entered into negotiations with the GNA government and sent Franclin Bouillon to Ankara in June for direct negotiations with Atatürk. The French representative offered to base the negotiations on the Treaty of Sèvres. Kemal turned down the offer pointblank. He declared: 'We cannot enter into sincere relations with the countries which have not taken the Treaty of Sèvres off their minds. In our view, this Treaty does not exist.' 'I have laid down the principle', Atatürk said, 'that it is the National Pact that must be the starting-point of our negotiations.' He emphasised that 'the new Turkey will be able to compel recognition of her rights, just as the rights of any other independent nation are recognised.'[38]

The French were the first in the West to realise that there could be no other base for negotiations with the Kemalists. A treaty whereby France recognised the GNA government and pulled her forces out of Cilicia, which thus enabled the Kemalists to drop the Southern Front, was signed in Ankara on 20 October 1921. That meant a breach in the common position of the West and a serious diplomatic success for Ankara. 'That was the first time our national aspirations were recognised and confirmed in a treaty with a Western Power,' Atatürk stated in that connection.[39]

The principles of the Kemalists' foreign policy with regard to the nations of the East came to light in the years of the national liberation movement. As to the Arab countries, which had earlier formed part of the Ottoman empire, the new Turkey, acting in compliance with the provisions of the National Pact, relinquished all claims to them, thereby opening up the way to establishing equal and friendly relations with them. Along with that, she had no reason to differ with independent Afghanistan, Iran and other Eastern countries. A Turkish delegation concluded a Treaty of Friendship with Afghanistan and established diplomatic relations with her in Moscow on 1 March 1921. The national liberation war in Turkey earned sympathy and support in Arab countries, Afghanistan, Iran and India.[40]

All these factors combined were certainly strengthening the Kemalists' international position. By that time it was the GNA government that began to be treated as a genuine representative of the Turkish nation. During 1922, the Kemalists made a series of attempts, by using their earlier military and diplomatic successes, to get the Entente to recognise the National Pact in a peaceful way and to withdraw the invading forces from Anatolia. Yet all those attempts were unavailing. 'True', Atatürk said in this connection, 'we did not have any particular certainty and hopes in the diplomatic sense until the adversary was driven out of our country by force of arms and until we had proved our right to exist, having demonstrated the force and power of the nation in practical terms.'[41]

The armed struggle for the implementation of the National Pact had to be continued by every means. It was only the crushing defeat of the invaders by the Turkish army in August 1922 that cleared the way to peace negotiations and forced the Entente to accept them. The Mudanya armistice treaty was signed on 11 October 1922, and the Lausanne peace treaty with Turkey in July 1923.

On 1 November 1922 the GNA passed an Act to abolish the Sultanate and on 29 October 1923, declared Turkey a republic. The Caliphate was abolished, too, in March 1924. That was the starting-point of a new period in the history of Turkey and, accordingly, in her foreign policy. The major objectives now were to consolidate her political independence won in the course of the liberation struggle, overcome economic dislocation and backwardness, and develop and strengthen the national economy as the base for political independence.

Kemalist foreign policy, 1923–1938

Following the proclamation of the Republic, the Kemalists' foreign policy was based on the same principles as had been put forward and motivated by Atatürk and his associates in the course of the national liberation movement, as related earlier. The only distinguishing feature of the foreign policy of the republican period was a certain shift of accent. There was a practice of combining peaceful and violent methods of resolving foreign policy problems during the years of the national liberation movement. After the Turkish people, faced by the grim necessity of upholding their independence by force of arms, had successfully resolved that problem, the centre of gravity shifted towards peaceful tactics. A review of Atatürk's foreign policy statements and his actual performance in this area during the republican period will make it clear that his major concern was to strengthen peace and to look hard for nothing but peaceful ways of resolving conflict situations.

Soviet-Turkish relations were further developed during that period. These included as important an act as the signing of a Treaty of Non-Aggression and Neutrality in December 1925, which envisaged that in the event of armed action against either of the contracting parties, the other contracting party undertook to observe neutrality. Both parties also undertook to refrain from attacking one another and from participating in alliances or hostile acts directed against the other, and to resolve all disputed issues through negotiation.[42] The protocols prolonging the 1925 Treaty were signed in Ankara in December 1929 and then in November 1935.

Soviet-Turkish relations in the 1920s and the first half of the 1930s developed against the background of the subsisting hostility of the Entente powers towards Turkey where their intervention had been defeated. Besides, there was still a set of outstanding problems to resolve. The Entente powers kept up the same kind of hostility towards the Soviet Union as well. That prompted both nations to draw closer together and to seek each other's support. The USSR and Turkey held identical views on a number of international issues during that period. For example, the Soviet government offered to invite Turkey to join the Preparatory Commission for the Disarmament Conference. This resulted in a Turkish representative attending the Fifth Session of the Preparatory Commission in March 1928 in Geneva where he spoke up in full support for the Soviet proposals on disarmament. That was the first international forum for republican Turkey to attend.

Yet another significant fact was that on 1 April 1929, the GNA ratified Turkey's accession to the Moscow Protocol on an early enforcement of the Brian-Kellogg Pact repudiating war as a means of national policy. In that way Turkey seconded the position of the USSR on the matter, opposed Western attempts at cutting the USSR off from international politics, and contributed, just as the other parties to the Protocol, towards strengthening peace and security in Eastern Europe and in Asia. Also in cooperation with the USSR, Turkey settled the question of her joining the League of Nations in 1932.

Cooperation developed not only in the political but in the trade and economic areas as well. The first Soviet-Turkish trade treaty was signed in March 1927. The 1934 Agreement providing for a Soviet credit to Turkey for the construction of two textile mills started off technical and economic cooperation which is so effectively developing today. That can be said to have been the first case of this kind of cooperation between a socialist and a developing nation. In the 1930s, the Soviet Union lent Turkey substantial assistance in drawing up her first five-year industrial development plan (1934–8) and in promoting her agriculture and industry.[43]

The essence of the Kemalists' political line in relation to the Soviet Union was largely expressed by Atatürk in his speech at the opening of the Assembly session on 1 March 1923. 'The foundation of our policy in the East', Atatürk said at that time, 'is the strengthening of sincere relations with the Russian Soviet Republic on the basis of the Moscow Treaty and the promotion of mutual economic ties in conformity with the existing laws in both countries.'[44]

Looking at Turkey's policy towards the Soviet Union in that period as a whole, there were, of course, some diplomatic zigzags in it, but this was not the main thing. As before, it was determined by Atatürk's firm principle of strengthening friendly relations and all-round cooperation. This line was the pivot of his policy. In that period, Soviet-Turkish relations were a major contribution to the strengthening of regional and world peace and international security. The experience of Atatürk's political course with regard to a socialist country is certainly topical and, in our opinion, merits a serious study on an international plane.

The shaping of Turkey's relations with the West in that period was characterised by the overcoming of hostility, a search for a settlement of remaining outstanding issues, and gradual normalisation. Addressing the Assembly on 19 September 1921, Atatürk noted the establishment of friendly relations with the RSFSR, and declared: 'If the powers of the Entente also recognise our right to existence and national independence, then there will be no reasons for divergences between us, and we shall be able immediately to establish peace and set up mutual relations.'[45] It can be said that this was the principle foundation of the Kemalists' relations with the West.

The keynote of the development of relations with Britain was a difficult search for a settlement of the question of Mosul, occupied by British troops in 1918 in keeping with the Mudros armistice. Britain took advantage of its influence in the League of Nations, as well as of the support of France and Spain, to settle this issue in its favour. In spite of the conclusion of the Lausanne Treaty, the imperialist powers once again bared their claws. In this matter, Turkey at that time could rèly only on the Soviet Union's support.

Since Mosul came within the boundaries established by the National Pact, Turkey had to start an armed struggle for it. However, as is justly noted by Turkish researchers M. Gönlübol and C.Sar, this could have served as a pretext for the implementation of schemes of the Republic's internal and external enemies. Besides, Turkey was exhausted by the War for Independence and had to rebuild its economy.[46] All this prompted it to sign a treaty with

Britain in June 1926 on Mosul on terms proposed by the League of Nations.

Following this, over a number of years, Anglo-Turkish relations remained strained. There was a sign of rapprochement only in the latter half of the 1930s in connection with the threat of war in Europe emanating from Germany and Italy. The 1930s marked the beginning of the development of trade and economic co-operaton between Turkey and Britain.

In spite of the treaty with Turkey, concluded in 1921, France was the most persistent of all the Entente powers in advocating the preservation of a regime of capitulations, of previous economic privileges of the West in Turkey. And on the question of compensation for the Ottoman empire's pre-war debts, the Entente powers came out in a united front against Turkey, exerting political and economic pressure on it. France's special interest in this matter was explained by the fact that the biggest capital investments in the Ottoman empire had been its own. Only in 1928, following lengthy negotiations, was an agreement signed regulating financial and economic matters. It was clarified and finally regulated by the agreement of 1933.

Another outstanding issue was the establishment of borders between Turkey and Syria, then a French-mandated territory. The matter concerned the so-called Iskenderun *sancak* (district), which came within the boundaries fixed by the National Pact and was populated mostly by Turks. Turkish diplomacy had to exert considerable efforts to settle this question. The Turkish-Syrian border issue was partly decided by the agreements of 1926 and 1930, but the *sancak* remained within the limits of Syria. The matter again became aggravated following the cancellation in 1936 of the French mandate in Syria. Kemal Atatürk personally attached great importance to this matter, believing it to be necessary to fight for this territory. Opening the statutory session of the Grand National Assembly of Turkey on 1 November 1936, he stated: 'The biggest question of this period for us, which takes our nation's attention day and night, is the fate of the areas of Iskenderun and Antakya, the real masters of which are the Turks. On this issue we are compelled, in all seriousness and determination, to insist on our stand. This is the only major divergence between us and France, to friendship with whom we have always attached great importance.'[47]

The Iskenderun *sancak* was joined to Turkey after Atatürk's death in 1939; however, this was a success of his foreign policy line. In general, he advocated a peaceful way of settling questions, even though the way might be long and difficult. He was opposed to the use of force and to a policy of *fait accompli*: this was one of the overall principles of his foreign policy. Trade and economic ties developed along with the normalisation of political relations with France.

Pursuing the line of improving relations with the West, Turkey gradually normalised its relations with Italy as well, as seen in the signing in May 1928 of an agreement on neutrality. By the beginning of the 1930s, Italy had become one of Turkey's main trading partners, but the further development of relations was held up by fascist Italy when it began manifesting its policy of international aggression at that time. This evoked a strong negative reaction from Atatürk.

Following lengthy and difficult negotiations, relations were normalised in the 1920s and '30s with Greece, the most active participant in military intervention. The sharpest issues were gradually settled.

In this same period, Turkey established diplomatic relations with the United States, with most of the European states, and with a number of other countries.

The Kemalists attached great importance to the strengthening of relations with the Balkan countries. Here, too, as with the Arab countries, while remaining loyal to the National Pact, they endeavoured to build relations with the former parts of the Ottoman empire on a basis of equality and friendship. The implementation of the Kemalists' policy in the Balkans proceeded in two directions: first, the promotion of bilateral relations and, secondly, the creation of an alliance of Balkan states. As for the first direction, Atatürk emphasised the following at the opening of the Assembly session on 1 March 1923: 'We have no contradictions with our neighbours on the European continent. . . We sincerely wish the earliest possible restoration of official relations with the Balkan states, which are friendly to us, and with whom we had long-standing ties. We want to open embassies and consulates there.'[48] A treaty of friendship with Albania was signed in December 1923, and treaties of friendship with Bulgaria and of peace and friendship with Yugoslavia in October 1925.

By 1929, relations in the Balkans had mainly become stabilised. On the other hand, at that same time, tension began to grow in Europe in connection with the aggressive aspirations of Germany and Italy. All this objectively brought the Balkan countries closer together. Atatürk sought such rapprochement and lent it every assistance, proceeding from the interests of strengthening peace and security in the region and resisting the possible aggressor. Addressing the Assembly on 1 November 1931, Atatürk stated: 'Owing to its geographic position, Turkey is especially interested in the preservation and strengthening of peace in the Balkans.'[49]

Four Balkan conferences took place in the period of 1930–3. This work resulted in the signing of the Balkan Treaty in Athens in February 1934. Greece, Romania, Turkey and Yugoslavia became members of the treaty, or, as it was called, the Balkan entente. The Kemalists exerted considerable effort to bring about this treaty. They had no special interests in the Balkans, and regarded the treaty as a collective guarantee of security for its members, as a barrier against danger from outside, which at that time, in the Mediterranean and Balkan areas, stemmed mainly from Italy.

The Balkan entente had a certain role to play in safeguarding peace in the region. Atatürk said in his opening address at the fourth congress of the People's Republican Party on 9 May 1935: 'The conclusion of the Balkan Pact was also an important event of the past four years. Four states, guided by sincere mutual trust, signed that pact to ensure their security. . . . Just a year has passed but the Balkan Pact has already become an important factor for maintaining international peace.'[50]

The extension of relations with the Eastern countries was an indubitable success of the Kemalists' policy. Parallels can be drawn both in goals and in means, between Atatürk's policy in the Balkans and his policy towards Turkey's eastern neighbours. Bilateral relations were developing successfully there as well. True, these relations, particularly those with Iran, were adversely affected to some extent by the abolition of the Caliphate in 1924; however, it was clear even at that time that the Caliphate had ceased to play an effective unifying role for the Muslim states, and that none of them would have actually agreed to any restriction of its sovereignty by recognising the Caliph's supreme authority. Apart from that, the progressive forces in Muslim countries supported Turkey as a country which had been fighting against imperialism and won a victory in that struggle.

In April 1926 a Treaty of Security and Friendship with Iran, and in May 1928 a Turkish-Afghan Treaty of Friendship and Cooperation were signed. Contacts with the Arab countries were developing as well: a friendship treaty with Iraq was signed in June 1926 and prolonged in April 1937, a friendship treaty with Egypt was signed in April 1937, and relations of friendship were established with Yemen and Libya.

That was one aspect of relations with the Muslim East. Another aspect of these relations, as in the Balkans, consisted in the Kemalists' striving to establish some sort of collective security system there as well. Turkey was prompted to do so by Italy's aggression against Abyssinia. Talks and contacts initiated in 1935 were crowned with the signing of the Saadabad Pact between Afghanistan, Iraq, Iran and Turkey in July 1937. The provisions of the pact stipulated, among other things, non-intervention in each other's internal affairs, non-violability of common borders, consultations on international affairs affecting the interests of the contracting parties, repudiation of acts of mutual aggression, etc.

Like the Balkan entente, the Saadabad Pact was concluded with Turkey's active participation, if not on its initiative, and also had the objective of ensuring peace and security in that region within the powers of the countries which had signed it. In a speech at the Assembly on 1 November 1937 Kemal Atatürk characterised the Saadabad Pact as follows: 'The policy of friendship and rapprochement with Eastern countries that is being pursued consistently by the government of our republic has achieved another major success. What I mean is the quadripartite Saadababad Pact, which we have signed with our friends, Afghanistan, Iraq and Iran. This peace document cannot help giving us much gratification.'[51] Both the Balkan and the Saadabad Pacts were manifestations of a principle of Atatürk's foreign policy, which favoured active efforts for peace and security rather than passive pacifism, and also the achievement of collective guarantees for this within the available possibilities.

The Kemalists' line for strengthening relations with neighbouring and other nations logically led them to the decision to join the League of Nations. As early as March 1924, Atatürk said in the Assembly: 'When the peace treaties have come into force, the question of Turkey's joining the League of Nations may arise. We wish success to the League of Nations. We wish it to become a body settling international conflicts on the basis of law and justice and ensuring friendship and harmony in relations between nations rather than to be an instrument of domination of the stronger.'[52]

In July 1932 Turkey was accepted into the League of Nations. The League failed to become an effective instrument of peace, and the Kemalists had no illusions on that score. However, they wanted to use the possibilities offered by that organisation to extend their relations with different countries, to enhance Turkey's position on the international scene and to strengthen universal peace. Turkey's constructive role in the League is illustrated by its support in 1935 of the economic sanctions taken by decision of the League against Italy because of its aggression against Abyssinia. Turkey took part in the sanctions against the aggressor, although its trade relations with Italy were damaged as a result.

It is not possible to analyse here in detail the Turkish Republic's foreign policy during Atatürk's lifetime. However, even a short examination of its major lines gives every reason to believe that its main content was a striving for establishing and developing relations of friendship and mutually beneficial economic co-operation with its neighbours and other countries and a comprehensive and active desire for strengthening peace and security in the region and throughout the world. Atatürk made this point on more than one occasion in his speeches. 'The foreign policy of the Turkish Republic', he said in his Assembly speech on 1 March 1924, 'is honestly aimed at safeguarding peace and observing treaties. It is the extension of relations and mutual respect for rights that constitute the line of our activity.'[53]

These words were matched by deeds, by energetic and purposeful actions, as has been shown above. 'Peace all over the world'[54] was the keynote of Atatürk's foreign policy activity.

Returning to the beginning of the present chapter, where the main directions of the developing countries' foreign policies were characterised, we believe there is every reason to characterise Atatürk's foreign policy as a policy of positive neutrality, i.e. effective co-operation for strengthening world peace and international security. Of course, we should take account here of the difference between the conditions of the 1920s and 1930s and those of the present time: there was no such extensive and powerful non-aligned movement then as we have today. Kemal Atatürk's foreign-policy principles and activities make it possible to presume that he could have become one of the leaders of this movement.

Today dozens of newly-free countries are facing the tasks, including those in foreign policy, which the Kemalists had to tackle half a century ago. The latter set an example of masterfully combining military actions and diplomacy during their war of national liberation. Their experience demonstrated that it is important to use all possible means for settling conflicts peaceably, but that in doing so it is even more important not to relinquish the basic interests of the national-liberation movement, such as independence, sovereignty and territorial integrity.

The Kemalists were the first, or among the first, to appreciate the full importance of co-operation with a socialist state (the only one in the world at the time) for the sake of the triumph of the national-liberation movement, and the consolidation of political independence and national economic growth.

Last but not least, the practice of the Kemalists' foreign-policy activities following the establishment of the republic is also important. This practice demonstrated that the path of effective positive neutrality was leading both to the growth of the international prestige of a young state and to more stable peace and international security.

NOTES

1. See *The Foreign East and our Time: Main Laws and Specific Features of Development of the Newly Free Countries*, Moscow, 1974, vol. 2, 487–8 (in Russian).
2. *ibid.*, 581–2.
3. Atatürk, *Söylev (Nutuk)*. Türk Dil Kurumu Yayinları. Birinci cilt, Ankara, 1974, 8–9.
4. *ibid.*
5. *ibid.*, 10.
6. *ibid.*, 11.
7. *ibid.*, 10.
8. A.M. Shamsutdinov, *The National Liberation Struggle in Turkey* (1918–1923).
9. Atatürk, *Söylev (Nutuk)*, *op. cit.*, 46–7.
10. *ibid.*, 47–8; Gönlübol Mehmet *et al.*, *Olaylarla Türk Diş Politikasi (1919–1973)*, Ankara, 1974, 10.
11. Atatürk, *Söylev (Nutuk)*, *op. cit.*, 65.
12. *ibid.*, 76.
13. *ibid.*, 78.
14. Jorge Blanco Vilialta, *Atatürk*, Ankara, 1979, 192.
15. Aptülahat Akşin, *Atatürk' ün diş politika ilkeleri ve diplomasisi*, (Birinci Kisim), Ankara, 1964, 33–5.
16. *ibid.*, 81.
17. A.M. Shamsutdinov, *op. cit.*, 92–5.
18. Muammer Aksoy, 'Atatürk' ün ışığında "tam bağımsızlık ilkesi" ', *Prof. Dr. Yavuz Abadan'a armağan*, Ankara, Siyasal Bilgiler Fakültesi, 1969, 726.
19. Aptülahat Aksin, *op. cit.*, 34.
20. Kemal Atatürk, *Selected Speeches and Statements* (Russian translation from the Turkish), Moscow, 1966, 186–9.
21. A.M. Shamsutdinov, *op. cit.*, 73.
22. Kemal Atatürk, *Selected Speeches and Statements*, *op. cit.*, 100–1.
23. A.M. Shamsutdinov, *On the Establishment of Diplomatic Relations between the Governments of the RSFSR and GNAT. Turkey: History and Economics*, Moscow, 1978, 7.
24. *PCFA Annual Report to 8th Congress of Soviets of RSFSR (1919–1920)*, Moscow, 1921.
25. A.M. Shamsutdinov, *On the Establishment of . . .*, *op. cit.*, 10.
26. *Soviet Foreign Policy Documents*, vol. 2, Moscow, 1958, 555; *The History of Soviet Foreign Policy*, vol. 1 (1917–45), Moscow, 1976, 143–4.
27. *The History of Soviet Foreign Policy*, *op. cit.*, vol. 1, 145.
28. Kemal Atatürk, *Selected Speeches . . .*, *op. cit.*, 101.
29. A.F. Miller, *Notes on Turkey's Recent History*, Moscow, 1948, 113–14.
30. For fuller information on the problem see Addenda to vol. 3 of *Soviet Foreign Policy Documents*, Moscow, 1959.
31. S.I. Aralov, *Memoirs of a Soviet Diplomat. 1922–1923*, Moscow,

1960, 87−8 and 102−4.

32. *ibid.*, 35.

33. Anatoly Glebov, *A Policy of Friendship*, Moscow, 1960, 21.

34. Kemal Atatürk, *Selected Speeches . . .*, *op. cit.*, 228.

35. Atatürk, *Söylev (Nutuk)*. Birinci cilt, 93−3.

36. A.M. Shamsutdinov, *The National Liberation Struggle . . .*, *op. cit.*, 235.

37. Mehmet Gönlübol and Cem Sar, *Atatürk ve Türkiye' nin dış politikası (1919−1938)*, Istanbul, 1963, 25−9.

38. *Mustafa Kemal: the Way of New Turkey*, vol. 4, *The Victory of New Turkey, 1921−1927*, Moscow, 1934, 42−3 (in Russian).

39. *ibid.*, 46.

40. A.M. Shamsutdinov, *The National Liberation Struggle . . .*, *op. cit.*, p. 272; Gönlübol and Sar, *op. cit.*, 84−6.

41. *Mustafa Kemal. The Way of New Turkey*, *op. cit.*, 64.

42. *The History of the Foreign Policy of the USSR*, *op. cit.*, 233−4.

43. P.P. Moiseyev, *USSR-Turkey: a Half-century of Economic Cooperation (stages and trends). Problems of the History of Turkey*, Moscow, 1978, 175−8 (in Russian).

44. Kemal Atatürk, *Selected Speeches . . .*, *op. cit.*, 292.

45. *ibid.*, 166.

46. Gönlübol and Sar, *op. cit.*, 117−18.

47. Kemal Atatürk, *Selected Speeches . . .*, *op. cit.*, 394−5.

48. *ibid.*, 293.

49. *ibid.*, 367.

50. *ibid.*, 387.

51. *ibid.*, 403.

52. *ibid.*, 327.

53. *ibid.*, 327.

54. Usually this principle is formulated as 'peace in the country, peace all over the world'. We believe, however, that its first part has a socio-political meaning related to domestic policy, while the second is immediately applicable to foreign policy. The formula was included in the preamble of the second Constitution of the Turkish Republic, adopted in 1961, and was written into the programme of the People's Republican Party, which was approved in 1931.

The Kemalist revolution in comparative perspective

S.N. EISENSTADT

The Turkish revolution and the institutionalisation of the Kemalist regime are approached here from the point of view of a comparative analysis of modern revolutions and post-revolutionary regimes.

Let us start with the basic historical fact that the 'real', 'true' great revolutions have occurred in only very few societies — the Great Rebellion and the Glorious Revolution in England; the American Revolution; the French, Russian and Chinese revolutions; possibly the revolt of the Netherlands; and the Turkish and the (North) Vietnamese revolutions — and that they all took place when their respective societies were at certain stages of historical transition.

It might be worthwhile, therefore, to see whether these societies, as well as the historical circumstances in which the revolutions took place in them, share some common characteristics. A closer look does indeed reveal, first of all, that all these societies belong to the imperial or imperial-feudal types of political systems, the most important of which have been the Roman and the Hellenistic, the Chinese, Byzantine, Russian, Abbasid and Ottoman, and the major regimes of Western and Central Europe.

Of special interest for our discussion is the fact that within those societies specific patterns of change developed which differed from those in other 'traditional' or historical societies, especially the so-called patrimonial societies and most city-states and tribal federations. It was only in some of the Near Eastern — above all the ancient Israelite and Islamic — tribal federations and the great city-states of Greek and Roman antiquity that a different pattern of change developed, more similar to the imperial one. The pattern of change that developed in these imperial and imperial-feudal systems also evinced some features relatively close to those envisaged as revolutionary change.

The outstanding feature of the patterns of change in these societies was that a relatively high degree of coalescence between changes and restructuring in the major collectivities (political, religious, national) and institutional frameworks (the economic, the religious and that of social stratification) tended to go hand in hand with a high degree of restructuring in the political system itself. These socie-

ties also developed strong connections among the various movements of protest and political struggle, and a very high level of
organisation and articulation of the issues of such struggle.

The conditions that account for the major differences in the patterns of change can, first of all, be found in some of the cultural
orientations which prevailed in these different types of societies.
They can also be found in the combination of these cultural orientations with structural characteristics of societies that cut across
similar levels of technology, on the one hand, or of structural differentiation or class composition, on the other. The most important
of these characteristics are the structures of their centres and of
centre-periphery relations.

It is important to remember that most of these empires — with the
partial exception of the Roman and Hellenistic ones — developed in
close relation to some of the great civilisation or traditions such as
the special Chinese blend of Confucianism, Taoism and Buddhism;
the Christian tradition in its variety, and the Islamic one. Most of
these, with the partial exception of the late-comer, 'Islam', emerged
in the so-called Axial age, that is around the first millennium B.C.
which saw the breakthrough of some of the great civilisations in various parts of the world, the respective historical 'leaps' affected by
various cultural innovations: the Hebrew prophets, the Greek
philosophers, Jesus and the Apostles, Confucius, the codifiers of the
Brahmin tradition, and the Buddha.

Most of the civilisations or traditions within which these imperial
or feudal-imperial societies developed shared several basic cultural
orientations or codes that distinguished them from other civilisations that emerged in the same period. First, they were characterised
by a conception of a high level of autonomy and distinctness of the
cosmic (religious) and mundane orders. Second, even though they
shared this emphasis on the tension between the cosmic and mundane worlds with other civilisations, such as the Hindu and the Buddhist, unlike those they included some kind of worldly activity, not
only in the political, military and cultural spheres, but especially in
the European case also in the economic sphere, as a bridge between
the transcendental-cosmic and the mundane worlds, or in Weber's
terminology, as a focus of salvation. In addition, there developed
within these civilisations a strong emphasis on the commitment of
the different sectors of the population to the cosmic and social
orders and a relatively autonomous access of at least some of the
groups of these societies to the major attributes of some representative orders.

At the same time, these societies were also characterised by specific properties of their centres, of centre-periphery relations, and of

the structuring of social hierarchies and collectivities. The major characteristic of the centre-periphery relations in the imperial and to a large degree also in the imperial-feudal societies was, first, a high level of distinctiveness of the centre and of the perception of the centre as a distinct symbolic and organisational unit and, second, continuous attempts of the centres not only to extract resources from the periphery, but also to permeate it and to reconstruct it. In addition, in many of these societies there also developed potential tendencies toward the impinging of at least part of the periphery on the centre or centres.

This higher degree of symbolic distinction of the centre and of strata formation was carried by a multiplicity of élites — both political and economic — as well as by representatives of the solidarity of different collectives having relatively autonomous bases and potentially autonomous access to the centre and to each other. These élites impinged on the centre and the periphery alike, shaping various movements of protest and of political activities and struggle which developed within them. Each of these élites could be a carrier of alternative conceptions of social order and could become a starting-point for movements of protest or political struggle with a high level of organisational and symbolic articulation, by mobilising the available free resources and organising them into new directions.

The combination of cultural and structural characteristics which can be found in the imperial and the imperial-feudal societies generates processes of change somewhat similar to those presented in the image of revolution. The 'problematic' cultural orientations inspired visions of new types of social order, while the organisational and structural characteristics provided the framework through which some aspects of these visions could be institutionalised and the two were combined by the activities of the different 'entrepreneurs' analysed above.

Through the interaction between these structural and cultural characteristics, the different conditions which have been singled out in the literature lead to revolution. These conditions of revolution are, as we have seen, inter- and intra-élite competition; their interweaving with the broader social movements; the political articulation of the feeling of relative deprivation of broader groups which become linked with one another and thus lead to the outbreaks of 'real' revolutions, and the concomitant institutional change. In other types of societies, these various types of 'preconditions' or of precipitants, while possibly also leading to the demise of regimes, to internal wars and to some far-reaching changes, will not lead in either 'revolutionary' direction and/or to the type of social transformation connected with it.

But the 'mere' prevalence within these societies of the above-mentioned cultural orientations and structural characteristics does not explain or assure their resulting in revolutions. Even in these societies the first 'true' modern revolutions constituted a sort of 'mutation', an entirely new type of process of change. These revolutions developed only in very specific socio-historical circumstances, which we should mention here, if only very briefly.

The most important circumstances are those of relatively early stages of transition of modern settings in which there occurs the coincidence of three major aspects of the breakthrough from a 'traditional' to a modern setting. These aspects are, first, transition from a 'traditional' or 'closed' pattern of legitimation of political authority, as well as possibly also in the definition of symbols of collective identity to an open one; secondly, the transition to an open system of stratification, to a 'class' system, rooted in or connected with a trend to a market economy in general and an industrial economy in particular, and, thirdly and closely connected with the former, the creation of and/or incorporation of the respective societal units into a series of continuously changing international political, economic and cultural systems.

The coincidence of these transitions raises a series of problems which call for a redefinition of almost all the major symbolic premises and institutional arrangements, above all inasmuch as they bear on the access to power and the structure of the political centres. The growing socio-economic change and differentiation provides the movements of protest and political struggle and innovation with a larger number of groups ready for 'social mobilisation'; and the intensification of processes of change generated a larger number of élites of institutional entrepreneurs to serve as agents of such mobilisation, as linkages between themselves and between the centres and broader strata.

Hence it is in these types of situations of change that the potentialities for symbolically and organisationally linking movements of protest, rebellions and heterodoxies, and central political struggle and institution-building could become actualised and focused on the reconstruction of the social order. Accordingly, it is in these circumstances that the potentialities of change through revolution become intensified and that the special mutations of revolution *may* develop.

The Islamic and Ottoman backgrounds of Turkey

From the point of view of our analysis of the conditions of revolutions, the Islamic civilisation or civilisations evince a very complex pattern (Eisenstadt, 1978). This pattern has been characterised by the continuous prevalence, within Islam, of cultural orientations which were indeed conducive to the development of revolutionary tendencies, but which often became only latent. The relative weakness of these orientations was strongly connected with the development, in the realm of Islam, of structural characteristics — above all of patrimonial as against imperial regimes — which minimised the structural conditions conducive to the development of strong potential revolutionary tendencies. The root of these rather contradictory tendencies lies in several aspects of the history of Islam, which we shall briefly analyse.

Several important cultural orientations crystallised in the Islamic realm: the distinction between the 'cosmic' transcendental realm and the mundane one; the stress in overcoming this chasm through total submission to God and through this worldly (above all, political and military) activity; the strong universalistic element in the definition of the Islamic community; the principled autonomous access to salvation, through submission to God, of all members of the community; the ideal of the *ummah* (the political-religious community of all believers distinct from any ascriptive, primordial collectivity); and the ideal of the ruler as the upholder of the purity of the *ummah* and of the life of the community.

Of special importance from the point of view of our analysis is the fact that in the Islamic realm the original vision of the *ummah* assumed complete convergence between the socio-political and the religious community. Many of the later caliphs (such as the Abbasides and Fatimides) came to power on the crest of religious movements which upheld this ideal, legitimised themselves in such religious-political terms, and sought to retain popular support by stressing the religious aspect of their authority and by courting the religious leaders and religious sentiments of the community. Political issues were the central problem of theology in Islam. At the same time, however, because of the historical patterns of the spread of Islam, there developed, at least during quiet periods of different Islamic regimes, a relatively strong segregation between this-worldly and other-wordly activities, with a generally stronger emphasis on the latter.

In close relation to these developments, the historical spread of Islam gave rise to a high degree of symbolic and organisational autonomy of the political élites; to a relatively high symbolic autonomy — but only a minimal organisational one — of the religious élite; and to a growing separation of the two. The religious leadership was greatly dependent on the rulers and did not develop into a broad, independent and cohesive organisation. Religious groups and functionaries were not organised as a separate entity, nor did they constitute a tightly organised body — except when, as in the

Ottoman empire, they were organised by the state. Thus there developed a strong dissociation between the political and the religious élites as well as between these élites and the local community, because of the strong ideological dissociation of the universal Islamic community and the various primordial ones. But there was always prevalent in Islam a strong latent religious-ideological orientation towards unification of these spheres.

The combination of religious orientations, structures of élites and the relations between élites and local ascriptive communities gave rise, in imperial and patrimonial Islamic systems alike, to some unique types of ruling groups, and to a distinct pattern of accountability of rulers. The most distinctive of such ruling élites were the military-religious rulers who emerged from tribal and sectarian elements, and from the system of military slavers, which created special channels of mobility such as the *qul* system in general, the Mameluke system and Ottoman *devşirme* in particular, through which the ruling group could be recruited from alien elements.

The combination of all these factors had several repercussions on the politics of accountability of rulers. On the purely symbolic level, the rulers were supposed to uphold the ideal of the *ummah* and to be accountable to it; but this ideal was given up quite early in the history of Islam and instead there developed the theological acceptance of any ruler as preferable to anarchy. And yet the older ideal was never fully given up, and it is the combination of the two that explains several crucial aspects of the political dynamics in Islamic countries. On the one hand there developed, in stable Islamic societies, rather effective routine checks — religious or otherwise — on the authority of rulers. At the same time it was the religious leaders, the *ulema* and the Sufi sheiks, who were the keepers of the law and, through it, of the boundaries of the community — thus not only being an indispensable partner of any ruling coalition, but also a very potent one in possible confrontations with the rulers.

It is true that, as Bernard Lewis has shown, a concept of revolution did not emerge in Islam. But at the same time, there developed, as indicated by E. Gellner in his interpretation of Ibn Khaldun, a less direct yet very forceful pattern of accountability of rulers, manifest in the possibility of rulers being deposed by the combination of sectarian groups with the resurgence of tribal revival against 'corrupt' or weak regimes.

Given all these historical processes, it was only under very special circumstances that imperial or quasi-imperial regimes developed in Islam. One of them has been the early Abbaside period — which was indeed often seen as being initiated by the Abbaside revolution. The Ottoman empire — despite the prevalence, as has been pointed out by Şerif Mardin, of many patrimonial features — has been another approximation to an imperial regime in the realm of Islam. Interestingly enough, these characteristics became predominant in the nineteenth century — during the period of reforms, and it was because of this that there developed in Turkey the revolutionary movement which led to the Kemalist revolution and the institutionalisation of the Kemalist regime.

The special background characteristics of the Turkish revolution have greatly influenced the pattern of institutionalisation of the Kemalist post-revolutionary regime and they distinguish it from other modern post-revolutionary regimes. However, before analysing these specific patterns, it might be worthwhile to stress the characteristics which the Turkish revolution shares with other modern revolutions.

The modern revolutions pushed the societies in which they took place in the direction of modernisation of their organisational and symbolic aspects. All post-revolutionary societies experienced growing structural differentiation and specialisation: the establishment of international organisational frameworks and markets, the development of market economies and of modern industrial or semi-industrial institutional frameworks in the economy, the elaboration of relatively open, non-traditional systems of stratification and mobility in which criteria of achievement — specifically economic, occupational and educational — become relatively predominant, and the weakening of traditional strata formation and its replacement by more open class formation in the structuring of social hierarchies and centralised political systems. These organisational changes were closely associated with the basic premises of the revolutionary image — that is, the premises of equality, freedom and solidarity — and with their basic institutional derivatives, the undermining of traditional legitimation, the restructuring of centre-periphery relations, the growing impingement of the periphery on the centre in the name of revolutionary premises, and the far-reaching transformation of the nature and contents of societal centres and of the rules of access to them.

Such social transformation, of course, took place in varying degrees in all the modern and modernising societies. In revolutionary societies they occurred by means of violent upheavals and through specific constellations of processes of change. Revolutionary transformation entailed first of all a considerable convergence between the restructuring of access to the centre, its symbols and the patterns of its legitimation, on the one hand, and changes in principles of distributive justice, legitimation and structure of institutional activities and/or delineation of the boundaries and symbols of membership in the collectivity, on the other. Furthermore, changes in the political sphere itself crystallised in a certain pattern. Thus, changes in the symbols and patterns of legitimation of regimes, in the composition of the ruling class, in the bases of access to the centre, in centre-periphery relations, and in positions of control over resources, coalesced.

But beyond this outcome, common to all modernisation processes in general and to revolutionary ones in particular, there developed among them some very important differences, such as that between democratic and autocratic results. The best way to understand the different outcomes of revolutions — and implicitly also of processes of transition to modern social and political systems — is to analyse them within the broader framework of their discontinuity from pre-revolutionary societies. What, then, are the most important aspects of such discontinuities? They seem to be, first, the degree of change in the symbols of collective identity and of the legitimation of regimes; secondly, the amount of violence and violent institutional and symbolic disruption with the past that the respective revolutions entailed and the degree to which such violence was symbolically upheld, and, thirdly, the degree of discontinuity in the organisation and premises of institutional structures.

The last discontinuity can be differentiated according to the following dimensions:

(*a*) The degree of discontinuity in the composition of the ruling élite or class and of the holders of the power and prestige — especially of the highest positions in the various institutional spheres. Such discontinuity ranges from complete (violent or non-violent) elimination of the previously uppermost groups to their assimilations in the new frameworks.

(*b*) Organisational changes in the scope of the principal units of the various institutional spheres, as for instance the transition from small-scale cliques to organised parties or from narrow to broader institutional markets.

(*c*) Changes in the 'meaning' of institutions, i.e. the avowed symbolic 'purposes' or ultimate goals through which the major institutional spheres are defined as contributing to the consequent mode of their legitimation, and to the articulation of new roles. In the economic sphere, such changes are manifest in what marxists call the mode of production. In the political sphere they are manifest in the type of regime and in the pattern of political articulation, in centre-periphery relations, and in the symbols and bases of political legitimation.

(*d*) The concomitant changes in the control over the access of different groups to the major resources and markets and the degree of dislocation of different groups from their bases of power and from their control over the use of resources, the degree to which changes in the composition of ruling and other classes were connected not only with changes in the relative position of these groups but also with the loss — especially by the middle and lower groups — of access to and/or control of resources, autonomous access to bases of power, as well as with the degree to which institutional restructuring was connected with coercive measures.

Different post-revolutionary societies varied greatly with respect to the sometimes paradoxical constellations of these discontinuities.

The outcome of the Kemalist revolution differed greatly from those of other modern revolutions. Its most salient characteristics from the point of view of the different discontinuities — and the subsequent patterns of institutionalisation of the regime — were first of all a shift in the bases of political legitimation and the symbols of the political community, together with the redefinition of the boundaries of the collectivity. The redefinition of the political community took place in a unique way: the society withdrew from the Islamic framework into that of the newly-defined Turkish nation. While this process appears similar to the path followed by the European nation-states, it in fact involved the negation of a universal framework: Islam. This was not the case in Europe. Thus the Turkish revolution rejected completely the religious basis of legitimation and attempted instead to develop a secular national one, as the major ideological parameter of the new collectivity, with very little emphasis on the social components of ideologies. This shift was connected with an almost total displacement of the former ruling class — political as well as religious — by the members of the secondary (bureaucratic and intellectual) élites. A parallel development was connected with the broadening of new markets and the opening up of the flow of resources. However, markets were initially controlled by the ruling élite. Moreover, attempts were made to crystallise new economic institutions modelled on the capitalist system but imbued with a strong étatist orientation.

The displacement of the ruling group was not connected with that of the stronger elements of the traditional social and economic spheres. In urban and rural settings displacements occurred in two seemingly contradictory directions. First, the élitist establishment and bureaucracy became stronger, formulating étatist policies and orientations. Secondly, there was a movement towards a somewhat more autonomous class formation based partly on the links between the bureaucratic elements and the stronger socio-economic ones.

These shifts in the principles of legitimation, the symbols and boundaries of community, together with the change in the ruling class, were connected with the ideological restructuring of centre-periphery relations towards modernity. Concomitantly, political participation was in principle extended to broader strata, although in the early years of the revolutionary regimes it was entirely controlled by the ruling group.

A comparison

These outcomes can be compared — even if very schematically — with two other 'extreme' cases — the English revolution on the one hand and the Russian one on the other. In some ways the Turkish revolution can be seen as a case between these two extremes.

The English revolutionary process — from the Great Rebellion to the Glorious Revolution — generated a relatively small degree of discontinuity in the symbols of the political community, although there took place a rather marked shift in the bases of legitimation. This shift was connected during the Great Rebellion with considerable violence, although the later European and Asian revolutions were far more violent. The revolutionary outcomes in England included major shifts in the importance and power of different segments of the ruling class. The new elements — landed and urban middle groups, lower echelons of the aristocracy, and especially the professional, religious and independent political entrepreneurs (closely related to but not identical with both aristocratic and middle-class rural and urban strata) — were incorporated into the centre without extensive symbolic or physical destruction of the more traditional aristocratic and court groups. At the same time there occurred far-reaching though gradual changes in some of the basic principles of hierarchisation of the social structure as well as in the criteria of access to resources and to the base of power which controlled the use of these resources. Criteria of economic standing slowly became more important, interweaving more closely with those of social status and political power. This development was connected with the increasing strength and autonomy of urban, agricultural, commercial and semi-industrial middle classes and economic activities. The growing control these groups exercised over the use of their resources was bound up with the autonomy of private property and civil rights.

The ascendancy of the rule of law was connected with the broadening of access among various, but especially middle, groups to the major markets, as well as with their growing control over the flow of resources among markets. The stress on private property and civil rights was initially instrumental in the dissociation of many of the lower (particularly rural) groups from the bases of their resources and in the creation of an urban proletariat. Such dissociation was only partial or temporary. The institutionalisation of civil rights, the rule of law, and the sovereignty of parliament later become starting points for the political organisation of these groups and for the crystallisation of their own rights of access to the centre after prolonged struggle. Thus access to markets and to control over them, so closely related to the legal system, was also extended to the proletarian groups that emerged in the wake of the dislocations caused by capitalistic developments in agriculture and later by the Industrial Revolution.

Concomitantly, England experienced an intensification of changes in the meaning of institutions and in the restructuring of roles. In the economic sphere, this meant that the capitalist system or mode of production constituted not only an organisational framework but also a new, self-legitimising system with new, autonomous roles and symbols. In the political field there took place, as indicated above, shifts in the principles of legitimation: the seemingly constant restructuring of relations between the socio-economic and political orders towards differentiation; and the growing articulation of the autonomous access of socio-economic groups to the centre.

Contrary to this pattern, the outcome of the Russian Revolution exhibits the largest degree of discontinuity from the pre-revolutionary structure. Under the Bolsheviks, Russia broke totally with the past in terms of the restructuration of the socio-political order. This took place first in the symbols of the polity and in its legitimation. Concomitantly, the ruling class was totally displaced and almost exterminated — by the new, revolutionary party élite, which constituted a unique type of modern ruling class, and by new upper (usually party and bureaucratic) social and economic groups. Even if these groups sometimes came from older, non-proletarian elements, they were organised according to entirely new principle of hierarchisation focused on the political dominance of the new ruling élites. Russia also witnessed the almost complete displacement of lower groups, especially the peasants, who lost whatever limited control they once had over their own resources.

Changes also occurred in the meaning and structuring (although not necessarily in the organisation) of the major institutional spheres. The movement was away from a partly capitalist economy to one regulated by the state, vaguely defined or legitimised in terms of contribution to the modernisation of the collectivist economy, placing a very strong emphasis on heavy industrialisation and controlled by the new party bureaucracy. The restructuration of the Russian economy was based on the expansion of markets, the flow of resources and on determined efforts on the part of the ruling class to control, through coercion, the access to markets and the flow of resources. Similarly, while centre-periphery relations were theoretically restructured according to the basic tenets of modernity (which emphasised participation of the broader strata in the centre and the accountability of the centre), the actual access to the centre was narrowly restricted by coercive measures. Unlike the traditional Russian centre, the Bolshevik one continuously mobilised the periphery — without, however, allowing it to get autonomously organised or to have access to the centre.

Historical roots of the structure and ideology of the Kemalist revolution

How can we then explain these variations — and what is their implication for the institutionalisation of the Kemalist regime? The most important variable which explains such differences in the outcome of revolutions is the structure of the revolutionary élite; and this in turn is influenced above all by the structure of the preceding centres and by the revolutionary situation itself.

The most important characteristics of the Turkish revolutionary groups are:

(*a*) the fact that the revolution was undertaken by military-official elements — among whom autonomous political leadership and autonomous religious and intellectual elements were relatively weak;

(*b*) that at the same time these officers had a modern educational background and evinced strong ideological and intellectual tendencies;

(*c*) that the ideology they carried was a secular, rationalist, nationalist, anti-religious, étatist one, with relatively weak social orientations or themes;

(*d*) closely connected with the former, a relatively low level of antagonism towards the upper and middle social classes — as distinct from the former political and religious élites;

(*e*) the fact that, at the same time, these classes were not allowed any autonomous access to the new centre — just as they were barred from the older one; and

(*f*) the relatively minor contacts between these revolutionary groups and lower classes and movements of rebellion among them.

These characteristics of the Kemalist revolutionary élite have their roots in the historical background and the structure of the pre-revolutionary centre — especially in its rigidity, openness and composition, in the degree of cohesion of the ruling élites and their solidary relations with different other groups in society, and in the revolutionary situation and experience itself. In general the most important aspects of the rigidity or openness of the centre are: first, the centre's tactical rigidity in the face of new demands; secondly, its structural rigidity, i.e. the degree to which the centre is based on denying autonomous access to other groups; thirdly, the degree to which the composition of the centre is homogeneous or hetero-geneous; fourthly, the relationship among groups and élites in the centre, among those aspiring for access to the centre, and between these groups and other social actors (secondary élites, social classes, broad ascriptive collectivities). These various aspects of the structure of the centre and its relations to other élites and broader strata influence the centre's ability to mobilise the resources needed for coping with the problems attendant on the transition to modernity, to incorporate new claimants (or potential claimants) to participation in it, and to establish links with the broader strata in order to effect institution-building. In this way, such aspects of the structure of the centre and of the major groups also influence the different outcomes of the revolutions.

The Ottoman centre represented a mixture of imperial and patrimonial elements. The imperial element was strongly rooted in the ideology of Islam and in the orientations of some of the groups in the centre; the patrimonial element was evident to some degree in the organisation of the centre, in the composition of the periphery, and in centre-periphery relations. The onset of modernisation intensified the development within the centre of a relative plurality of elements: the rulers, different groups of bureaucrats, semi-professional groups, and the military. Some of these elements established relatively solidary relations with upper groups of the rural periphery and in a sense provided an important link between some of the stronger and internally solidary elements of the periphery with the centre.

This Turkish centre was based — like the Russian but not the English one — on the principled denial of the autonomous access of broader groups to the centre, thus giving rise in the post-revolutionary situation to a much more far-reaching pattern of discontinuity. Not only did rupture and discontinuity occur here in the symbols and legitimation of the political regime to an extent unknown in the preceding cases, but these trends were also connected with the displacement of the ruling class and the upper classes, with the dislocation of other classes, and with drastic changes in most principles of the distribution of resources. At the same time, however, the Turkish centre was relatively pluralistic, and this tendency grew stronger as it responded to modernisation. Accordingly, in the Kemalist Revolution, discontinuity in the symbols of political legitimation and removal of the former ruling group were not connected with drastic changes in the composition of the upper social groups, with far-reaching dislocations of other groups, or with any marked shift in their access to the centre. All these developments attested to the more general tendency that the more pluralistic the centre and the more politically open it is to at least certain broader groups, the greater the chances that the tendency toward restructuring the principles of political legitimation as well as the principles of access to the centre will not be connected with total restructuring of the basic principles of the major institutional spheres.

This was closely related in Turkey to relatively solidary relations of the newer groups within the centre, and hence also to a relatively small degree of coerciveness in the institutionalisation of the post-revolutionary regime. At the same time, because, as we have seen, these solidary relations were not based on new autonomous political or, above all, religious orientations or activities, and the revolutionary experience itself was not connected with mass movements, there did not develop in Turkey stable institutional complexes with new meanings which promoted or maintained extensive organisational changes in institutional spheres — beyond the general étatist orientations.

It was the combination of these various factors that explains some of the additional features of the problems of long-term institutionalisation of the Kemalist regime. The relative weakness of the coercive element in the institutionalisation of this regime explains how the relatively peaceful transition from the initial autocratic to the later democratic regime was possible. At the same time, one of the most important results of the combination of the weakness of the autonomous religious elements, the relatively secluded culture of the secular revolutionary élite, and the weakness of social ideology, was the relatively weak institutionalisation of legitimation in terms which would be acceptable to all groups, and hence the relative instability of the post-revolutionary regimes. Closely connected with this was also the relative oscillation between, on the one hand, independent institution-building by more autonomous strata which started to develop during the post-revolutionary period, and, on the other, the more étatist, semi-patrimonial policy which remained very much in line with some of the older Ottoman patterns.

BIBLIOGRAPHY

On the conditions of revolutions: S.N. Eisenstadt, *Revolutions and the Transformation of Societies,* New York, 1978.

On the basic tenets of Islam: G.E. von Grunebaum, *Medieval Islam: A Study in Cultural Orientation,* Chicago, 1946; *idem* (ed.), 'Studies in Islamic Cultural History', *American Anthropologist Memoir,* no. 6, Menaska, Wisc., 1954; B. Lewis, *The Arabs in History,* London, 1937; M.G.S. Hodgson, *The Venture of Islam: Conscience and History in a World Civilization,* 3 vols., Chicago, 1974; B. Lewis, 'The Concept of an Islamic Republic', *Die Welt des Islams,* 4, no. 1, 1955, 1 – 10; *idem. Islam in History: Ideas, Men and Events in the Middle East,* London, 1973.

On sectarian tendencies and processes of change is Islam: H. Laoust, *Les schismes dans l'Islam: introduction à une étude de la religion musulmane,* Paris, 1965; B. Lewis, *Islam in History,* 217 – 66; C. Cahen; 'La changeante portée sociale de quelques doctrines religieuses', *l'Elaboration de l'Islam, Colloque de Strasbourg, 12 – 14 June, 1959,* Paris, 1961, 5 – 22; and M.S. Stern, 'Isma'ilis and Qarmantians', *ibid.,* 99 – 108; B. Lewis, 'Islamic Concepts of Revolution', *idem, Islam and History, op. cit.,* 253 – 67; E. Gellner, 'A Pendulum Swing Theory of Islam' in R. Robertson (ed.)., *Sociology of Religion,* Baltimore, 1969, 127 – 41.

On the structure of the Ottoman empire: H. Inalcık, *The Ottoman Empire: The Classical Age, 1300 – 1600,* London, 1973; idem, 'The Nature of Traditional Society: Turkey' in R. Ward and D. A. Rustow (eds.), *Political Modernization in Japan and Turkey,* Princeton, 1964, 42 – 63; Ş. Mardin, 'Power, Civil Society and Culture in the Ottoman Empire', *Comparative Studies in Society and History,* 11 (June 1969), pp. 258 – 81; Ç. Keyder, 'The Dissolution of the Asiatic Mode of Production', *Economy and Society,* 5, no. 2 (1976), 178 – 97; K.H. Karpat (ed.), *The Ottoman State and its Place in World History,* Leiden, 1974; B. Lewis, *Origins of Modern Turkey,* London, 1961.

On the modernisation process in Turkey: Ward and Rustow, *op. cit.;* M. Ma'oz, *Ottoman Reform in Syria and Palestine, 1840 – 1861,* New York, 1968; Ç. Keyder, *loc. cit.;* Ş. Mardin, *The Genesis of Young Ottoman Thought,* Princeton, 1962.

On the Kemalist revolution: Ş. Mardin, 'Ideology and Religion in the Turkish Revolution', *International Journal of Middle East Studies,* 2, no. 3 (1971), 197 – 211.

On some aspects of the Kemalist and post-Kemalist regimes: M. Heper, 'Political Modernization as Reflected in Bureaucratic Change', *International Journal of Middle East Studies,* 7 (1976), 507 – 21; *idem,* 'The Recalcitrance of the Turkish Public Bureaucracy to "Bourgeois Politics": a Multi-Factor Political Stratification Analysis', *Middle East Journal,* 30, no. 4 (Autumn 1976), 485 – 500; *idem,* 'Transformation of Charisma into a Political Paradigm: Ataturkism in Turkey', mimeo., Boğaziçi University, Istanbul, 1976: K. H. Karpat, *Turkish Politics: The Transition to a Multi-Party System,* Princeton; 1952; I. Sunar, *State and Society in the Politics of Turkey's Development,* Ankara, 1974.

Part II:
Economic and Cultural Change

The political economy of Kemalism

FEROZ AHMAD

The ideology that came to be described as Kemalism was unveiled in 1931 at the congress of the Republican People's Party (RPP). It was defined in terms of six principles, namely nationalism, republicanism, populism, secularism, statism and revolutionism, which would thenceforth guide the destinies of the Turkish nation. They were first made part of the party's programme, and then in 1937 inserted into the constitution and institutionalised. Though unveiled only in 1931, Kemalism had been evolving throughout the previous decade, in fact ever since the start of the national struggle in 1919, re-adjusting to events and circumstances. However, if we consider the late nineteenth- and early twentieth-century trends of Ottomanism, Pan-Islamism, and Pan-Turkism, the search for ideology was much older. But these were limited ventures with aims which hardly went beyond the search for identity for the Muslim-Turkish community; they did not seek to provide an ideological framework for the development of state and society as a whole. Kemalism, on the other hand, not only provided an identity defined by the revolutionary concept of nationalism, but the other five principles became the basis for the new regime and the society it set out to create.

Despite the original character of Kemalism, it did have antecedents for both its ideas and its social foundations. It would be unhistorical to conceive of such an ideology without recognising the contribution of the Young Turk era (1908–18), when some of the ideas refined by Mustafa Kemal were first put forward and discussed. Nor must we forget that Kemal Paşa played an active role during the decade when the Ottoman empire was undergoing a most rapid and radical transformation. He witnessed and engaged in the debates of the period, and later some of the most prominent intellectuals and ideologues — Ziya Gökalp and Yusuf Akçura, to mention only two of the most important — joined the Kemalist movement and participated in the development of its ideology.[1]

Perhaps even more important than ideas was the social and political transformation of the Young Turk era. Not only did the old ruling class of the Palace and the Sublime Porte lose much of its power, but the Young Turks began to take active measures to create a new social basis for the Turkish polity. Modernisation and western-

isation were now defined as the establishment of capitalism with all
the features of a capitalist society, and no longer as the implementation of institutional reforms. That meant creating a class capable of
sustaining capitalism — the bourgeoisie — without which, Yusuf
Akçura warned, 'the chances of survival of a Turkish society composed only of peasants and officials will be very slim.' By the end of
the war, such a class, still very much in its infancy, had begun to
emerge, as had a new but small group of capitalist farmers. Both
groups had acquired great wealth through wartime profiteering
encouraged by the Young Turk government, and were more confi-
dent of the political role they would play. As a result, by 1919 when
the national struggle was launched, Turkish society was no longer
composed only of peasants and officials, though they were still
numerically dominant. The journalist Falih Rıfkı Atay, a spokesman for the Kemalists, might well ask in 1922: 'The bourgeoisie? I
wonder, where is this Turkish class?'[3]

The question of Turkey's political economy, however, ought not
to be considered merely in terms of numbers. It is true that there was
hardly a strong indigenous business or industrial class — capitalists
or workers — worth talking about: in the 1915 industrial survey,
only 284 workplaces employed more than five workers, of which 148
were in Istanbul, 62 in Izmir, and the remaining 74 in western
Anatolia. Of the capital employed in these ventures, 85 per cent was
Greek, Jewish, Armenian or foreign.[4] The situation improved in the
years 1915–18 but not in the sense of bringing about a numerical
breakthrough or a take-off to bourgeois industrial society. Nevertheless, psychologically there was an important change in attitude
during the war years;[5] there was a realisation within the Turkish
ruling élite that without the reorganisation of social and economic
life, it would not be possible to modernise the political and cultural
life of Anatolia or gain the acceptance of Europe. The first step in
this direction was the abolition of the capitulations in September
1914; this, *inter alia*, permitted the Turks to raise tariffs on imported
goods so as to be able to protect and develop local commerce and
industry. The existence of free trade had not only been a factor in
discouraging the growth of local industry, it had also provided a
small segment of the commercial community, predominantly non-
Muslim, with better opportunities for money-making by handling
foreign trade rather than by trying to develop local markets and
manufactures. The Kemalists, who succeeded the Young Turks,
accelerated the protectionist trend and accomplished what may perhaps be described as a bourgeois revolution from the top or, stated in
another way, a bourgeois revolution by proxy. This was often done
against the wishes of the infant class which seemed to prefer the

easier route of foreign collaboration to Kemalist autarchy. But it still lacked the power to influence state policy, directed as the latter was by an élite of autonomous vested interests.

This is not to suggest that the Kemalists set out consciously to carry out a revolution; in a sense such a process had already been set in motion by the Young Turks, and the Kemalists were partly carried along by the momentum thus created. The collapse of empire and foreign occupation of the most valuable parts of Anatolia brought into question the very existence of a Turkish nation and state, even while these were mere ideas waiting to be translated into reality. Thus in the summer of 1919 it was conceivable that Anatolia might go the way of Greater Syria and be partitioned into small states for the convenience of Western control. There were local groups of notables organising themselves to safeguard their own interests, and they seemed willing to do this by compromising with one great power or another, accepting its tutelage and, if necessary, agreeing to sacrifice other parts of Anatolia. In their minds, the notion of a national struggle was of secondary importance. Such were the 'Defence of Rights Societies' founded in Thrace and Izmir and then in other parts of Anatolia.[6] In the capital, the Sultan and his entourage, who might have provided the focus for national resistance, threw themselves upon the mercy of the Allied powers, especially Great Britain. They accepted, under protest, any outcome that was decided for their future so long as they were permitted to retain the trappings of power. In their minds there was no concept of nation or national sovereignty, let alone national economy; on the contrary, they found the idea of national sovereignty subversive, for it challenged the very basis of their power, based as it was on archaic tradition. Istanbul therefore resisted the national movement in Anatolia with cunning and fanaticism. But once the capital had been occupied by Allied troops on 16 March 1920, that was the *de facto* end of the Ottoman state and the Sultan's claim to lead the people as the 'shepherd leads his flock.'[7]

It is instructive to examine the social groups which either actively supported the Sultan, or sat on the fence waiting to see whether he would succeed in retaining control of the delicate situation. As one would expect, die-hard support for the Sultan came from his palace entourage as well as from the high bureaucrats of the Sublime Porte, who had sided with the pro-British liberals during the Young Turk era. The Sultan had everything to lose if the nationalist ideas of sovereignty and populism were allowed to prevail. The men of the Sublime Porte, like Tevfik Paşa and Ali Kemal, depended on British support to maintain a reformed traditional order in which a monarch, restrained by constitutionalism, would reign while they, the high bureaucrats, ruled. Such a formula meant political and economic subordination to Britain. They were willing to accept that, as were the bourgeoisie who were content merely to replace the ousted Christian minorities in the economic order. These Turkish groups were rather like the liberal faction in the Indian National Congress in the same period who preferred dominion status within the British empire to full independence. They were willing to settle for a British mandate so long as it guaranteed a viable Ottoman-Turkish state; others among them believed that an American mandate would be better suited to Turkey's needs. All the pro-Istanbul factions were convinced of the need for a period of foreign tutelage before Turkey could stand on its own feet.

Even as Mustafa Kemal Paşa began to give shape to a nationalist movement at the Sivas Congress in September 1919, he heard voices among his supporters favouring a mandate. This was partly a symptom of general demoralisation caused by all the setbacks the empire had suffered, ever since it was described by Europe as 'the sick man' whose demise was a matter of time. It was also due to the belief among the bourgeoisie and the landlords in the nationalist camp that the Allies might permit the creation of a nationalist Turkey if they, in turn, were permitted to enjoy economic privileges. Thus Bekir Sami Bey, the Kemalist foreign minister at the London Conference in 1921, made substantial economic concessions to the European Powers whereby 'the French were to have preference in enterprises for the economic development of districts evacuated by France, as well as the provinces of Mamuretülâziz, Diyarbakır and Sivas, and, in addition were to be granted mining concessions in Ergani, etc. . . .'[8]

Italy agreed to support Turkish claims at the conference for the restitution of Thrace and Izmir, and in return the nationalists would cede to Italy the right to exploit the regions of Antalya, Burdur, Muğla, Isparts, as well as parts of Afyonkarahisar, Kütahya, Aydın and Konya. Bekir Sami went as far as to agree to cede to Italian capitalists those enterprises which could not be carried on by the Turkish government or by Turkish capital, as well as to transfer the coal mines of Ereğli to a Turco-Italian company.[9] Bekir Sami was convinced that the agreements he had signed were in accord with the highest interests of the nation. He appealed to the National Assembly to support him, arguing that 'while the opportunity is still given us, prudent policy might save the country from the abyss into which it has fallen. . . . If this is not done, none of us will be able to withdraw from the responsibility imposed upon him before history and the nation. . . .' The continuation of the national struggle, he contended, 'will destroy and annihilate our country to such a degree that its existence as well as that of the nation will be jeopardised.' He advised Kemal Paşa to take this opportunity to make peace on the terms he had negotiated, his conclusion being that the Allies would give nothing better.[10]

Mustafa Kemal described Bekir Sami as 'an adherent of peace at any price.' The terms he was asking the Assembly to accept were the same as the ones the 'powers had concluded among themselves, under the name of the "Tripartite Agreement" and which divided Anatolia into three spheres of influence.' The Kemalists found such terms totally unacceptable, for they contradicted the very principles of the national movement. As a result of these differences, the foreign minister was forced to resign.[11]

Bekir Sami's views, however, were shared by significant factions in the bourgeoisie and among the landowners. Such groups viewed the national struggle as primarily a struggle for political sovereignty and control of the state. Economic sovereignty was not of such significance since both groups believed that they had much to gain from economic subservience to Europe. Its capital investment was expected to develop the infrastructure while its factories would supply goods for the Turkish market. In return, Turkey would export agricultural goods and raw materials. But the Kemalists made no distinction between political and economic sovereignty, arguing that the one could not exist without the other. The Minister of the Economy, Mahmut Esat, stated this quite categorically in his speech before the Economic Congress of Turkey: 'I understand national sovereignty to be national economic sovereignty,' he declared. 'If that is not the case, then national sovereignty becomes a mirage.'[12]

In the early years of the national movement, the emphasis of the Kemalist leadership was on change, even revolutionary change. There was an acute awareness that the Turks were in the process of making a fresh start and abandoning their decadent Ottoman past. This attitude was in keeping with the influence of the French revolutionary tradition on radical thought in Turkey. Thus the Allied occupation of Istanbul in March 1920 was seen as not merely the *de facto* end of the Ottoman state but the beginning of a new age marked by what Mustafa Kemal described as the 'first national year' or *'birinci millî sene'*.[13] This fresh start was expected to lead to the creation of a totally new state and society. In order to carry out this metamorphosis, the Kemalists realised that they would have to create even 'a new type of Turk very different from the "Ottoman" '.[14] Given this propensity for revolutionary change, the dependent political economy of the old order would have to be the first to go. This becomes quite clear if one reads contemporary nationalist writings.

In his speech before the Grand National Assembly in March 1922, Kemal Paşa noted that the Turkish economy had been unable to defend itself against European competition ever since free trade was permitted by the 'Reorganisation' or *Tanzimat* regime (1839–76). To make matters worse, the competitive edge had been blunted even more 'by the chains of economic capitulations'.[15] After this period, foreign capital had acquired an extraordinary position in the empire, reducing Ottoman state and government to the status of 'the gendarmes of foreign capital'. The Ottoman empire was now nothing more than 'a colony of the foreigners'. Turkey, like any other new nation, concluded Kemal Paşa, could not consent to the continuation of such a state of affairs.[16] It was true that they were now living in a different age, but in many respects the situation remained unchanged. Mustafa Kemal noted that there were millions of unemployed in Britain and that they would influence Britain's policy towards Turkey. Britain would try to establish open markets in order to solve the problem of unemployment created by the general post-war economic crisis prevailing in Europe.[17] Turkey therefore had to be on her guard and insist on the right to impose tariffs, without which the creation of industry would be virtually impossible. The Kemalists differed from their bourgeois supporters insofar as they had a long-term vision of a new Turkey, of which industry was an essential component. The bourgeoisie, on the other hand, viewed the situation from their own narrow perspective, content to profit from the role of commercial middlemen in an economy controlled by Europe.

Thus during the war of independence the Kemalists were anti-imperialist, not only because they wanted to prevent the partition of Anatolia, but also because they refused to allow the new Turkey to remain an economic colony of the West. This aspect of the struggle is sometimes lost sight of because some critics have cast doubt on Kemalism's anti-imperialism, claiming that the Kemalists were making concessions to foreign capital while indulging in rhetoric against it at the same time. Such critics miss an important point about the political economy of Kemalism, namely that it was capitalist yet at the same time anti-imperialist. There was no contradiction in this policy, though it was undoubtedly most difficult to follow. It became the stated policy of almost all the new nation-states in the period of de-colonisation. Foreign capital was welcome so long as it did not come with political or economic strings. It was realised that Turkey, ravaged by war and starved of capital, would have to rely on foreign investment if it were to build an infrastructure for a modern economy. Mustafa Kemal explained this to the Assembly in March 1922: 'If we want to bring happiness and prosperity to our nation in a brief period of time, we will have to obtain foreign capital as rapidly as possible, and benefit to the maximum from whatever foreign know-how is necessary to achieve our country's well-being and prosperity, and our nation's happiness and welfare; our own present financial position is inadequate to build, install, and operate public utilities.'[18] But the representatives of the nation were quickly reminded that 'we cannot think of anything other than achieving our national goal which consists of guaranteeing, before all else, our life and liberty; . . . the aim of our present crusade is total independence. Total independence is possible only with financial independence.'[19]

Perhaps nothing illustrates the aspirations of Kemalist political economy better than the proceedings of the Economic Congress of Turkey, held in Izmir in February 1923. The war of independence was over and peace was in the process of being negotiated in Lausanne. The nation's boundaries, stipulated in the National Pact of 1919, had virtually been won on the battlefield, but the struggle for economic sovereignty was still being waged at the negotiating table. One aim of the Economic Congress was to show the world that there was a unity of purpose between the political leadership and the various economic groups, particularly the commercial community which, in the empire, had been the instrument of foreign penetration, and whose nationalist sentiment was still suspect. But at the congress this group, represented by the 'National Turkish Commercial Union', adopted a strong nationalist platform. It demanded the right to impose tariffs against foreign goods, opposed concessions to or monopoly rights for foreign capital in Turkey, proposed monopoly-free cabotage for Turkey's coastal waters, and called for a national bank of emission to be established as soon as possible. Foreign capital would be welcomed only provided that it was deemed beneficial for the economy of the nation.[20] Almost all the measures proposed at the congress were designed to achieve one fundamental goal: to further the establishment of a national economy and to strengthen those economic forces in the country which, within a short time, would provide the socio-economic basis for the emerging republican state.

There was unity of purpose between the new state created in 1923 and the principal economic classes, the infant bourgeoisie and the landlords. But that ought not to disguise the fact that the Kemalist state was essentially autonomous, and not subservient to the dictates of those classes. That is as one would expect in a situation in which society was essentially pre-capitalist, and modern classes such as the bourgeoisie, capitalist farmers and workers existed in a most rudimentary form and were very much in the process of growth. Far from being in a position to direct the state, these classes had to be nurtured by it.

The new state was dominated by an intelligentsia (*münevverler, aydınlar*), military and civilian in composition, which formed the hard core of the Kemalist movement. For convenience, we may appropriate Arthur Koestler's description of the intelligentsia and the historic role it has played, for it approximates closely to the role of the Turkish intelligentsia: 'The intelligentsia in the modern sense thus first appears as that part of a nation which by its social situation not so much "aspires" but is *driven* to independent thought, that is, to a type of group-behaviour which debunks the existing hierarchy of values (from which it is excluded) and at the same time tries to replace it with new values of its own. This constructive tendency of the intelligentsia is its second basic feature. The true iconoclasts always had a prophetic streak, and all debunkers have a bashfully hidden pedagogic vein.'[21] By 1923, the Kemalist intelligentsia was actually in power. It was determined to replace 'the existing hierarchy of values' and take the country far beyond the vision of the bourgeoisie, let alone the landlords and the tribal chiefs. These old classes would have preferred a constitutional monarchy with its traditional religious ideology; instead, the Kemalists established a republic which was rapidly secularised, against the opposition of even some of the most prominent leaders of the national movement. This was the logical outcome of a struggle which had emphasised nationality and national sovereignty, as well as the striving for Western civilisation. But the old classes found the new order difficult to swallow. Nevertheless the reforms were carried out 'for the bourgeoisie in spite of itself', to corrupt the more familiar Kemalist adage. The reforms of the mid-1920s and 1930s were more acceptable to these classes for they destroyed many of the institutional and juridical obstacles of the traditional, pre-capitalist order to the emerging modern structure, while maintaining existing property relations.[22]

For the next quarter-century, the political economy continued to evolve in the shadow of the state. Aware of the weakness of the private sector as well as public interest, Kemal Paşa informed the Assembly as early as March 1922: 'One of the most important goals of our political economy is to place under state control, as far as our financial and technical ability allows, economic institutions and enterprises which directly involve public advantage.'[23] This goal remained fundamental to the economic philosophy of Kemalism and it was to become one of the main planks of the statist policy of the 1930s.

If we have emphasised the relationship between the new regime and the main urban class, the bourgeoisie, it is because the Kemalists were convinced that the urban economy would be the driving force for development while the rural sector would provide the fuel. The countryside was not being taken for granted and there were no illusions about its importance for the nation's future. 'Gentlemen, our nation is agrarian', Kemal Paşa said to the Assembly. The peasant was 'Turkey's real master and owner, and the true producer . . . The quintessence of our political economy is to use the results and the fruits of the peasant's labour for his own highest advantage.'[24]

These statements should not be dismissed as mere rhetoric. The Turkish intelligentsia had a genuine appreciation of the peasant's contribution to the economy — and to the army as cannon-fodder — as well as sympathy for his tragic plight. The intelligentsia followed the example of the Russian *narodniks* and tended to idealise the peasantry. Influenced by such sentiments, the Young Turks had intended to destroy the *status quo* in the countryside, and to save the peasant from the clutches of the feudal lords (*derebeys*), tribal *ağas*, and notables (*eşraf*). Despite their good intentions, they failed to carry out any measures to improve the lot of the wretched peasant; on the contrary, his situation actually became worse during the turbulent decade which ended in 1918.[25] In the Republic, the condition of the peasantry improved to some degree — the burden of the tithe was removed — but there were no structural changes in the countryside. More specifically, no land reform was carried out. We need to ask why.[26]

To begin with, the Turkish Republic was not confronted with a land question of the type which confronts so many newly-independent Third World nations, resulting from a large population and insufficient land. In Turkey, the value of land had been going up since the turn of the century, leading to increased demand. This rising demand led to some regional tensions, but in general there was sufficient land available to meet the demand. Thus, except for pockets of large holdings in parts of Anatolia, Turkey remained a land of smallholders.

The real problem of agrarian Turkey was not the shortage of land, but the shortage of labour, aggravated as it was by constant warfare and the loss of population. The shortage of farm-labour became so critical during the First World War, the government was forced to institute the *corvée* so as to provide cheap labour and maintain vital farm production. By 1923, the population within the borders of the new state — and with it the productive capacity of the nation — had declined by about 20 per cent.[27] The re-distribution of land at this point would have sharply reduced the size of the agrarian labour force available to the landlords; they would have been forced to pay higher wages while land rent would have fallen. On both counts, the landlords opposed land reform or any structural change in the countryside. Scarce and costly labour might, however, have forced the landlords to adopt modern farming methods involving the use of machines, thereby making Turkish agriculture capital- rather than labour-intensive. That is how the Young Turks, and the Kemalists after them, envisaged solving the problem of under-population. Kemal Paşa observed: 'as our population is small in relation to the size of our country, there is a much greater need here than in other countries to use machines and scientific tools for farming.'[28] The government hoped to nudge the farmers in this direction by demonstrating the efficacy of scientific farming on some model farms. But that method did not work and mechanised farming became widespread only after farm machinery was imported under the Marshall Plan.

The agrarian question in Turkey was primarily political and not economic in nature. Its solution may well have depended on whether it was the peasants or the landlords who supported the national movement. As it turned out, it was the landlords who gave their lukewarm support while the peasants remained generally apathetic. How is that to be explained?

The peasants may have been exploited and abused by the notables in the countryside, but they held the state responsible for their oppression. It was from the state that they expected succour. They hoped that the revolution of 1908 would bring change to the countryside, but they were bitterly disappointed. The Kemalists simply inherited the sullen bitterness of the Anatolian peasantry. One has a sense of the peasantry's hopes and expectations, its disappointment and frustrations, from reading the reports of the journalist Ahmed Şerif from Anatolia in 1909. One report in particular which chronicles the complaints of an old peasant bears quotation at length. It describes a situation which was serious in 1909, but which must have become desperate a decade later, just as the Kemalists were preparing for their life-and-death struggle:

Liberty was a word we only began to hear recently. From what we have heard, and from some activities, we understand that it is something worthwhile. . . . But we thought that everything would be rectified; taxes would be collected peacefully and justly; murderers and thieves in the village would be reformed; our children who go for military service would not be kept hungry and naked for years, but would be discharged on time; officials would not do things as they pleased and everything would be changed. So far nothing has happened. In the past some things used to even function better; today everything is in a mess. If we go to a government office we do not know who is in charge. . . . The government still does not look into our problems. . . . Several people hold a deed for a particular field and we are not sure whether the ground we till belongs to us or not. Because of that there are fights every day and sometimes people are killed. We go to the state office and the court but we cannot explain our problem. They think only of collecting taxes when they are due. . . . We work all the year round and we pay our taxes annually; if we don't they take them by force, even selling our pots and bedding. Thus we are always in debt. During the past few years there have been many peasants in the village who have not had seed to sow. Since there is no help from anywhere else, we have had to buy seed from the *aga* at either 100 or 125 *kuruş* per *kile* or return him three *kile* for one. Those *ağas* became a menace; they can have a peasant beaten by their toughs, have him jailed, or sometimes have him frightened by having the state come in. In this way they collect their debts from those who cannot pay. As a matter of fact, the Agricultural Bank is giving loans, but that does not help us. That money runs out before it reaches our village.[29]

This long list of grievances suggests that the peasantry was more alienated from the state than from the village notables. This alienation became even more acute during the World War. The peasants saw the national struggle as a continuation of the war and having fled from one they fled from the other. The nationalists found it very difficult to recruit peasants into the army. The peasants were most receptive to the propaganda of the Sultan's government when they were told that they did not have to serve in the ranks of the nationalists. In the turmoil of those years, there was no peasant movement to seize land; most peasants remained passive, though some joined local guerrilla forces often led by bandits, already in rebellion against the state. It is difficult to see what issue the Anatolian peasantry could have been mobilised around and therefore bad history to hold the Kemalists responsible for not mobilising it.[30] Compare and contrast the situation in Anatolia with that of India. There the peasantry was so inflamed against the oppression of British rule that it was beginning to act spontaneously, crying out to be mobilised; the Indian National Congress had to restrain the peasants and channel their activities in a non-revolutionary direction through the mediation of Mahatma Gandhi and Gandhism. No such problem existed for the Kemalists.

Had there been a peasant movement capable of being rallied to the nationalist cause, it is conceivable that the Kemalists would have turned to it rather than to the landlords. At the critical juncture when the survival of the Turkish people was at stake, Kemal Paşa sought

the support of any class: one has that impression from his brief conversation with Aralov, the Soviet ambassador to Ankara: 'In Russia
you have a combative and veteran working class. It is possible to rely
on it and it ought to be depended on. We have no working class. As
for the peasant, he carries very little weight.'[31] Does not that suggest
that a politicised peasantry might have been a different story? But
such a class did not exist, fragmented as it was by ethnic and religious
loyalties and totally dependent for its very survival on local forces.
Therefore the Kemalists had no choice but to reach the peasants
through the agency of their traditional leaders, the local notables
and the men of religion, the *ülema*. These people were often the local
landowners and they exerted a strong pressure to increase the size of
holdings as much as possible. The Kemalists succumbed to such
pressures as though to a natural process, just as they might have
succumbed to the peasantry's demand for land. The price of the collaboration between the Kemalists and the notables was the tacit
agreement to maintain, and even strengthen, the *status quo* in the
countryside. This was done through the formation of the People's
Party in which the landlords were a powerful element, by an electoral law which guaranteed the existence of an effective landlords'
lobby in the Assembly, and by the inclusion of Article 74 in the new
constitution which virtually closed the door to land reform.[32] Thereafter, the government tried to improve the lot of the peasantry
through education, hoping that in time general enlightenment would
transform the situation in rural Anatolia.

The origins of Kemalist political economy are to be found in the
social structure the new regime inherited, and the way in which it
defined this social reality. The new state was described as 'a People's
State, the State of the People' (*Türkiye Devleti bir Halk Devletidir,
halkın Devletidir*) while its predecessor, the Ottoman state, had been
'a personal state, the state of individuals' (*Müessasatı maziye ise bir
şahıs Devleti idi, eşhasın Devleti idi*).[33] During the national struggle,
the people or *halk* came to be identified by the Kemalists as all those
who supported the nationalist cause against the imperialist powers
and the old order. Like the Third Estate in France before the 1789
Revolution, the term '*halk*' included the vast majority of the nation,
with an array of socio-economic groups and only members of the old
order excluded. The principal task of this collective was to defeat the
old order and its allies and to create a new order of their own. Above
all else, this task required solidarity and united action by all the components of this entity, the people. Class conflict was therefore
implicitly excluded.[34]

The problems that the Kemalists faced and the revolutionary solutions they proposed arose out of the national struggle against

imperialism and the cosmopolitan institutions of the Ottoman-Islamic structure, rather than out of class struggle. These struggles, especially against the latter, implied stressing the unity of the people as a nation rather than the conflicts and the differences that divided them. That explains why the Kemalists attacked the universalist ideology of the old regime which paralysed and froze all classes, rather than act on behalf of the oppressed against their oppressors. To have done both would have been to court disaster; Mustafa Kemal was too astute politically to fall into that trap.

The Kemalists denied the possibility of class struggle in Turkey at that stage of development, precisely because there were no developed classes in the country capable of waging such a struggle. When he discussed this question with Kemal Paşa, Ambassador Aralov was told: 'In Turkey there are no classes. . . .there is no working class as there is no developed industry. As for our bourgeoisie, it is necessary to raise it to the level of a bourgeoisie. Our commerce is extremely puny because we have no capital. . . .' The government would give priority to the development of 'national trade, [it would] open factories, bring underground wealth to the surface, aid the merchant of Anatolia and make him wealthy. These are the problems facing the state.'[35] Initially, therefore, the aim of Kemalist political economy was to create a nation with a class structure worthy of a modern capitalist society. When that had been accomplished and class conflict ensued, the state would then step in and mediate.

If the Kemalists did not recognise the existence of developed classes in Turkey, they were aware that interest groups were quite capable of organising political parties and indulging in activities detrimental to the nation's interest. The country had suffered from chronic instability during the Young Turk period caused by the activities of political parties. The new regime refused to permit such activities and declared that the new Turkey would be served by a single party, the People's Party, which 'includes within it the whole nation, and not just a section'.[36] This was yet another sign of the Kemalist regime's sense of autonomy *vis-à-vis* classes, as well as its paternalism, based on the belief that it was the impartial guide of the people and knew what was best for them.

Throughout the 1920s, Turkey experimented with the free-enterprise economic model, constrained as it was by the temporary limitations imposed by the Treaty of Lausanne. During these years the government played an important role in the economic reconstruction of the country, and members of the Kemalist élite participated in economic ventures like the founding of major institutions such as the Business Bank (*Iş Bankası*), which remains to this day the largest commercial enterprise of its type. The government's aim was to create an infrastructure without which the internal market would remain pitifully undeveloped.

Perhaps this experiment with economic liberalism would have continued for longer if the great depression had not exerted an immediate effect on Turkey, where the economic crisis in the capitalist world, ushered in by the Great Crash of 1929, gave a sharp impetus to state intervention. The impact of the depression on the economy was sufficient to force the government to take counter-measures. The crisis came to be seen as a failure of the free-enterprise system, identified with Western capitalism. The Soviet Union, with its system of state controls, seemed to have escaped the crisis. It was therefore seen by the Kemalists as a model that might be usefully copied in certain areas of the Turkish economy.

State intervention in economic affairs was in no sense a novel experience for the Turks. It had been tried during the First World War when it was described as 'state economics' or *devlet iktisadi-yatı*; in the 1930s the term was streamlined and called statism or *devletçilik*. But its fundamental features remained virtually unchanged: to help the private sector to grow and mature by showing the way and by carrying out economic measures it was too weak to carry out for itself.[37] This time, however, the policy was soon institutionalised; this alarmed Turkish business circles. Statism became one of the 'six fundamental and unchanging principles' adopted by the Republican People's Party in 1931 and incorporated into the constitution in 1937. These six principles defined the ideology of Kemalism, and thus its political economy; they therefore deserve to be quoted at some length.

It is one of our main principles [read the 1935 Congress minutes] to consider the people of the Turkish Republic, not as composed of different classes, but as a community divided into various professions according to the requirements of the division of labour for the individual and social life of the Turkish people.

The farmers, handicraftsmen, labourers and workmen, people exercising free professions, industrialists, merchants and public servants are the main work groups constituting the Turkish community. The functioning of each of these groups is essential to the life and happiness of the others and of the community.

The aims of our Party, with this principle, are to secure social order and solidarity instead of class conflict, and to establish harmony of interests. The benefits are to be proportionate to the aptitude and to the amount of work.

Although considering private work and activity a basic idea, it is one of our main principles to interest the State actively in matters where the general and vital interests of the nation are in question, especially in the economic field, in order to lead the nation and the country to prosperity in as short a time as possible.

The interest of the State in economic matters is to be an actual builder, as well as to encourage private enterprises, and also to regulate and control the work that is being done.

The determination of the economic matters to be undertaken by the State depends upon the requirements of the greatest public interest of the nation. If the enterprise, which the State itself decides to undertake actively as a result of this necessity, is in the hands of private entrepreneurs, its appropriation shall, each time, depend upon the enactment of a law, which will indicate the way in which the State shall indemnify the loss sustained by the private enterprise as a result of this appropriation. In the estimation of this loss the possibility of future earnings shall not be taken into consideration.[38]

Despite the corporatist rhetoric evident in this document and influenced by the prevailing fascist mood of the 1930s, the Kemalist denied any affinity with fascism. Unlike the regimes in Rome and Berlin, Ankara accepted liberal principles and the nineteenth-century idea of progress. It recognised the rule of law and the importance of the constitutional state. Unlike fascism, there was no denial of the universality of civilisation, nor a rejection of rationalism, individualism, and the fundamental equality of man and ethnic groups. The Kemalist regime continued to be transitional in character, preparing the ground for a liberal political and economic system which would replace it in the near future.

In the early 1930s, there was a danger that the bureaucratic elements in the state and the party might become dominant and strive for state rather than liberal capitalism. The 1935 Congress, whose minutes are quoted above, reflected this danger. This bureaucratic threat was most real under the influence of the journal *Kadro*, which was patronised by premier Ismet Inönü. But strong and determined opposition led to the closure of this journal in late 1934. Meanwhile Celâl Bayar, the leader of the Business Bank group, was appointed minister of the economy in 1933, suggesting the regime's opposition to extreme statism. Bayar held this portfolio until 1937 when he was made prime minister. Although a committed liberal, he recognised the weakness of the Turkish bourgeoisie and the need for the state to play the leading role in the economy. Bayar feared that under the extremists, statism might assume such proportions as to lead to the eclipse of the emerging private sector. He warned against that and pleaded that private enterprise be given a larger share of the national economy. Thus if there were any controversy, it was over the state's failure to define the extent of its intervention to the satisfaction of Turkey's business community.[39]

The businessmen need not have worried, for prime minister Inönü reassured them that state intervention was only designed to create a viable industrial base, something the bourgeoisie was incapable of doing on its own.[40] Most of the measures of this period — the first five-year plan for 1934–8, the founding of Sümerbank in 1933 and Etibank in 1935, for example — were designed to achieve this purpose, and directly benefited the private sector.[41] The state was still playing its autonomous role on behalf of the bourgeoisie, despite the latter's fears and criticism.

In these years of controversy, the trend towards a mono-party state, in which party and state coalesced, is worth noting. This trend, which derived from the example of the fascist states, was favoured in the RPP by a faction led by the party's secretary-general, Recep Peker. This faction railed against liberalism, forecasting its imminent doom which would be followed by the universal reign of statism. Although their voice was loud and alarming, their following in the party was limited. They succeeded in alienating the business community as well as many influential republicans. As a result, President Kemal Atatürk intervened and Peker was forced to resign in 1936 for trying to gain control of the party and for holding extreme views on all subjects, including economics.[42] The following year, the economy was liberalised and this trend continued until it was halted by the pressures of wartime neutrality.

The success of Kemalist political economy was seen only after 1945 and the triumph of the liberal democracies. It was marked in Turkey by the establishment of multi-party politics and a mixed economy in which the state sector was subordinated to the private. The infant bourgeoisie, which according to Kemal Atatürk had to be nurtured to the level of the bourgeois class, had grown strong enough to challenge the ruling party and defeat it in the first honest general election. Thereafter this class continued to grow, enlarging both the commercial and the industrial sector of the economy, creating at the same time the other class of capitalist society, the proletariat. Even the countryside, which the Kemalist regime had neglected for political reasons, was affected by the post-war transformation and integrated more rapidly into the expanding market economy. Yet whenever the country ran into a structural crisis — as in 1960, 1971 and 1980 — the interim regime which seized power invariably spoke of returning to the path of Kemalism. This suggests that ever since the Second World War, the political economy of

Turkey has lacked firm ideological foundations. The search for those foundations continues.

NOTES

1. Yakub Kadri Karaosmanoğlu, *Atatürk*, Istanbul 1961, 64, claims that Kemalism was totally original, and he does not think that these thinkers, whom he names specifically, influenced Atatürk.

2. From, *Türk Yurdu*, no.14, 12 Aug. 1333 (1917), quoted in Niyazi Berkes, *The Development of Secularism in Turkey*, Montreal, McGill University Press, 1964, 426.

3. F.R. Atay, *Eski Saat*, Istanbul, 1933, 95, quoted by Taner Timur, *Türk Devrimi ve Sonrası 1919–1946*, Ankara, 1971, 21.

4. See Timur, *op. cit.*, 21.

5. See Feroz Ahmad, 'Vanguard of a Nascent Bourgeoisie, the Social and Economic Policy of the Young Turks 1908–1918' in Osman Okyar and Halil Inalcık (eds.), *Social and Economic History of Turkey (1071–1920)*, Ankara, 1980. Yıldız Sertel, *Türkiye'de ilerici akımlar*, Istanbul, 1969, 17, gives figures for the workforce in 1921 which suggest an increase from that figures for 1915.

6. On these societies, see T.Z. Tunaya, *Türkiye'de Siyasi Partiler 1859–1952*, Istanbul 1952, 481 ff.

7. On the role of the Istanbul governments in this period, see Sina Akşin, *Istanbul Hükümetleri ve Milli Mücadele*, Istanbul, 1976. For the Sultan's claim to be the 'shepherd of his flock' see Şevket Süreyya Aydemir, *Tek Adam: Mustafa Kemal (1919–1922)*, vol. 2, Istanbul, 1966, 226.

8. *A Speech delivered by Mustafa Kemal Atatürk 1927*, Ministry of Education Printing Plant, Istanbul, 1963, 498. This is an improved edition of the English translation, published in Leipzig in 1929; it is certainly more readily available.

9. *Ibid.*

10. *Ibid.*, 500–1.

11. *Ibid.*, 498.

12. A. Günduz Ökçün (comp. and ed.), *Türkiye Iktisat Kongresi 1923-Izmir*, Ankara, 1968, 259.

13. Kemal Paşa uses this term at least three times in his speech opening the new session of the Grand National Assembly. See Kazim Öztürk, *Cumhurbaşkanları'nın T. Büyük Millet Meclisini Açış Nutukları*, Istanbul, 1969, 105, 108 and 113. The analogy with the fall of the monarchy in France in 1792 seems obvious.

14. See Vedat Nedim Tör, *Kemalizmin dramı*, Istanbul, 1980, 20.

15. Kemal Paşa's Assembly speech of 1 March 1922 in Öztürk, *op. cit.*, 86.

16. Kemal Paşa's speech inaugurating the Economic Congress of Turkey, 17 February 1923, in Ökçün, *op. cit.*, 248 and 253.

17. Öztürk, *op. cit.*, 103.

18. *Ibid.*, 88.

19. *Ibid.*, 89.

20. Ökçün, *op. cit.*, 406 ff; and Doğan Avcıoğlu, *Türkiye'nin Düzeni*, Ankara, 1969, 229–33. By 1926, Kemal Paşa could proudly inform the Assembly that cabotage had been placed under the Turkish flag. See his speech of 1 November 1926 in Öztürk, *op. cit.*, 190.

21. Arthur Koestler, *The Yogi and the Commissar*, Danube edition, New York, 1967, 73.

22. For an account of the reforms see Bernard Lewis, *The Emergence* of *Modern Turkey*, 2nd edn, London, 1968, 261–74 *et passim*.

23. Öztürk, *op. cit.*, 86–7.

24. Both quotations are from the speech of 1 March 1922 in *ibid.*, 84–5.

25. See Feroz Ahmad, 'The Agrarian Policy of the Young Turks 1908–1918' to be published in the proceedings of the Second International Congress on the Social and Economic History of Turkey, Strasbourg University, 1–5 July 1980, edited by Irene Melikoff and Jean-Louis Bacquet-Grammont.

26. See Avcıoğlu, *op. cit.*, 233.

27. Vedat Eldem, *Osmanlı imparatorlugunun iktisadi şartları hakkında bir tetkik*, Istanbul, 1970, 63.

28. Assembly speech of 1 March 1923 in Ozturk, *op. cit.*, 128.

29. Ahmet Şerif, *Anadolu'da Tanin*, Istanbul, 1977, 46–7. The original edition was published in 1910. Earlier, at 25. Ahmet Şerif commented: 'What the peasant cannot understand is that even though he has been hearing a great many promises during the past year, he has not seen them kept, not even those which would have been easy to carry out. He wants to see the venal and corrupt official removed; he wants to know that there is no need to quake any longer with fear before the gendarmes whom he feeds free of charge, and provides fodder for his beasts. He wants to see those things change which seem unimportant to us but are very important to him.'

30. The unwillingness to mobilise the peasantry that would alienate the landlords is the most general criticism of the Kemalist regime. While that may be true, the critics never establish that there was a peasantry to be mobilised through land reform. It is ironic that later, the peasantry failed to support the party which favoured land reform but voted for the party, the Democrat Party, that opposed land reform but promised to liberate the peasant from the tyranny of the state.

31. S.I. Aralov, *Bir Sovyet Diplomatının Türkiye Hatıraları*, Istanbul, 1967, 92.

32. See Avcıoğlu, *op. cit.*, 235.

33. Kemal Paşa's Assembly speech of 13 August 1923 in Öztürk, *op. cit.*, 166.

34. Kemal Paşa's speech at the Economic Congress in Ökçün, *op. cit.*, 255–6. This speech may also be read in *Atatürk'ün Söylev ve Demeçleri*, vol. ii, Ankara, 1959, 112.

35. Aralov, *op. cit.*, 234–5 (both quotations).

36. Kemal Paşa's Balikesir speech delivered from the pulpit of the Paşa

mosque, 7 February 1923, in *Atatürk'un Söylev ve Demeçleri*, vol. ii, 97. With this sentiment prevailing, the two brief experiments with multi-party politics were bound to fail. See Walter Weiker, *Political Tutelage and Democracy in Turkey*, Leiden, 1973.

37. The early definition of statism is from Tekin Alp, 'Harbden Sulha Intikal Iktisadiyatı — Devlet Iktisadiyatı' in *Iktisadiyat Mecmuası*, vol. 2, nos. 62 and 64, 16 Aug. and 14 Sept. 1917, 1–3. For a later discussion of statism see Korkut Boratav, *Türkiye'de Devletçilik (1923–1950)*, Ankara, 1962.

38. The quoted passage is an excerpt from the official translation of the programme of the RPP, reproduced in Donald Webster, *The Turkey of Atatürk*, Philadelphia, 1939, 308–9.

39. Korel Göymen's, interview with Celâl Bayar, 2 March 1970, cited in his article 'Stages of Etatist Development in Turkey', *Gelişme Dergisi/Studies in Development*, no. 10, Winter 1976, 91.

40. Basvekil Ismet, 'Fırkamızın Devletçilik Vasfı', *Kadro*, no. 22, Oct. 1933, 4–6.

41. Göymen, *loc. cit.*, 97 ff; and Z.Y. Hershlag, *Turkey: the Challenge of Growth*, Leiden, 1968, 61 ff.

42. Göymen, *loc. cit.*, 105.

Kemalist economic policies and étatism

KORKUT BORATAV

1. *Introduction*

The new Turkish Republic inherited a seriously handicapped economy from the ruins of the Ottoman empire in 1923. It was, first of all, an economy almost without a modern industrial basis. Existing 'industrial' production materialised predominantly within establishments of an artisanal character. Indeed, the Ottoman Census of Industry for 1915, covering almost all the provinces where significant industrial activity (if any) existed, all within the geographical limits of present-day Turkey, reveals a very weak industrial sector: there were only 182 operating industrial establishments of a non-artisanal character,[1] employing a mere 14,060 workers and employees. Of this labour force, 70 per cent were engaged in the production of wool and cotton yarn, cloth and raw silk, in flour mills and in tobacco processing. These activities, which represented 78 per cent of industrial production, were the main body of Ottoman industry.[2] The lack of faith in any form of national industry was reflected in a popular saying of the times: 'If you want to hang yourself, do it with English rope!'

The Turkish economy of 1923 was also a disarticulated one, in the sense of a lack of organic complementarity between its parts. A striking symptom of this could be observed in the area of transportation. The railway network, totally under foreign ownership, was oriented only towards the requirements of external markets: areas producing primary commodities for Western markets were linked to the main export centres, whereas commodity flows between the vast cereal-growing regions of inner Anatolia and the consuming cities were either practically non-existent or extremely weak due to the lack of transportation facilities. This state of things led to an unbelievable situation in which the cost of transporting one tonne of wheat from central Anatolia to Istanbul in 1924 was $8.8 whereas it was only $5 from New York to Istanbul;[3] and, hence, it seemed more rational to feed the population of Istanbul from Iowa rather than Ankara and Konya and let the Anatolian peasant vegetate in subsistence farming.

The final collapse of the empire had been a very painful one, through a decade of almost uninterrupted wars which had brought the nation to the very limits of endurance. The demographic consequences of the war years were severely aggravated by large-scale population transfers between Turkey and Greece, as agreed to in the Lausanne Peace Treaty, creating serious dislocations. Nobody seemed to have any idea how many people were living within the boundaries of the new Turkish state. The dependent and semi-colonial status of the Ottoman empire had resulted in relatively developed statistical systems on external trade and foreign debts, whereas elementary quantitative information on the state of the nation was lacking. Even in 1926–7, estimates of the population of Turkey varied between 6 and 10 millions — Mussolini was speaking of a Turkey of 6 million people in 1927 — but the first Census of Population in 1927 produced the surprising result of 14 millions.[4]

The financial dependence of the Ottoman empire is a subject too well-known to need elaborating here. But republican Turkey had inherited an economic structure with chronic external deficits and the bulk of the Ottoman debt to be repaid in the coming years; factors, seemingly, to perpetuate the financial and economic dependence of Turkey in the following period. If we look retrospectively at the path which the new Republic had to follow in the next fifteen years, under the constraints of the economic legacy of the empire, some examples of which were briefly discussed above, we will see that external conditions contributed to make this path a very rough one: the difficult years of post-war adaptation were followed by the Great Depression and its grave repercussions on the delicate Turkish economy; and by the preparations for the new war which was going to ravage mankind at the end of the period in question.

But if we also examine the state of the nation at the time of Atatürk's death, or immediately before the Second World War, it will be apparent that the economy had done unexpectedly well under these difficult, seemingly impossible, conditions. It was by then a society which had taken the first, but decisive steps toward industrialisation and modernisation, and it was also an economy which seemed to sustain a state of external equilibrium, something which had been unthinkable in 1923. In other words, the Turkish economy appeared to be following a dynamic path of self-reliant growth and industrialisation, the quantitative indicators of which will be examined in the following sections of this chapter.

If this assertion on the surprisingly positive performance of the Turkish economy under such unfavorable conditions can be shown to be true, it raises some challenging questions for the economist. Were particular policies, i.e. 'Kemalist economic policies', related to this process of development? And are we justified in speaking of a strategy, or even a model of development incorporating these policies and their implications, which may have a bearing for other nations and other periods, particularly for contemporary developing economies?

It is our conviction that affirmative answers can be given to these questions in relation to the economic policies adopted in Turkey soon after the Great Depression. Étatism is the label usually used to characterise these policies. The factors leading to the gradual adoption, or rather, discovery of this model and its consequences and implications are the subject-matter of this chapter.

2. *Main sub-periods of 1923–1939*

(a) *Problems and Criteria in Periodisation*

From the viewpoint of economic policies, the conventional periodisation of republican Turkey between 1923 and 1939 divides these years into two distinct time-intervals. The first sub-period, labelled the 'liberal' one, is considered to cover the years from 1923 to 1930 or 1931; and the second, so-called 'étatist' sub-period covers the remaining years. Some writers, while following the same convention, tend to qualify 1930–1 (or 1932) as a transition period, but we believe that this is not particularly illuminating. Instead, we propose to insert a new sub-period, namely 1930–2, in this scheme and revise or qualify the label used to depict the two conventional periods. We shall attempt to show that, despite the relative brevity of the sub-period, the set of policy tools implemented from the end of 1929 up to the second half of 1932 had a consistent logic of its own, and that therefore 1930–2 should be considered a distinct policy model in its own right.

As for the 'liberal' and 'étatist' labels, the former seems to be a misnomer while the latter, as is inevitable for all shorthand expressions, is unable to reflect some important, and external-oriented, characteristics of the relevant period. Despite these qualifications, considerations of expediency may lead us to use the conventional 'liberal' and 'étatist' terms, bearing in mind that these terms actually contain more than they suggest, and partly different from it.

Our own periodisation[5] is the following: *1923–9*: an open economy and active state support for private accumulation; *1930–2*: protectionism and import substitution based on private capital; and *1933–9*: the synthesis of protectionism and étatism. The starting dates of our sub-periods are based not on the *implementation* of new policies, but rather on the year when the first *measurable effects* of these changes on the national economy are perceived, a time-lag of one year being assumed between these two phenomena. Thus, although the first protectionist measures were implemented in 1929 and the first decisive steps towards étatism were taken in July 1932, the relevant sub-periods are considered to begin in 1930 and 1933 respectively. The use of quantitative economic indicators in the comparative evaluation of our periods has induced us to adopt this practice.

(b) State support for private accumulation in the open economy

The economic resolutions of the Lausanne peace treaty (1923) included a number of elements which were to act as constraints on the economic policies of the Republic. Apart from the engagement to pay approximately two-thirds of the Ottoman debt, the most important among these concerned the customs tariffs to be applied by Turkey. The treaty froze the Turkish tariffs at the adjusted specific Ottoman tariff scale of 1916, which corresponded in value terms more or less to the same rate of nominal protection as the 1914 tariffs. Differential rates of excise taxes for imported and locally produced commodities were also prohibited, the only significant exception being in the area of government monopolies where, for revenue purposes, higher prices could be charged.[6] Turkey also undertook to eliminate the existing quantitative restrictions on foreign trade and refrain from introducing new ones. These limitations were to last, in practice, up to the end of 1928. Against these economic concession to the Western powers, the legal and political 'capitulations' which had reduced the Ottoman state to the status of a semi-colony were abolished.

There are a number of indications that those provisions of the peace treaty reducing, if not altogether eliminating, the possibilities of implementing an effective and protective foreign trade policy were considered as trivial concessions, if concessions at all. Indeed, the predominant economic philosophy of the period reflected a state of mind which minimised the risks of economic domination by imperialism, to which, despite political independence, a poor country like Turkey could be subjected. Direct foreign investment, as long as the investors refrained from seeking *political* concessions, was encouraged; particularly in partnership with Turks. There were a number of joint ventures in this sense, in which influential political figures played a prominent role.[7] About one-third of the corporations established between 1920 and 1930 were partnerships of Turks with foreign capital.[8]

This positive and optimistic attitude towards foreign capital had its counterpart in the policies regarding local private capital. This was the period not of liberalism, but of wide-scale state support for private enterprise. The Law for the Encouragement of Industry

(1927) is without parallel in the history of republican Turkey in the variety of subventions and incentives it provided for new industrial establishments. State monopolies in sugar, tobacco, oil, explosives, alcohol, matches and harbours and docks, constituted — paradoxically — another area in which private entrepreneurs were able to benefit from government support. The monopoly rights established over these activities were not directly exercised by the state; rather, the authority to produce, import or export the commodity or to operate the activity on which a monopoly was established was usually given to a local or foreign firm under favourable conditions. Although the official justification for this procedure was based on revenue considerations, utilising an escape clause of the Lausanne treaty concerning restrictions on excise taxes, the actual exercise of monopoly rights by private firms generated substantial profits — something which was the subject of violent criticism during the political controversies of 1930.[9]

A similar development took place in banking. At the beginning of our period, the Turkish banking system, which still lacked a central bank, was predominantly under foreign control. In 1924, with the direct initiative and contribution of political leaders, a private national bank (*Banque d'affaires*) was established. This was originally envisaged as a national finance institution to counter-balance the influence of foreign banks. Prominent political figures were appointed to its board of directors, and in the following years the bank acted as an influential lobby, through its holdings in various economic activities in favour of private interest groups and as a mediator between business and government circles. Respected writers on the period have commented upon 'personalities of profiteering inclination . . . coming from the ranks of officers, administrators and politicians of the liberation period, . . . using their connections with the government, . . . acting as middlemen in various activities', who 'found a refuge for themselves' in the so-called 'Bank of Politicians' and 'used it for their own benefit'.[10]

These observations, which go beyond an evaluation of the Bank's activities as such, give a realistic portrait of the period in question. A process of accumulation *via* the contribution of external capital, but with the active participation and partnership of indigenous elements, was being envisaged. In this partnership, with what was hoped would be a more equal character, the traditional non-Muslim and comprador bourgeoisie was to be replaced by an authentic national one. But this national bourgeoisie was either non-existent or extremely feeble. The most painless method of producing a truly national bourgeoisie seemed to pass through a process of active state support for private accumulation. Where Turkish merchants or industrialists were lacking, it was necessary to create them *via* the enrichment of particular individuals through state resources and support, and the natural candidates for this role were to be found within the ranks of the leading cadres and politicians. This was the philosophy on which the economic policies of the so-called 'liberal' period were based.

(c) *The passage to a protected economy*

The year 1929 was a critical moment for the Turkish economy for more than one reason. It was the year when the period of obligatory application of Ottoman tariffs had expired, and thus a new scale of import duties could be implemented. Preliminary work on the new tariffs had been in progress since 1925,[11] and the government finally adopted them in June 1929 which provided an average nominal protection rate of 46 per cent, compared with the 13 per cent of the previous tariffs. This was one of the first steps in the transition to protective policies; and, the new system was adopted, despite a proposal for a much more moderate tariff scale put forward by the Istanbul chamber of commerce.[12]

1929 was also the year when the first instalment of the Ottoman debt was to be paid by the republican government. Technical negotiations on the modalities of repayment had been going on since the conclusion of the Lausanne treaty, and an agreement was finally reached in 1928 whereby the Ottoman debt was to be liquidated between 1929 and 1953. However, the first two instalments proved such a heavy charge on external finances that the government had to suspend repayments at the end of 1930. Nevertheless, the debt problem was a contributing factor to the emergence of 'the monetary crisis of 1929', as it was called. The Turkish 'monetary crisis' preceded the first impacts of the Great Depression on the Turkish economy by a few months. The main manifestations of the Turkish crisis were a sudden deterioration of the balance of trade and a corresponding depreciation in the Turkish lira *vis-à-vis* the pound sterling. The official explanation of the crisis pointed to speculative inventory-building through excessive imports, induced by prior knowledge of the new import duties by profiteers and corrupt individuals in privileged positions. Possible pressure on the Turkish lira due to the beginning of debt repayments was another factor contributing to the flight away from the lira.

It is beyond the scope of this chapter to discuss the official diagnosis of the crisis, but the important new variable in this picture was in the serious reservations and lack of confidence which the Kemalist leadership started to feel towards the commercial bourgeoisie, particularly those elements dealing with foreign trade. This evaluation created a state of mind favouring stronger government control of external trade and financial operations.

Thus, even before the first repercussions of the Great Depression reached the Turkish economy, the year 1929 had brought a number of new elements inducing the Kemalist leadership to revise the 'open door' policy of the previous years. The impact of the Depression strengthened the proponents of this new thinking — which, in turn, led to a swift adoption of defensive mechanisms against the crisis. What were these economic measures, steps and actions the impact of which dominated the national economy during 1930–2? The most important, in chronological order, were the following:[14] the law on foreign exchange markets (1929), the establishment of the semi-official Society of National Economy and Savings (1929),[15] the establishment of a consortium of banks in which the treasury and the national banks owned the majority share (58 per cent) and which was to act as a central bank in the area of foreign exchange transactions (1930), the law on the protection of the value of the Turkish lira (1930), the establishment of the Central Bank (1930), the law on export control, particularly on quality and standards (1930), and the law authorising the government to use quantitative controls and quotas on imports (1931). To this list, should be added two official economic policy documents, both dated 1930: *The Report on the Economic Situation* (the so-called 'Şakir Kesebir Plan') and *The Economic Programme*.[16] The main theme dominating these two documents was the establishment of external equilibrium through import substitution and, where possible, through increased exports.

An analysis of the content and actual operation of the measures and activities connected with the preceding list clearly shows that they were only concerned with the control of foreign trade and foreign exchange transactions, thus setting up the mechanisms and tools of a protectionist economic model. Indeed, by 1931 almost all the policy tools for controlling the external economic relations of the national economy were fully established; tools which were to be powerful defensive mechanisms in the hands of various governments for several decades to come. On the other hand, the policy measures of 1929–31 are wholly devoid of étatist or interventionist elements *within* the national economy. The policy-makers of the period have made a clear distinction between state intervention on external economic relations and state intervention in the internal market; fully developing the former, but carefully refraining from the latter. It is therefore a model of protectionism, wholly based on the free play of the market forces within the limits of the internal market.

It is true that the term 'étatism' came into circulation in 1930 and was incorporated into the programme of the Republican People's

Party (RPP) in 1931. But it is equally true that until the second half of 1932, étatism was a term without any clear content,[17] and that apart from public investment in railways there was no significant state activity in the productive field, and public intervention in the economy was carefully limited to the area of foreign trade. This was clearly a period of a protected internal market, where the state was assigned mainly to safeguarding the mechanisms of protection with no other new functions to play in the running of the economy.

(d) The search for a new model and the transition to étatism

In a quantitative assessment of the period 1930—2, particularly from the viewpoint of industrial growth, one would be likely to arrive at a positive conclusion. The average growth rate of industry for these three years in constant (1938) prices is 14.8 per cent, while imports show a dramatic drop from the level of 256 m. lira in 1929 to 101 m. lira in 1932, thus generating a positive trade balance for the first time since the proclamation of the Republic.[18]

These data can be interpreted as a distinctly positive process of import-substituting industrialisation, and thus the attainment, at least in broad lines, of the objectives which the Kemalist leadership had set for the economy. Yet by the end of 1930 Atatürk himself had become increasingly dissatisfied with the economic and social situation of the country and had started thinking about the modalities of further change which were finalised nearly two years later. This apparent paradox has to be explained by further analysis.

First, in spite of an apparently impressive tempo of industrial growth, the *quality* of industrialisation left much to be desired. The free play of market forces behind protective walls created a vast area for short-term profiteering. Many activities, classified as 'industrial' according to statistical conventions, in fact consisted of minimal transformations of imported materials, then sold at monopoly prices in the internal market. A well-known writer on the period, A.H. Başar, writes sarcastically of these 'national industries' which nobody had any right to criticise 'since they are working for the salvation of the country.' Başar's observations on the new 'class of industrialists' are eloquent enough: 'A primitive but shameless industry, taking refuge behind the new tariffs and selling at many times the world prices' consisting of so-called 'factories' located either 'within the ruins of an old religious school' or 'under a booth in a vacant plot in Galata', or 'in an old stone house in [the writer's neighbourhood] emitting soot from its sheet-iron chimney' and poisoning the environment; 'industrial (!) establishments making nails by simply cutting iron wires, and selling the nails at ten times the external market price, but importing the iron wires duty-free', or those 'which simply galvanise the duty-free imported bars and sell them at exorbitant prices'.[19]

These observations should be interpreted as reflections of two basic features of the industrialisation process in these years: the primitive character of private 'industry' and the uncontrolled appropriation of the rent of protection by this same class of industrial capitalists. This latter fact, jointly with the well-established practices of active state support for private accumulation of the preceding years, contributed to the generalisation of the atmosphere of corruption and profiteering in political circles.

The consequences of these developments on income distribution in favour of particular segments of the bourgeoisie and bureaucracy are evident. But, the deterioration of the economic conditions of low-income groups was accelerated by the disastrous effects of the Great Depression on wide sections of the peasantry. The price index for wheat fell from 100 in 1929 to 32 in 1931 whereas the corresponding fall for industrial goods was from 100 to 65.[20] Farmers facing this unprecedented deterioration in prices for their products had to finance fixed obligations such as interest charges to moneylenders undertaken during the preceding years or fixed taxes on land and animals. This naturally created situations of economic collapse and expropriation for wide sections of poor and middle peasants. The dramatic shift in the internal terms of trade in favour of industry was not reflected in any improvement in the relative position of the urban working class. Although we lack reliable data on wages, all indirect evidence show that this was a period when urban real wages were more or less at subsistence level and that the fall in prices of wage goods immediately resulted in corresponding falls in money wages.[21] Therefore, the improvement of the internal terms of trade for industry during 1930–2 can be interpreted as the appropriation of the rent of protection by industrial capital strengthened by lower money wages, thanks to the collapse of the wheat price.

The popular reaction to these adverse developments was quickly transmitted to the political leadership under the particular political conditions of 1930. This was a year of experimentation with a bi-party system. The Liberal Party — founded in 1930 at the instigation of Atatürk, who nevertheless remained as Chairman of RPP — met with unexpected support in various areas of the country. This was particularly evident in the rich farming areas of Western Anatolia and in some coastal towns, such as Samsun and Izmir where strikes and workers' demonstrations against the government were on the verge of taking a violent turn. These were developments which the leadership of the Liberal Party, composed of trusted collaborators and colleagues of Atatürk, did not wish but could not control, and which finally led to the dissolution of the Party by the end of 1930.

It was Atatürk's strong sense of realism and critical perception which led the Kemalist leadership to realise that the economic measures taken in 1929 and 1930, mainly as defensive action in face of the crisis situation of 1929, were not only insufficient, but that some of their consequences were gradually undermining the very foundations of the new regime. A radical reorientation of economic policies seemed necessary, but in which direction? This was the main preoccupation of the leadership in 1931 and 1932. Atatürk decided to go to the country in November 1930 in an extended tour, which lasted with some minor interruption until March 1931 and in which a number of political leaders and experts accompanied the leader. The economic hardships against which wide sections of the population were struggling in order to survive were directly observed by Atatürk during this expedition, and intense discussion on the observed problems and on strategic alternatives immediately followed.[22]

Étatism seems to have emerged as the strategic concept to lead the country out of the impasse. In January 1931 Atatürk proclaimed: 'In the economic area . . . the programme of the Party [is] étatism.'[23] In May 1931, the Third Congress of the RPP accepted étatism as one of the basic principles of the Party programme. But these developments were taking place at a time when the economic policy measures launched at the end of 1929 were being continued on the same lines without any 'étatist' modifications, and with no significant state intervention on the operation of market forces. Only in July 1932 did the government introduce the new model in its concrete form. Eight bills were submitted to parliament, all concerning economic policies and reflecting a very radical reorientation in the management of the economy. That particular moment in the economic history of the republic should be considered as the beginning of the étatist subperiod in the strict sense.

(e) *Main elements of étatist policies*

It is beyond the scope of this paper to undertake a concrete analysis of individual policy measures, but a brief survey of the main groups of economic policies may be fruitful.

First, as has been pointed out earlier, the protective measures controlling foreign trade were continued, and even strengthened during these years.[24] This was also the period of restrictions and controls on foreign capital. Most of the nationalisations of foreign investments — mainly in the areas of public utilities, mining and railways — took place in the 1930s,[25] although there was never an exclusion of capital imports in principle. The Soviet Union and Britain supplied credits for some of the major government investment; there was, as always, some trickling in of Western capital through partnerships with local firms, and the special trade relations with Germany in the second half of the 1930s brought in a number of complications in Turkey's external economic relations.[26] Nevertheless, this was the time of balanced external accounts when minimal resort was had to capital imports.

Secondly, some degree of government control of internal markets was employed. A number of agricultural commodities were subjected to direct or indirect government support policies, a measure with implications we shall investigate below. The prices of industrial goods were also under government supervision, and interest rates on financial transactions and on banking activities were, in principle, fixed by public authorities.

But the most characteristic feature of étatist policies was the emergence of the state as the major productive and investing agent. Most of the state monopolies of the 1920s, which were then administered by private firms, were gradually transferred into effective government management; and maritime transport between Turkish ports was transformed into a state monopoly. But it is the ambitious programme of state investment in industry and mining which characterises this period. Although private industry and mining was never prohibited, the licensing of new major investment and the granting of mining rights rested with the government.

Turkey can thus boast of one of the earliest experiences in national planning in the world. Work on the first five-year industrial plan started late in 1932 with assistance from Soviet advisers, and the Plan was adopted in 1934. Although it was a list of investment projects in detail, rather than an elaborate planning text in the strict sense of the term, it was for that period the major document guiding investment decisions. Despite a number of deviations, the targets of the Plan were considered to be achieved by 1938. A new plan, implementation of which was interrupted by the war, was launched in that year.[27]

By 1939, Turkey had gone a considerable distance along the road to industrialisation. A country which had imported its flour, sugar and cloth in 1923 was now at a stage when a wide variety of basic consumer goods, as well as a quantity of capital goods, were being produced in its factories — mostly established by state investment of the post-1932 years. Thus it was a period of close control of foreign trade, and of attempts at some control of internal markets and an active role by the state in capital accumulation, particularly in industry. These can be considered elements of the Kemalist model of development; a model which, we think, can only have been relevant for that period. The internal logic, if there was any, and the implications and consequences of this model have to be further analysed.

3. *An evaluation of alternative economic policies*

(a) *The alternatives in the early 1930s and a 'pure' model of étatism*

At the time of the first impact of the Great Depression on the Turkish economy early in 1930, what were the possible policy alternatives facing the Kemalist leadership? If we exclude a Soviet-type socialist alternative, which was unfeasible for obvious political and social reasons, three alternative models can be envisaged, all of which were discussed, tried and implemented in one way or other.

The first alternative was the continuation of the 'open door' and 'liberal' policies of the 1920s. Historical circumstances, which we have investigated above, had already compelled the leadership to take a number of steps signifying departures from that model in 1929, even before the repercussions of the Great Depression were felt; and, there is no evidence to suggest that the ruling circles seriously visualised the elimination of protective measures as a *response* to the Great Depression in 1930. One can conjecture that a return to the 'open economy' model of the 1920s would have dragged the Turkish economy into a chronic state of depression in the footsteps of the capitalist metropoles for at least a decade. The drastic deterioration in the external terms of trade, coupled with the gradual withering up of capital inflows — all as a result of the world crisis — would have undermined the import capacity of the economy: a situation which could not have served as an inducement to industrialisation, due to the lack of protective barriers.

The second alternative comprised the policies tried during the years 1930–2. It was, as we have shown, a protective model in which the initiative for accumulation and industrialisation was left to private capital. The favourable market conditions emerging as a consequence of protective policies would serve as the impetus for growth. The rent of protection to be appropriated by the local industrial bourgeoisie would constitute the basic source of accumulation. This process would be reinforced by the low prices of agricultural inputs (cotton) to industry and the depression of money wages (due to cheap wheat). It is not easy to visualise the course of events had this model been pursued up to the end of the 1930s. But the distributional consequences of these policies had political and social implications which the leadership, as we have seen, considered extremely risky. The model might have been able to create the mass of surplus necessary for growth, but the pattern of utilisation of the surplus would inevitably have escaped centralised control, something which the leadership considered undesirable from the viewpoint of the quality and dynamics of industrialisation.

Étatism was the strategic new element, the addition of which to the protective policies of the second model resulted in a new synthesis, and which was in fact the third viable alternative of the 1930s. What were the potentialities that this alternative offered to the Kemalist leadership which were lacking in the first two alternatives? In attempting to tackle this question, it seems fruitful first to analyse the implications of a 'pure' model of étatist industrialisation, and then investigate the deviations of the actual policies of 1933–9 from this pure model and their consequences.

Under a 'pure' model of étatist industrialisation, the state would be in a position to appropriate the rent of protection as a whole, since the industrial sector would be under state ownership. Moreover, in a pure étatist model of market control, effective government marketing policies on agricultural commodities would enable the state to occupy the totality of the area between primary producers and final (retail or export) markets. In the conditions of the 1930s, this would have created the possibility of state appropriation of the potential surplus resulting from the dramatic fall in agricultural prices.

The economic surplus thus generated could conceivably be utilised in a variety of ways by the state. The state, as the main industrialist, could charge high prices for industrial goods, and as the major purchaser of agricultural goods it could pay low prices to farmers; the large resulting margin would constitute the instrument for further industrial accumulation. Alternatively, the state could use this potential surplus as a fund for social and welfare purposes or for redistributive policies, while accepting a lower growth rate — a number of choices being available in this respect. Priority for public expenditure in health, education and social services; application of low prices for wage goods, but high prices for non-basic industrial goods, while paying high prices to poverty-stricken sections of farmers — only an industrial sector under public ownership without the constraint of the profit motive could continue functioning under such circumstances. Or a mixture of these growth and welfare policies, differentiated according to crops, branches and economic groups, could be implemented.

These were all new possibilities which transition to a pure étatist model would bring about — possibilities which were either totally lacking in the alternative policy models, or which would be completely outside the sphere of state control. The question is to what extent and in what manner these possibilities were actually exploited during 1933–9.

(b) Deviations from the pure model

Étatism, as actually implemented in the period 1933–9, contained a number of critical deviations from the pure model outlined above.

First, the state was never in a position to occupy the whole area between agricultural producers and final markets. The only significant agricultural commodity in which government had a trading and manufacturing monopoly (for the internal market only) was tobacco. In wheat, government agencies were authorised to buy and market the commodity from 1932 onwards, but with no monopoly powers. As for the markets of agricultural inputs for the newly-established industries (cotton, sugar beet), the relative size and importance of public ownership within the textile and sugar industries equipped the state with quasi-monopolistic powers to act as the price leader. But in most other agricultural products, price formation was left to the free play of market forces. Under the circumstances of *partial* public intervention in agricultural markets, the state cannot determine agricultural prices freely. The existence of a rival marketing network of private merchants brings a *lower barrier* for prices, below which farmers would refuse to sell to government agencies, whereas no such limit exists for support prices *above* equilibrium prices.

Secondly, in manufacturing industry, despite a *de facto* monopoly of public ownership in heavy industry, military production and a few other branches, in many sub-sectors state enterprises existed side-by-side with private industry; and there was also a wide area of industrial activity with no public sector at all. This resulted in a situation in which advantages, such as favourable price and cost structures created for the benefit of state industry, were shared by private enterprises in the same branches. This can be characterised as *partial* acquisition of the rent of protection and of the agricultural surplus by private industry. This partial private appropriation of the surplus generated as a consequence of public policies and for the benefit of the state sector was a matter of concern for the Kemalist leaders, and there were attempts, not altogether successful, to prevent or control this process.[28]

Apart from this domain of intra-branch co-existence, there was also the sphere of complementarity between the public and private sectors — a fruitful relationship for certain sections of the bourgeoisie, particularly for government contractors or small industrialists providing inputs for the modern productive sectors. The first five-year plan, defending the étatist strategy against 'liberal' criticism, was explicit on this point: 'With the industrial development of the country . . . a number of industrial branches surrounded by private enterprise will emerge, and they will survive under more favourable conditions than exist today. . . . The incremental volume of business will result in an accumulation of wealth which should subsequently flow into industrial investment and we will certainly witness the development of an ancillary [private] industry.'[29] It should be kept in mind that the most probable alternative to an étatist model of industrial growth was a chronic state of stagnation, and that gains and profits accruing to the type of intermediate and ancillary activities deriving from a high level of government expenditure would not materialise at all in a stagnant economy.

These observations lead us to conclude that étatist industrialisation was also a process in which state economic activities were at the origin of private capital accumulation. That is why étatist industrialisation cannot be characterised as a non-capitalist path; in the final analysis, it is rather a process of capitalist development in which the state functions *also* as the strategic agent for private accumulation.

(c) An overall view of economic performance

We shall now compare the economic performance of the étatist sub-period with the previous two sub-periods. Six economic indicators will be utilised for this exercise: (a) growth-rate of GNP; (b) growth-rate of industrial production; (c) share of industrial output in GNP; (d) share of investments in GNP; (e) share of imports in GNP; (f) balance of trade. The first four are evidently positive success indicators, while the last two should be interpreted as indices of economic dependence on the part of the national economy, and hence as negative success indicators, at least under the conditions of the period under review.

Table I gives the annual average values of the six categories mentioned above for our main sub-periods. A summary comparison of

Table I. ECONOMIC INDICATORS OF THE MAIN SUB-PERIODS, 1923–1939 (*annual averages*)

		1923–9	1930–2	1933–9
(a)	GNP Growth Rate	10.9*	1.5	9.1
(b)	Industrial Growth Rate	8.5*	14.8	10.2
(c)	Share of Industry in GNP	11.4	13.6	16.9
(d)	Share of Investments in GNP	9.1	9.7	10.7
(e)	Share of Imports in GNP	14.5	8.9	6.6
(f)	Exports — Imports	−56.6	+6.6	+12.4

Source: Calculations based on Tables 8.2.C, 8.3.A, 9.3 and 9.5 in Bulutay, Tezel and Yıldırım, *Türkiye Millî Geliri 1923–1948*, Ankara, 1974.
Notes: Rows *a – e* in percentages; row *f* in millions TL; rows *a – c* calculated in 1938 prices, rows *d – f* in current prices.
* 1924–9.

the economic indicators for our main periods leads us to the following generalisations:

1. The étatist period (1933–9) is superior to 1923–9 from the viewpoint of all our indicators excepting GNP growth rate; but it should be kept in mind that the relatively high growth for the 1920s is largely a reflection of the reconstruction process of a devastated economy.

2. The étatist period is superior to 1930–2 in all respects except the industrial growth rate.

3. The most striking feature about the positive economic performance of 1933–9 is the fact that it took place simultaneously with the elimination of the trade deficit and a significant fall in the share of imports in GNP. Indeed the annual trade balance, which registered a deficit for every year between 1923 and 1929, attains the highest positive average values during the étatist years — a development which results from the dramatic drop in imports. The average annual level of imports was 215 m. TL in 1923–9; whereas it was 120 m. in 1930–2 and slightly above 100 m. in 1933–9.[30] The average annual share of imports in GNP is thus reduced from 14.5 per cent in the first sub-period to 8.9 per cent in the second and to 6.6 per cent in 1933–9.

Thus at a time when the capitalist world economy was passing through the most serious crisis of its history, the Turkish economy, as it closed itself to the external world to a significant degree and attempted to rely on its own strength, was able to sustain significant rates of accumulation and growth. This picture of a dynamic and growing underdeveloped economy, side-by-side with a stagnant, crisis-ridden but powerful and dominant capitalist world system can probably provide important lessons on development strategies in the twentieth century. This point will be taken up in our last section (page 182, below).

(d) Mechanisms of accumulation and relations of distribution

What was the mechanism of accumulation which made this development possible, and what were the distributional consequences of this mechanism? A detailed analysis of individual policy measures and direct investigation of income distribution data (which are in fact unavailable) is required for a rigorous answer to this question. We shall have to be satisfied instead with using data on relative prices for some major commodities and sectors, and hence on the internal terms of trade — something which, we believe, can provide important insights on the appropriation and pattern of use of the economic surplus as well as on changes in income distribution.

The price index for industrial goods and the indices constructed from the time series of prices for wheat, cotton and tobacco will be used in this analysis.[31] All the three agricultural commodities selected for this investigation were, as we have shown above, susceptible to government price policies in one way or another; and hence their price movements may be interpreted as reflecting government objectives in some degree. But it should be emphasised that the price levels of each of these commodities had different implications for relations of distribution and for processes of accumulation.

Wheat, in which Turkey had become self-sufficient during the 1930s, was probably the most strategic commodity. The price of wheat, apart from influencing the standard of living of the mass of Anatolian peasantry, also determined the trade-off between money wages and profit margins in industry. This elementary economic relationship, which was among the main preoccupations of classical economists, was well grasped in the early years of the Republic. 'When bread gets cheaper, the wages of labourers also fall,' wrote a prominent Istanbul newspaper in 1925, supporting the statement with examples.[32]

Cotton was both an export commodity and the major input for the newly-established textile industry; the bulk of cotton production was for internal consumption.[33] Its price was the major cost element for the textile industry — something which had different implications for the state and private sectors, since the two sectors would follow different behaviour patterns in pricing and *vis-à-vis* the profit motive. Cotton was also a crop which was predominantly produced in big holdings. Tobacco, on the other hand, was a typical crop of a small but market-oriented peasanty. It was mainly produced for external markets, and therefore the price received by farmers was mainly a demand and income element with a negligible effect on industrial costs.

The price indices and the important price ratios for 1924–39 are shown in Table II. Because 1923 was a year of extremely low prices for agricultural commodities, 1924 — as a reasonably normal year — is taken as the base period in this Table. In order to permit a better understanding of the consequences and of the distribution implications of étatist policies, we have constructed Table III which takes the average indexes and ratios of 1931 and 1932 as the base year and transforms the data into 1933–9.

What are the main conclusions which can be drawn from an analysis of the price ratios given in Table II and III?

(*a*) Table II clearly demonstrates the deterioration of the terms of trade against agriculture in the early 1930s. The price ratios of wheat and cotton with industry fall sharply after 1928 and reach a trough in 1931, whereas tobacco/industry price ratios follow a more balanced, and a rather cyclical pattern.

Table II. PRICE INDICES AND PRICE RATIOS (1924 = 100)

	1924	1925	1926	1927	1928	1929	1930	1931	1932	1933	1934	1935	1936	1937	1938	1939
(a) Price Indices																
Industry	100	102	100	95	95	98	76	64	50	47	50	54	63	65	60	61
Wheat	100	136	117	111	127	118	69	38	40	35	34	43	44	44	41	42
Cotton	100	103	75	104	107	102	81	52	49	50	54	62	67	62	56	62
Tobacco	100	103	94	106	83	105	105	52	51	44	66	79	77	70	63	68
(b) Price ratios																
Wheat/Industry	100	133	117	117	134	120	91	59	80	74	68	80	70	68	68	68
Cotton/Industry	100	101	75	109	113	104	107	81	98	106	108	115	106	95	93	102
Tobacco/Industry	100	101	94	112	87	107	138	81	102	94	132	146	122	108	105	111
Wheat/Cotton	100	132	156	107	119	116	85	73	82	70	63	69	66	71	73	68
Wheat/Tobacco	100	132	124	105	153	112	66	73	78	80	52	54	57	63	65	62

Source: Calculations based on Tables Ek. 1, 10, 12, 25 in Bulutay, Tezel and Yıldırım, *op. cit.*

Table III. PRICE INDICES AND PRICE RATIOS (1931–2 = 100)

	1931–2	1933	1934	1935	1936	1937	1938	1939
			(a) Price indices					
Industry	100	83	87	95	111	115	105	107
Wheat	100	90	88	112	115	115	105	107
Cotton	100	100	107	123	132	123	108	123
Tobacco	100	86	127	152	150	135	123	131
			(b) Price ratios					
Wheat/Industry	100	108	100	118	104	100	100	100
Cotton/Industry	100	120	123	129	119	107	103	115
Tobacco/Industry	100	104	146	160	135	117	117	122
Wheat/Cotton	100	90	82	91	87	93	97	87
Wheat/Tobacco	100	105	69	74	77	85	85	82

Source: Table II.

(*b*) In this respect, the most dramatic deterioration in price ratios is observed for wheat: by 1934 the price index falls to 34, and the wheat/industry price ratio to 68. If one takes 1927–8 average as the base period instead of 1924, the corresponding indicators for 1934 are 29 and 54 respectively. Since wheat is the only agricultural commodity in our sample which scarcely enters external trade at all in this period,[35] its price can be considered a purely internal one; not *directly* influenced by world market prices, particularly after 1930. Therefore, it may be significant to compare external terms of trade for the Turkish economy as a whole with the 'pure' internal terms of trade represented by wheat/industry price ratios (see Table IV). This Table clearly shows that in the relevant period the internal terms of trade as represented by wheat consistently stay below the external terms of trade for Turkish exports. The explanation for this phenomenon probably lies in the *relatively* high prices for industrial goods in the internal market; or rather in the rent of protection implicit in industrial prices and which is thus a component of the internal terms of trade. This observation can also be interpreted as demonstrating the two potential sources of accumulation in the 1930s: high prices paid by consumers of industrial goods (rents of protection) and low prices paid to (wheat) farmers.

(*c*) A close investigation of the price ratios as a whole during the étatist period, 1933–9, as possible reflections of policies of accumulation, brings forth wheat again as the strategic commodity. The mechanism for government intervention in the wheat market, which was set up in 1932, seems to have arrested further *absolute* falls in wheat prices by 1933-4. But it was never used to *improve* the terms of trade for wheat in the following years. Indeed, relative prices for wheat show a striking stability during the étatist years, as can be

Table IV. EXTERNAL AND INTERNAL TERMS OF TRADE (1927–8 = 100)

	External Terms of Trade	Wheat/Industry Price Ratios
1929	84	95
1930	80	72
1931	78	47
1932	69	65
1933	61	57
1934	65	54
1935	72	65
1936	81	56
1937	78	54
1938	61	54

Source: Column 1: Paasche price index for Turkish exports divided by the same index for imports as calculated by Tezel, '1923–1938 Döneminde . . .', *op. cit.*, Table 2.
Column 2: Transformed from Table II above.

observed in Table III. In other words, the adverse terms of trade for wheat in the early 1930s were kept more or less constant until the war, with favourable consequences for the creation and appropriation of a surplus to be used for industrialisation.[36]

(*d*) This observation on wheat for the étatist years cannot be generalised for other crops: relative prices for cotton and tobacco follow a different course from wheat prices. There are significant improvements in cotton and tobacco price ratios during the étatist period, and this shift is not due to a corresponding improvement in export prices of these commodities. This assertion is particularly true of tobacco, for which unit export prices in 1933–9 stay consistently below the average prices for exports of 1931–2, whereas prices received by tobacco farmers are, from 1934 onwards, always above their 1931–2 levels. Taking the 1931–2 averages as 100, the unit export price for tobacco rested at 74 by 1939, while prices received by tobacco farmers reached 131. For cotton, on the other hand, export and internal prices both followed an upward but unidentical movement.[37] We can broadly conclude that relative prices earned by cotton and particularly by tobacco farmers were *mainly* determined by internal market conditions and/or government price policies.

(*e*) As to the underlying causes behind the significant improvement in the relative prices of these two commodities, each probably has a different explanation. A strong and dominant state sector in the textile industry was in a position to pay relatively high prices for cotton (compared with wheat, for example) and either to allow for a narrowing of profit margins, or to pass them on partly or totally to consumers. C. Bayar, minister of the economy in the étatist years, clearly explained the situation as follows: 'Local raw materials are expected to appreciate . . . as a result of industrialisation. Prices of many of our agricultural products, which had fallen to very low levels because of the Depression, are now above international prices thanks to our process of industrialisation. . . Cotton is a case in point . . . which shows that when a new industry whose raw material is produced in the country is established, farmers will gain.'[38] Although Bayar's assertion on internal prices exceeding international cotton prices is not totally corroborated by quantitative data, there was no necessity for state industry even approximately to follow international prices in what it paid to cotton farmers. It was in a position to pay, relatively, as low prices as government agencies paid to wheat farmers. But instead, a deliberate policy of high prices seems to have been followed. An additional, but probably important factor in the choice of this policy was the influence which the economically strong cotton farmers could exert, which also led to a generous allocation of credits and physical resources in favour of cotton production.[39]

(*f*) Tobacco, on the other hand, was not a strategic or basic commodity like wheat or cotton from the viewpoint of the industrialisation process as such. Therefore, the government, through its tobacco monopoly, could afford to use a relatively generous populist price policy in favour of the small and medium tobacco farmers. Whenever prices paid to farmers exceeded the export price, redistributive adjustment mechanisms could be used without undue difficulty, although the existence of private agents in the export market could create complications.

(*g*) It seems safe to assume that real wages were kept more or less constant during the period. A strict control of the labour market was institutionalised,[40] and it was possible to keep money wages at low levels thanks to the low price of wheat (and possibly of cotton textiles), although a temporary and contradictory measure of financing government wheat purchases through a tax on bread was implemented for a time.

The picture which emerges from the interconnection of these policies is one in which the potentials which the protectionist and étatist policies produced were mainly used for the creation and utilisation of an accumulation fund, the major contributors to which were the wheat farmers and the urban working class, as well as the urban middle classes paying higher-than-international prices for non-basic commodities. Distributional preoccupations were of a secondary nature, although certain sections of the farming population and of the bureaucracy seem to have been favoured by deliberate policies.

The policies of 1930—9 seriously handicapped the interests of the powerful foreign-oriented commercial bourgeoisie; but, on the other hand, the favourable conditions created for the benefit of the state industry were, to some degree, shared by the small, but emerging industrial bourgeoisie; and groups specialised in carrying out deals and contracts with the government benefited as well. Despite these facts, this period, by its very nature, did not reproduce the social tensions of the previous years resulting from the unbridled appropriation of the rent of protection by private interest groups and the profiteering activities which are inevitably present in such an economic environment.

It was, as a whole, a process of capitalist accumulation in which the state sector was the dynamic force. It was also a period of surprisingly positive economic achievements, despite (and perhaps also thanks to) thoroughly unfavourable external conditions. The rate of accumulation reached record levels in the étatist years, and by the beginning of the war the country had already passed the critical first threshold on the difficult road to industrialisation. The Kemalist economic policies of 1933—9 were the strategic instrument in this remarkable progress.

4. *Conclusion: Étatism as a model of self-reliant industrialisation for the Third World*

The following statement is taken from the introductory paragraphs of the first five-year industrial plan:

It was the Western areas of Europe and the Eastern coasts of North America where Western culture, technology and big industry were located. These areas, functioning as the workshop of the world, dispatched manufactures to the non-industrialised nations [where] the existing means of production, inundated by this big industry, were destroyed and the independent communities of yesterday were thus subjected to the hegemony of big capital and were transformed into legally independent, but economically dependent entities. This relation of dependence between the industrial countries of the West and the agricultural and primary producing countries created a state of affairs in which the industrial countries developed further and the primary producers gradually disintegrated. [. . .] The role of Turkey in the world commodity trade is to serve as an outlet for the industrial products of the West and, as an agricultural country, to provide raw materials to the same industry. [. . .] Despite the political and economic troubles and disagreements between them, the powerful industrial countries are basically in agreement in subjecting agricultural countries to a permanent status as primary producers and in dominating their internal markets. For this reason, they will sooner or later unite to use their political influence to prevent the present movements [towards independence] in the agricultural countries. And some of the agricultural countries may be resigned to accept this in return for minimal concessions. This fact, in particular, should compel us to establish the industry we require without any delay.[41]

A reader well-versed in the current 'dependence and underdevelopment' controversies is likely to find these views rather commonplace in the 1980s. But they are taken from an official document of an underdeveloped country, written fifty years ago, in the early days of the Great Depression. This fact, by itself, brings a highly original significance to the foregoing text. Indeed it is difficult, if not impossible, to find another official Turkish document of the past fifty years which has so correctly diagnosed the historical trend of the time.

First of all, the statement clearly shows that the writers of the First Plan considered the imperialist *metropoles* and the dependent *periphery* — in other words, *development* and *underdevelopment* — as components or parts of the same entity; and thus they anticipated the well-known theoretical explanation of the phenomenon of backwardness as a consequence of the development of the capitalist world system by at least three decades. Secondly, Turkey's place within the world economy is identified with precision. In this bi-polarised world system, Turkey is located, not within the ranks of the Western metropoles but within the dependent and underdeveloped pole, and thus shares the fate of other primary-producing, agricultural and oppressed nations. Thirdly, the writers of the Plan make a number of interesting observations on the effects of the Great Depression on both the imperialist centres and the periphery. They have perceived 'the political and economic troubles and disagreements' within the imperialist centres, emerging largely as a result of the world economic crisis; but they evaluate this situation as a favourable one for the backward countries, even as creating an *opportunity* for 'movements towards independence' in the economic sense. This reasoning is a logical extension of the explanation of the phenomenon of underdevelopment as a consequence of the development of imperialism. Thus a weakening at the metropoles due to the crisis of world capitalism had created a historical opportunity for industrialisation and development in the backward areas of the world economy.

And, finally, the authors are rather pessimistic about the future. What has emerged is only an opportunity which must be used immediately. They emphasise the necessity 'to establish the industry we require *without any delay*'. This sense of urgency derives from the perception that when the crisis of the imperial system is overcome, the industrialised countries will once again join forces to 'subject the agricultural countries to a permanent status of primary producers'; 'they will *sooner or later* unite to use their political influence to prevent the present movements' towards industrialisation and economic independence in the backward countries. And it seemed highly probable that the backward countries, and perhaps Turkey too, would give in 'in return for minimal concessions'. The consciousness that any loss of time would imply a very heavy future cost dominates the whole text.

The previous analysis of the early Depression years has shown that this sense of urgency, this feeling of immediate necessity for change, was not peculiar to the authors of the Plan but was shared by the Kemalist leaders as a whole. It is true that these were people of action, not theoreticians; and thus one rarely encounters clear-cut formulations on alternative development strategies in the economic controversies dominating the 1930s. But a careful analysis of the economic policy changes effected by the Kemalist leadership, which we have attempted in this paper, clearly shows a step-by-step evolution of a model of development which was finalised by the end of 1932: the synthesis of protectionism and étatism, as we have characterised it in this paper.

The *protectionist* element in this magnificent synthesis provided the correct defence mechanism against the world crisis; it enabled the partial 'delinking' of the Turkish economy from the imperialist system when the latter was in a depression. The *étatist* element, on the other hand, enabled the leadership to exercise economic and centralised control over the potential surplus emanating from the objective conditions of the period in question and to use this surplus as an accumulation fund for industrialisation. Thus the Kemalist leadership correctly perceived the conditions of the early 1930s as an historical opportunity for industrialisation. The lack of precedents forced them to follow a painful and forced march of trial and error through which they were able to discover the set of economic policies which served their objectives most effectively.

The experience of Kemalist Turkey in economic policies demonstrated for the first time in the twentieth century that for a backward and dependent country, self-reliant industrialisation without external deficits and without chronic indebtedness and the concomitant financial enslavement was not altogether utopian fantasy; in other words, the Kemalist experience can be interpreted as a serious endeavour to overcome backwardness and dependence within a *national* capitalist pattern. But the same experience, particularly its extension and consequences in the aftermath of the Second World War, also showed the limits and handicaps of such a model, the analysis of which is beyond the scope of this paper.

Kemalist economic policies thus provide a rich and untapped reservoir of positive and negative lessons for contemporary Third World countries, present-day Turkey included, all struggling to break the chains of economic dependence. We believe that in this respect the positive contributions of Kemalism far outweigh its negative lessons.

NOTES

1. For coverage, exclusions and definitions see A.G. Ökçün, *Osmanli Sanayii, 1913, 1915*, Ankara, SBF Yayınları, 1970, 2, 6.

2. *ibid.*, 14–25.

3. O. Silier, 'Türkiye'de Tarımsal Yapının Gelişimi, 1923–1938', mimeo, Boğaziçi Üniversitesi, Istanbul, 1979, 29n.

4. I. Tekeli and S. Ilkin, *1929 Dünya Buhranında Türkiye'nin Iktisadi Politika Arayişlari*, 1977, 59.

5. See K. Boratav, '1923–1939 Yıllarının Iktisat Politikası Açısından Dönemlendirilmesi', *Atatürk Döneminin Ekonomik ve Toplumsal Tarihiyle ilgili Sorunlar Sempozyumu*, Istanbul, 1977.

6. S. Meray (ed.), *Lozan Barış Konferansı*, part II, vol. 2, Ankara, SBF Yayınları, 1973, 9, 79–80; Tekeli and Ilkin, *op. cit.*, 67–8 O. Kurmuş, '1916 ve 1929 Gümrük Tarifeleri Üzerine Bazı Gözlemler', *Gelişme Dergisi/Studies in Development* Ozel Sayısı, 1978.

7. Y.S. Tezel, 'Birinci Büyük Millet Meclisinde Yabancı Sermaye Sorunu: Bir Örnek Olay', *SBF Dergisi*, 1970, xxv/1; Tezel, 'Birinci Büyük Millet Meclisi Anti-Emperyalist miydi? Chester Ayrıcalığı', *SBF Dergisi*, 1970, xxv/4; T. Timur, Türk Devrimi ve Sonrası, Doğan Yayınları, Ankara, 1971, 58–9; D. Avcioğlu, *Milli Kurtulush Tarihi* (I), Tekin Yayınevi, Istanbul, 1974, 377; S. Ilkin, 'Türkiye Milli Ithalat ve Ihracat Anonim Şirketi', *Gelişme Dergisi/Studies in Development*, Sayı 2, 1971.

8. A.G. Ökçün, *1920–1930 Yılları Arasında Kurulan Türk Anonim Şirketlerinde Yabancı Sermaye*, SBF Yayınları, Ankara, 1971.

9. K. Boratav, *Türkiye'de Devletçilik*, Gerçek Yayınevi, Istanbul, 1974.

10. F.R. Atay, *Çankaya*, Istanbul, 1969, 455–6; Ş.S. Aydemir, *Ikinci Adam* (I), Remzi Kitabevi, Istanbul, 1966, 446–7.

11. Tekeli and Ilkin, *op. cit.*, 69–74.

12. Kurmuş, *op. cit.*, 196.

13. Tekeli and Ilkin, *op. cit.*, pp. 43–5; Boratav, *Türkiye'de Devletçilik, op. cit.*, pp. 48–9.

14. See Boratav, *ibid.*, 47–50; Boratav, '1923–1939 Yıllarının. . .', *op. cit.*, 44; Tekeli and Ilkin, *op. cit.*, 92–139.

15. This society aimed mainly at discouraging the consumption of foreign goods which competed with local products.

16. These two documents are fully reprinted in Tekeli and Ilkin, *op. cit.*

17. For detailed evidence sustaining this assertion see Boratav, *Türkiye'de Devletçilik, op. cit.*, 78–89.

18. See T. Bulutay, Y.S. Tezel and N. Yıldırım, *Türkiye Millî Geliri: 1923–1948*, SBF Yayını, Ankara, 1974, Tables 8.II.C and 9.5.

19. A.H. Başar, *Atatürk İle Üç Ay*, Istanbul, 1945, 43–5, 91–2.

20. Calculations based on Tables Ek 1 and Ek 25 in Bulutay, Tezel and Yıldırım, *op. cit.*

21. See Silier, *op. cit.*, 30.

22. For a vivid account of this organised journey see Başar, *op. cit.*

23. B. Kuruç, 'İktisat Politikasının Resmi Belgeleri', mimeo, SBF, Ankara, 1963, 14.

24. Laws no. 2054 and 3018. See Boratav, *Türkiye'de Devletçilik, op. cit.*, 245–6.

25. M. Selik, *Türkiye'de Yabancı Özel Sermaye, 1923–1960*, SBF, Ankara, 1961.

26. Y.S. Tezel, '1923–1938 Döneminde Türkiye'nin Dış İktisadi İlişkileri', *Atatürk Döneminin . . ., op. cit.*, 1977.

27. Boratav, *Türkiye'de Devletçilik, op. cit.*, 154–7; E. Günçe, 'Early Planning Experiences in Turkey', *Planning in Turkey*, ODTÜ, Ankara, 1967.

28. Law no. 3003 is a case in point. See Boratav, *Türkiye'de Devletçilik, op. cit.*, 251–6.

29. A. Inan (ed.), *Raporlar, Kısım I, Sınai Tesısat ve İsletme*, Ankara, 1933, 13.

30. Averages based on Table 9.5 in Bulutay, Tezel and Yıldırım, *op. cit.*

31. Calculations based on Tables Ek 1, 2, 10 and 25 in *ibid*. See also Boratav 'Büyük Dünya Bunalımı iginde Türkiye'nin Senayileshme ve Gelişme Sorunları', *1976 Sanayi Kongresi*, Makina Mühendisleri Odası, Ankara, 1976, and Boratav, '1923–1939 Yıllarının. . .', op. cit. . . .

32. *Cumhuriyet*, 1.VIII.1925, quoted by Silier, *op. cit.*, 30.

33. *Ibid.*, p. 36.

34. The prices of wheat, cotton and tobacco increased by 38, 42 and 108 per cent respectively from 1923 to 1924.

35. The share of wheat exports in total wheat production changed between 0.6 per cent and 3.2 per cent in the 1930s. See Silier, *op. cit.*, 118.

36. This conclusion contradicts the analysis of Birtek and Keyder, 'Agriculture and the State', *Journal of Peasant Studies*, vol. 2, no. 4, 1975, in which, without using data on relative prices, the authors draw a picture of populist government policies in favour of wheat-growing peasantry in the étatist period.

37. Calculations made by the author using data in *Foreign Trade Statistics* and in Bulutay, Tezel and Yıldırım. *op. cit.*

38. Quoted by Kuruç, *op. cit.*, 40, 47.

39. See Silier, *op. cit.*, 119.

40. In this respect see S. Ilkin, 'Devletçilik Döneminin ilk Yıllarında İşçi, Sorununa Yaklaşım ve 1932 İş Kanunu Tasarısı', *Gelişme Dergisi/Studies in Development*, Özel Sayisi, 1978.

41. Inan, *op. cit.*, 8–10.

Religion and secularism in Turkey

ŞERIF MARDIN

Few categorical assertions can be made in the social sciences, but certainly one of them is that social thought never starts with a clean slate. The contributions of social innovators, therefore, become fully meaningful only when their proposals are set in the framework of their institutional and intellectual inheritance.

This also holds true for a series of reforms which were carried out in Turkey in the 1920s and the 1930s, due in large measure to the single-minded drive and determination of Mustafa Kemal Atatürk, the architect of the Turkish Republic and its first president. These reforms established the principle of laicism — or secularism — as the foundation stone of Turkish constitutional theory and political life. The principle has endured to our day despite changes in régimes and constitutional renovation.

Laicism was a concept which emerged from French constitutional practice in the nineteenth century and referred to the necessity that the state refrain from lending its positive support to any one religious denomination. It was considered to have been fully achieved in France in 1905 with the definitive separation of Church and State. In Turkey, laicism amounted to more than the official disestablishment of religion, since Muslims did not dispose of an autonomous religious institution such as the Catholic Church which could carry its religious functions independently of the state. In France, religion and the state already operated on two distinct institutional registers and were eventually separated in the law of the land. In Turkey a limb of the state was torn out of its body when laicism became the state policy. This is the reason why Turkish secularisation is considered a momentous achievement.

To say that Atatürk's policy is better understood when observed against his own background does not minimise this achievement, but it enables us to place this accomplishment in the frame of that celebrated meeting of East and West about which so much has been written. The historical context also brings out features which are crucial to an understanding of the future of laicism in Turkey. 'Cultural background' or 'historical context' as used here means not only the events of Atatürk's lifetime but the long-standing traditions and institutional arrangements in which he was rooted. It is these which provide the latent guidelines for the structuring of social relations in any society, even though they are also in constant flux.

Atatürk's secularising reforms show at least two facts which had antecedents in Ottoman history, namely his opinions as to the functions of religion in society and the methods which he used to translate his ideas into policy. His ideas on religion bore the stamp of the empiricism of Ottoman secular officialdom, and the method that he used to implement his ideas — legislation — was foreshadowed by the policies of the nineteenth-century Ottoman modernising statesmen.

Ottoman bureaucracy and modernisation

The Ottoman state, which emerged with its full outlines between the fourteenth and the sixteenth centuries, was an institutional achievement of major dimensions. As builders of an empire, the Ottomans confronted a number of obstacles which earlier Middle Eastern empires had only partly surmounted. One major task they faced was to establish effective government in a geographic setting which comprised a large variety of religious communities, ethnic groups and sub-cultures ensconced in ecological niches that were difficult of access. The Ottomans had to make nomads and city-dwellers contribute to a common purpose transcending their individual interests; they had to reconcile the requirements of imperial taxation with the autonomy of local magnates, who were often residual élites of earlier independent territories incorporated into the empire; and they had to find the means of integrating millions of Christians into a Muslim empire. In these tasks they seem to have succeeded better than their predecessors, an achievement which was, in great part, due to their ability to build a sultanic state. They created a class of military and administrative officials whose unstinting allegiance went to the Ottoman dynasty and sometimes even gave precedence to the state over the dynasty. They established a network of judicial and administrative positions staffed by district judges (*kadıs*) trained in Muslim law. They devised means of mobilising the land resources of the empire, which were now integrated with a system of taxation and with military organisation. They elaborated complex sets of regulations for commerce, and established control over a network of roads linking garrisoned cities. Subject populations such as the Christians, which the Ottomans had incorporated during their drive through the Balkans, were classified by their religious affiliation. The settlement of their civil concerns was delegated to their own ecclesiastical authorities — which the government used in order to secure access to their non-Muslim subjects.

Having added the Arab lands and Mecca and Medina to the

empire in the sixteenth century, the Ottomans began to see themselves as heirs to the Islamic Caliphate, and the Ottoman sultan
assumed the role of protector of the entire Muslim world.[1] In
consequence, even though the Turks had been converted to Islam
long before and had given a central place to Islamic institutions in
their state, religion now acquired a new 'imperial' dimension. However, Islam was far from a unitary concern. A central Islamic tradition, which in its essentials showed great similarities, prevailed in
cities throughout the Islamic world. But in the wider span of that
world, as in many regions in the Ottoman empire proper, this unity
disappeared, and heterodox doctrines, charismatic leaders and cults
with deep local roots and only an Islamic veneer became items to
reckon with. This religious heterogeneity was a source of deep worry
for Ottoman statesmen — a pattern which, as I shall try to show,
had changed very little even by the twentieth century.

One feature of Ottoman Islam was particularly galling to
Ottoman officials. The Shiite form of Islam had been adopted in
Iran in the sixteenth century by rulers who were engaged in a rivalry
with the Ottomans for the mantle of leadership in West Asia.
Ottoman Shiites were therefore considered by the Ottomans to be a
dangerous fifth column working to undermine their hegemony. But
quite apart from the dangers of Shiism, Ottoman officials evaluated
the practice of Islam from a perspective which they shared as officials, namely the fear that the Ottoman empire, already made up of a
mosaic of unwieldy components, would fragment. Faced, at the time
when they were trying to consolidate the empire, by what amounted
to a congerie of brotherhoods, sects and cults; confronted by a
succession of millenarian movements; and, furthermore, pitted
against potentially subversive magnates and what survived of
erstwhile princely dynasties, Ottoman bureaucrats felt the need to
get a grip over religion which would minimise the dangers that
religious movements spelled out. To this end they used a number of
policies. First, they tried to impose orthodox, Sunni Islam and were
constantly on the lookout for traitorous Shii. Secondly, they
deported to the far corners of the empire heterodox groups which
they considered dangerous. Thirdly, and most important, they
engaged in building a religious élite and an educational system controlled by this élite, both of which were in turn controlled by the
state. The higher religious functionaries, the doctors of Islamic law
(*ülema*) were, in effect, transformed into officials, for their
livelihood was granted them by the state, and the path they travelled
in their career was fixed by the state. The higher-ranking *ülema* also
acquired an understanding of the conduct of Ottoman politics in
positions which demanded that they participate in policy-making.

For those at the top of the hierarchical pyramid, politics — as would be expected — was ubiquitous.

Because the rulers of Islamic societies had been designated heads of the community of believers, and because the law of the land in these societies was basically law drawn from the Koran, the Muslim religious hierarchy did, theoretically, have an organic connection with what may be termed the constitutional law of Islamic states. In the Ottoman empire, *ulema* were much more clearly integrated with the apparatus of the state. Through their control of education, of the judiciary and of the administrative network, they acted as agents of the state and thus indirectly ensured the state's control of social life.

Ottoman government was therefore both 'Islamic' and 'bureaucratic'. It was Islamic in the sense that Islam was the religion of the state and that the Sultan's primordial role was that of the leader of the Islamic community; it was 'bureaucratic' in the sense that working for the preservation of the state coloured the practice of Ottoman officials. Endangering the state was what — by definition — made a movement heretical. At times, such as during the seventeenth century, the style of government was more 'Islamic', but by the middle of the eighteenth century the pendulum had swung to a more bureaucratic style.

What I have described as the 'bureaucratic style' of government was the product of a special attitude among a group of secular officials who concentrated on the power dimension of social relations as the most important aspect of life. They were hard-headed, empirically minded and pragmatic. Their ideology was that of the 'reason of state'. This stance was in great part the result of their training, which differed from that of the *ülema*. The latter went through a three-tier *cursus honorum* in schools known as *medrese*. The preparatory classes of the *medrese* taught general subjects such as rhetoric and grammar, but as one proceeded to higher levels, religious studies predominated. Graduates of the *medrese* were expected to have specialised in one of the religious sciences. They were trained to draw out of religious texts knowledge that would be applicable to ritual, to the interpretation of legal problems, and — of primary interest for us — the conduct of social life. They showed considerable ingenuity in finding Islamic justification for many activities — such as the charging of interest — which were prohibited in the strict application of the law. There was, nevertheless, an idealistic aspect to their thinking, a feeling that the commands of religion came first and that human concerns had to be adapted to this pattern. Without letting the contrast run away with us, we may say that the reverse was true for the secular officials. The usual pattern here was that after elementary training at the tender age of eleven or twelve, the aspiring bureaucrat was apprenticed to a government 'bureau'. It was here that the real education of the bureaucrat would take place, and this feature becomes increasingly marked towards the end of the eighteenth and the beginning of the nineteenth century. It is this background which seems to have been the source of the primacy which the secular bureaucrat gave to realistic appraisals of power factors in society, relegating idealism to the background.

When the Ottoman empire began to decline, two divergent perceptions of the causes for this decline emerged among the bureaucrats and the *ülema*. For the doctors of Islamic law, the reason for the decline was religious: the Ottomans had neglected their duties as Muslims, and therefore they had lost the power they commanded when their faith had been strong. For the military and the central bureaucratic apparatus, the empire had declined because the machinery of the state had deteriorated: incompetents had been placed in positions of responsibility; prebends had been distributed to the undeserving; bribery had become common practice. Again, the contrast in attitudes does not appear with as clear an outline as I give it here, but in general such a dichotomy can be observed. It will be remembered that a third category of officials also existed: *ülema* who, by the very nature of the posts they occupied, had acquired a sophisticated knowledge of governmental affairs: these tended to give discreet support to the secular thesis.

To arrest the decline of the empire, the secular bureaucracy and the military officials undertook reforms which gave highest priority to military reorganisation and the building of a new tax structure which would support it. At the beginning of the reform movement, some of the *ülema* sided with the reformists, and such an alliance was not unknown even in later years. Two reformist Sultans, Selim III (1789–1807) and Mahmud II (1807–39), were clearly out of the same mould that had established the tradition of *realpolitik* in the bureaucracy. They had little patience with arguments against the partial reform they were undertaking.

Although the body of Ottoman secular bureaucracy had shared the elaboration of policy with the higher *ülema*, they had long since disagreed with them on a number of issues. Now, at the beginning of the nineteenth century, they seized the initiation of change and embarked on a program which had the aim of introducing into Turkey administrative institutions and economic incentives which European enlightened despotism had used for some time. The changes thus brought about were eventually to undermine completely the prestige and position of the *ülema*: progressively eased out of the central processes of decision-making after the middle of the nineteenth century, they were eventually to be denied all but marginal roles in administration, the judiciary and the educational system.

Before the middle of the nineteenth century, in theory, the law of the land in the Ottoman empire was the *Şeriat*, the religious law based on the Koran. Verses from the Koran, the tradition of the Prophet Muhammad and the rationalistic expostulations of the great Muslim jurists were the sources of this law. In fact, bureaucratic practice had created a fund of secular legislation which even the circuit judges — trained as they were in the *medrese* — had to take into account. This practice predisposed the architects of the reform movement (*Tanzimat*) to visualise statutory regulations as the lever which would ensure that their reforms would become part of the law of the state. The *Tanzimat* was therefore characterised by a flood of statutes, regulations, ordinances and by-laws. The practice was inaugurated by the proclamation by Sultan Abdulmecid of a basic charter, the so-called *Hatt-ı Hümayun* of Gülhane (1839). This document legitimised the entire enterprise of reform and outlined the direction it was to take. An already existing rift between statute law and religious law thus deepened during the *Tanzimat*.

The new regulations of the *Tanzimat* were, by their very nature, secular. They originated in the bureaux of the Porte and set very specific targets for the implementation of administrative, financial and educational policies. In the years which followed — known as the era of the *Tanzimat* (1839–76) — a new administrative law and a rationale for administration were gradually secreted in the insterstices of change, a development Max Weber and Justice Holmes would have rightly appreciated. The religious underpinning of administrative practice was on its way out. Central to this transformation was the transfer of the functions of the circuit judge, trained in the *medrese*, to a new type of employee, the administrative official. A new school, the School of Administration (*Mülkiye*), was established in 1859 to train these cadres. Gradually, also, a system of secular courts came into being where the cases adjudicated were largely those which arose in relation to the new reform policy. A codification of commercial and criminal law was initiated. By the end of the nineteenth century, even religious law had been codified and systematised. But it was quite clear that the codification which had taken place was the product of a defensive move so that it could not be argued that the problems which could be solved under the *Code Napoléon* had no solution in Muslim law. This derived, mirror-image, nature of the new Muslim code, the *Mecelle*, did not show that Islamic law had triumphed but rather that it too had to bend to the exigencies of a Western European mode of posing legal problems.

The reform of public instruction followed the same course. It was placed in a new secular frame by the creation, in 1846, of a Ministry of Public Instruction.[2] In 1847 the state extended its direct grip on the educational process by replacing the system of neighbourhood schools financed by private support or by charitable grants by a system of state-financed primary schools.[3] In the 1850s and 1860s a system of post-primary education inaugurated by the state began to spread throughout Turkey. This major educational achievement of the *Tanzimat* was the *Rüşdiye*, the corner-store of its policy for training cadres. The graduates were required to master advanced arithmetic, to learn from their courses on Turkish composition to write a clear report, and to be able to draw on their knowledge of world geography and history. The speed in the propagation of the *Rüşdiye* was not equalled by the next wave of educational development, the spread of *lycées* to the provinces; however, between 1882 and 1900 most provincial capitals acquired a *lycée*.[4] Secularisation had started even earlier at the higher levels of education with the founding of the School of Medicine (1827)[5] and the Military Academy (1834, 1846).[6] A new, secular law school began to function in 1880.

All these developments were the consequence of the characteristic attitude of the Ottoman secular bureaucracy in matters which concerned the restoration of the power of the state: if Western institutions could rejuvenate the state, they would be adopted. It would be difficult otherwise to explain the ease with which Ottomans slid into westernising reform. Again, it is in this light that we understand how, already in the 1880s, the Ottoman statesman Saffet Paşa (1814–83) could urge Turkey to adopt 'the civilisation of Europe in its entirety, in short, to prove itself a civilised state'.[7] This statement was made privately, but Saffet Paşa also put himself on record publicly with similarly strong statements on the subject[8] and his statement is a fair summary of the thoughts of many of his colleagues. The distance travelled by Saffet Paşa in relation to his educational background should be noted since he had received a *medrese* education. But the reason for his eagerness to model the empire on Europe becomes clear when we isolate the formative influence of his youth; he acquired his values and world-view when, as a very young man, he was apprenticed to the Ministry of Foreign Affairs.

A more colourful picture of the way in which Ottoman bureaucrats of the *Tanzimat* could step out of what they considered to be the 'backwardness' of some Islamic practices, may be found in a

number of reports about Ahmad Vefik Paşa, an outstanding statesman of the era. Among his achievements Vefik Paşa could count the
translation of Molière into Turkish. At one time he was the governor
of Bursa province, the capital of which, the town of Bursa, was
deeply imbued with religious traditions; undeterred, Vefik Paşa
established a theatre in the town for the production of his translations of Molière and demanded that his employees buy season tic-
kets. The local recorder of the Descendants of the Prophet, the
Nakib ul Eşraf Asim Bey, claimed that he could not attend such
lighthearted entertainment because of his exalted status as an Islamic
official:[9] Vefik Paşa thereupon had Asım Bey's stables walled in by
the municipality. On another occasion, during a tour of inspection,
hearing that the lodge of a mystic order (*tekke*) was used as a refuge
for brigands, he had the building torn down on the spot. During his
renovation of Bursa he found that to implement his plans he had to
demolish the tomb of a saint known as the 'walking saint'. Vefik
Paşa went to the tomb, called three times 'O Saint, walk away!' and
then had the sanctuary demolished, remarking 'He must have
walked away by now'.[10]

The institutional secularisation achieved by the men of the
Tanzimat was paralleled by their favourable attitude towards the
practical applications of modern science. This was one of the reasons
why military medicine had such an early start in the empire.
Medicine for civilian purposes was also placed at the head of their
priorities, and when 'positivism' and 'materialism' began to
influence Ottoman intellectuals at the end of the nineteenth century,
it was through the channel of medicine and biology. Students of
Claude Bernard brought back ideas derived from his *Introduction to
the Study of Experimental Medicine*, and in the 1890s Büchner's
Kraft und Stoff became an influential source of 'materialistic' ideas.
A Turkish journalist, who was associated with the growth of a
periodical publication which acted as a channel for the transmission
of late nineteenth-century bourgeois optimism to Turkish audiences,
recounts how his own scientific world-view was shaped in the years
when he was a student at the School of Public Administration; the
course on botany given by the imperial physician Salih Efendi
'cleansed' his mind and the minds of the other students of 'supersti-
tions' through crystal-clear explanations of the life of plants,[11] I shall
try to show below that this new pattern for learning, which had to
emphasise clarity and internal consistency, was to have a striking
effect in changing the attitudes of the new generation of bureaucrats
which graduated from higher schools in the 1890s.

Secular as they would be, the architects of the *Tanzimat* could not
escape the impingement upon their policies of an aspect of the reli-

gious structure of the Ottoman empire. They still were not taken in by the religion-oriented theory of the decline of the Ottoman empire. This in itself may be considered an achievement, since the old theory emerged in a much more sophisticated version, one which seemed much more reasonable than the earlier explanation. This new viewpoint, which took shape in the 1860s, stated that every society was kept from disintegrating by the strength of its moral fibre; what kept moral fibre strong was a society's culture. Islam was the culture of the Ottoman empire and Ottomans only neglected this culture at their peril. This theory, which was stolen from the arsenal of Western romanticism, did not meet with much approval on the part of the *Tanzimat* statesmen, even though it was beginning to find supporters among constitutional liberals. With one exception, leading to the codification of Muslim 'civil' law, the statesmen dismissed such arguments. What the statesmen of the *Tanzimat* could not dismiss so easily was the old Ottoman classification of populations on the basis of religious affiliation.

Like a number of Middle Eastern empires before them, the Ottomans had a system of administration which was two-headed. In one respect it was territorial — the Ottoman empire was divided into provinces — but in another respect the system was based on religious distinctions. According to this classification non-Muslims were dealt with on the basis not of ethnicity or languagè but of their religious affiliation. Thus, for instance, one basic Ottoman administrative unit was the Orthodox church through which Ottomans had access to a large number of their Christian subjects. The state left the internal administration of persons belonging to the Orthodox church to the Orthodox patriarchate.[12] Armenian Gregorians and Jews were also governed in their civil affairs by their highest religious dignitaries. In this sense, the Muslim community too was conceptualised as one unit, even though it incorporated Arabs, Turks, Albanians, Kurds and Circassians.

During the nineteenth century, the European great powers increased their influence in a role they had assumed for some time, that of the protectors of the various Christian populations of the Ottoman empire. This was a political manoeuvre aimed at gaining a foothold on the territory of the 'sick man of Europe'. The states who actively participated in this policy were seeking a share in the division of spoils which would follow the sick man's demise. Beginning with the middle of the nineteenth century, internal developments in the religious communities in the empire changed the structure of their internal administration. The laity increased its power, and lay assemblies took over many of the functions which till then had devolved upon the ecclesiastical hierarchy. One by one, also, the communities obtained the recognition of their new 'civil constitutions' by the Ottoman state.[13] These communities were granted corporate personality in the law of the *Tanzimat*. The underlining of community boundaries in this fashion gave a new relief to the religious heterogeneity of the Ottoman empire. The *Tanzimat* statesmen were hoping that they could arrest this process, which set religious communities in a harder mould and which became the source of ideas demanding separation of these communities from the Ottoman empire. Indeed some of the states carved from Ottoman territory at the beginning of the nineteenth century such as Greece and Serbia had such antecedents.

The very process of community cohesion led a number of Ottomans to think of their own future in terms of a more cohesive Muslim community. We now encounter a third variant of the Muslim attitude towards the decline of the Ottoman empire. This was the idea that Ottoman Muslims should begin to look after their own interests *qua* Muslims. Such a policy might provide the 'cement' that would at least keep the Muslims of the empire unified; together, Muslims might keep the empire from further disintegration. By the year 1871, and the death of the Grand Vizier Ali Paşa, two factions had already formed among statesmen, one supporting the continuation of the institutional modernisation of the Ottoman empire as a means of providing the allegiance of all Ottomans towards an Ottoman state, the second ready to use Islam as a new political formula.

From then on — and this is crucial for an understanding of Atatürk's attitude towards Islam — Islam was to be judged by men belonging to either faction as viable to the extent that it provided an effective political formula, a means of rallying the population of the empire. Atatürk rejected this option in the second decade of the twentieth century because he believed that attempts to implement it had proved a mirage. Part of his reaction had to do with the dissonance between his own conception of time span and that of the Islamists. He thought in terms of decades — Muslim propagandists were thinking in terms of millenia. This sensitivity to a time-dimension is one of the aspects of the thinking of his generation which places it in a different category from the reformism of the early *Tanzimat*. I shall have more to offer on this subject below. What could and what could not be done with Islam as a political formula was demonstrated during the reign of Sultan Abdülhamid II (1876–1909).

By the time the treaty of Berlin had been signed in 1878, more territory had been whittled away from the Ottoman empire. In the remaining territories, the Muslims constituted a clearer majority than before. Faced with this demographic pattern and the growing antagonism of the Muslim and Christian populations, the Sultan decided to steer a middle course among the contending formulas for the empire's salvation. He continued the work of the *Tanzimat* statesmen for the rationalisation and the modernisation of the state apparatus. He lent his support to the expansion of the system of secular courts and secular education. He left the *medrese* to stagnate: by the end of his reign they were poorly staffed, poorly financed institutions which served as a refuge for draft-dodgers.

Abdülhamid also believed in science and its practical applications, but he opted for the use of Islam as a lever which would instil some consciousness of a collective goal into his subjects. He realised that a modern state could not function with the tacit allegiance which had been sufficient to get the machinery of the state to function in the time of his predecessors. To raise agricultural productivity — to provide only one example — was one of his targets, but he realised that this could only be achieved by a series of measures comprising railroad expansion, agricultural training and the participation of the peasant in the scheme. But more important even than participation was to forge some identity among the rural masses which would enable them to give meaning to their own allegiance to the distant figure of the Caliph. To this end the Sultan implemented an extremely intelligent policy, establishing contacts with sheikhs and dervishes, using propaganda to mobilise the town populations — here the building of a railroad to the Hidjaz occupied a strategic place — and trying to reconcile the Arab population to an Ottoman identity. At least in the Anatolian peninsula, the policy did have some results, as is attested by a number of contemporary observers. What the Sultan was grappling with were two characteristics of the rural personality of his realm: the lack of autonomy of individuals and the absence of a conception of a unit transcending the village or the hamlet. Millions of Ottomans fell in this category, and the extent to which they were bereft of collective identity was to be observed much later, during the First World War, by a young officer. This is the way he describes his first experiences in training Anatolian recruits:

At that time, as far as I was able to understand, our soldiers rather than being persons whom one could deal with as individuals, were better conceptualised as cogs in a community, as components of a group. In a community and in a group they could easily follow everything that was required of them. But whenever one of them would stray from the group and become isolated, he would be unable to determine an independent course of action for himself, of his own volition. Also, in collective undertakings, he would always look for someone to become dependent on or to follow. This often affected the conduct of war by my unit. A group of soldiers which had lost its sergeant or officer or directing agent would quite easily come apart. In moments of danger, a unit, instead of dispersing carefully at a moment's notice, would tend on the contrary to bunch up, to fall upon each other, and always in the direction of the centre of command.

As for danger, its resonance was for them non-existent. They did not need any preparation to go to sleep. They could go to sleep within a minute, possibly within a second. They would even be asleep at the time we thought them to be awake. At a time when you thought everything was perfectly ordered, a sentinel you trusted, standing in his trench, with his weapon at the ready, his eyes looking ahead, could have fallen into a deep sleep. That a person from whom you could demand everything at a time when he was subject to a unified command and in a group could become so remote from any form of social responsibility was something which left one gasping.

The same author describes the responses he received when he began asking his men questions relating to their religion:

When I asked the question 'What is our religion?' 'What is the religion which we follow?' I thought the answer I would receive would be 'Praised be the Lord, we are Muslims.' But this was not the responses I received. Some said 'We are of the religion of the Great Imam.' Others said 'We are the followers of the Prophet Ali.' Some could not solve this problem. Some did, indeed, say 'We are Muslims' but when the question was asked 'Who is our prophet?', they too became confused. Names of prophets that would never come to one's mind were mentioned. One said 'Our prophet is Enver Paşa.' Again when the question was asked of the few who had identified the Prophet, 'Is our Prophet alive or dead?', the matter once more became insoluble. Some said he was alive, some that he was dead . . .

The young officer who could not disguise the anguish he felt at the quality of the human material with which he was asked to conduct a war knew one thing: despite their crass ignorance of Islam, religion was still one of the ways by which they could acquire an 'internal gyroscope', a conception of the self which at the same time could be used to relate their selves to a national purpose. In contemporary Latin American usage, we would refer to what both the Sultan and the officer were seeking as *conscientización* or consciousness-building. What the Sultan did not realise was that the political message of Islam was not sufficiently focused to keep the many Muslims who made up his empire united around a common purpose, even though he did succeed in building some sense of Muslim identity and even of Ottoman identity among some of his subjects. Islam had thus been found to have a diffuse effect in building a social identity of sorts, and a solidarity of sorts, among the more isolated areas of the Ottoman empire. But even today the nature of the Islamic bond as a form of proto-nationalism is not understood.

Nevertheless, it is a sign of the hardiness of the idea of consciousness-building through Islamisation that the Young Turks who dethroned Sultan Abdülhamid did not entirely abandon experimentation with this formula, although their scepticism as to its effectiveness was growing.

Neither did the Sultan realise that the second part of his program, his continued support for institutional modernisation and the upgrading of institutions for professional training, would run into trouble. In the end these educational reforms gave rise to new, unanticipated attitudes which encouraged the radicalisation of persons trained in these institutions. These new tendencies were to take Turkey into laicism, for the new generation which emerged from the educational structure sponsored by the Sultan were marked by an uncompromising opposition to what they saw as the useless remnants of the *ancien régime*. The hardening of attitudes appeared both in the demand that reality should be made to fit an abstract plan or theory, and in the view that the time-span for a project was 'now'. This attitude differed fundamentally from that of the officials of the *Tanzimat*, ready as the latter were to live with compromises, half-measures, hybrid systems and conflicting values. From now on the word 'fossil' (or 'residue' — *müstahase*) was to appear with increasing frequency in the vocabulary of Ottoman progressive intellectuals. It is this sense of unease in operating with a system which was a mixture of the old and the new which appears most clearly in the ideas of Kemal Atatürk.

The reform of higher educational institutions and Sultan Abdülhamid II

It may come as a surprise to discover that the first years of Sultan Abdülhamid's reign were marked by outstanding achievements in education. In particular, beginning with the 1880s a system of military schools which took in boarding students immediately after primary education was inaugurated. These schools, the military *Rüşdiye*, could lead all the way to the military academy for those who had decided on a military career. The system had been promoted by one of the Sultan's greatest enemies, his director of military education, Süleyman Paşa, who had engineered the deposition of Sultan Abdülaziz in 1876. Sultan Abdülhamid, who succeeded to the throne shortly afterwards, had Süleyman Paşa court-martialled but this did not prevent him from implementing the system of education devised by the general. In 1895 there were twenty-eight of these military middle schools functioning in the empire, eight in the capital and twenty in the provinces.[14] The total number of students in these schools was 6,000 and by 1898 it had reached 8,000. There also existed seven military preparatory schools of *lycée* level which prepared students for entrance into the military academy or the military medical school. The same pattern of preparatory school was available for students who desired to enter the school of administration.

The educational standards of the military *Rüşdiye* were high. Many of the students who opted for a military career came from families of low socio-economic background and their profession was necessarily the focus for their self-image. As they moved upward in the system of military education they acquired a view of the world which stressed the positive sciences. The students were also constantly reminded that the fate of the empire depended on their own contributions to its salvation. It was through an understanding of the forces that had made the Western states powerful that they would save the empire. There was therefore a continuity between the student's world-view and that of the bureaucrats who a few generations back had started reform. But there was also an outstanding difference: the new generation not only knew more geography, more modern history and more mathematics than their predecessors, but they also acquired a new vision of reality from their knowledge. The most talented among them developed a conception of the ways in which one could shape society which made the action of the *Tanzimat* statesmen appear dated and over-hesitant.

The new impatience of the graduates of the Ottoman *grandes écoles* — both military and civilian — becomes apparent when one contrasts the type of pedagogy prevailing in the traditional system with the new system of book learning and classroom studies. If the term 'apprenticeship' provides the key to the old education, the conception of 'utopian mentality' explains the hidden spring of the new system and the stamp with which it marked the graduates.

In the traditional system, knowledge was a limited thing: the basic outlines of Islamic knowledge had been established once and for all. This fund of knowledge was transmitted, like that of a form of artisanship, through a mastery of known techniques. The new knowledge — geography, physics, chemistry, biology — was an expanding body with its own momentum which one had to keep up with in order to be well informed. Techniques for its use were constantly changing. Thus, change came in at the beginning as a datum of Western positive science. In this light, the *ülema* who had not kept up with the expansion of the intellectual horizons came increasingly to be seen as ignorant charlatans rather than as repositories of ancient wisdom. This was one of the factors which propelled the students into a clear confrontation with religion. In the future, references to the need for change and to the way that religion was an obstruction to progress was to become a *leitmotif* in Atatürk's writings.

In the traditional system, initiation into the world of knowledge through the guidance of a mentor was central. In the bureau, the mentor had been the sponsor of the new employee, or the experienced official who took an interest in his career. In the *medrese*, the mentor was the tutor to which the student was assigned for the duration of his studies. Personalities, thus established, together with the idea that knowledge was a limited fund which could only be approached through known techniques, limited the extent to which the initiate could go off on a tangent and dare to make new interpretations of matters already explored by his predecessors. In the new system, books which were distributed to the entire class were the foundation of knowledge; they became the reference-points for learning, and those published in France allowed one to be in advance even of one's teachers, who had gone to France only at an earlier stage.

Another, possibly more important, feature of the new learning was that the book, the classroom and the school now operated as what Irving Goffman terms a 'total institution'.[15] Each school was a self-contained universe in which students were segregated from Ottoman everyday life. In the training system of the bureau, students had culled their knowledge from actual official transactions. They were immersed in a complex skein of knowledge, practice, intrigue and planning. The new generation of officials was cut off from all this; they were studying principles and laws which were abstractions from reality, and had an artificial internal consistency. It was as if the generation of the 1890s thought that life as described in books was more real than life itself.

Here again, we get a better sense of what was involved in the change if we go back to the textbooks the students were using. The textbooks of geography, physics, mathematics and military science represented the systematisation of knowledge as applied to a given field. This systematisation proceeded by abstracting certain phenomena from the undifferentiated mass of impressions which made up the 'stuff' of everyday life. A model of the interaction between certain of these phenomena, selected as 'significant', was built and finally the model was made to run faster than reality. Science then appeared to the students in the form of abstract models of reality, a characteristic also emphasised by the lack of experimentation and the parlous state of laboratories. It was through an assimilation of theory that science was gaining a foothold among them.

By means of a similarly schematic presentation, students acquired their image of Western societies. Internally consistent systems, neat models and blueprints thus acquired a great importance in the minds of the generation of the 1890s. Thus it is no surprise to find out that the earliest protests of the Young Turks were concerned with what they considered the lack of consistency of their own system of education. For the most talented and idealistic, an interlocking of smoothly integrated parts became an obsession. What did not fit this interlocking pattern could be thrown out as irrelevant or harmful. Ottoman society with its trams operating in the midst of crumbling houses, newspapers which had to heed strange rules imposed by an ignorant censorship and regiments where graduates of the military academy took orders from officers promoted from the ranks, exemplified the type of dissonance that was most galling to the students. The ideal slowly began to emerge that it was either one or the other of the systems which had to emerge, not a mixture or a rickety compromise.

To 'run' a model of social reality faster than reality itself, one had to project oneself into a hypothetical future. The model of social reality constructed from the school vision of the world had, therefore, an additional element: that of a hypothetical future which could be shaped at will. This was also new compared to the ideas of the *Tanzimat* statesmen. The reformist of the *Tanzimat* was an activist, but he saw himself primarily as shaping the present, albeit for future use. The idea of a structured historical future developing out of the present with new features due to human intervention was not a datum of *Tanzimat* thinking. By contrast, the generation of the 1890s began to think of society in terms of both an abstract model and a blueprint for the future, albeit in the direction of 'progress'. Social 'projects' now became an intellectual exercise. A striking example of the centrality of hypothetical situations and of projects may be seen in a prefiguration of modern Turkey by the Young Turk, Abdullah Cevdet, entitled 'A Very Wakeful Sleep'.[16]

While the outline of a new type of social thinking began to emerge with the generation of the 1890s, the generation of the Young Turks, it does not become effective until the Young Turk revolution of 1908. Even then we see the Young Turks impelled to work with the familiar pieces of the Ottoman mosaic: various ethnic and religious groups, and Islam as the thin thread keeping the populations of the Ottoman empire together. As to the second use of the Islamic formula, its role as a 'raiser of consciousness', we see them become increasingly sceptical of this approach. It is because of this scepticism that the Young Turks — in keeping with their 'scientific-utopian' world view — entrusted one of their colleagues, Ziya

Gökalp, with research carried out to find an alternative formula to Islam. The Young Turks were thereby doing something the *Tanzimat* statesmen had never dreamed of: they had initiated a search for a systematic, internally consistent theory of reform.

Ziya Gökalp's investigations made him focus on two ideas, that of the 'nation' and that of 'civilisation'. According to him, 'civilisation' consisted of the technological and cultural implements which a number of societies could share. Modern western civilisation, for instance, marked by industrialisation and a number of new social institutions, was shared by many Western nations. Nationality was another component of the Western system of states, and this Ziya Gökalp linked to the concept of 'culture'. A 'culture' was the latent pattern of values, beliefs and institutions which defined a people. Whenever such a people had been incorporated within a multi-ethnic, plural state, its values had remained in the background. A modern state was a state which coalesced around one of these peoples and boldly made use of its characteristic institutions. Turks were such a group whose specific cultural values had receded into the background when they had established the Ottoman empire. As to Islam, Gökalp indicated that a number of items which were accepted as integral aspects of religion — particularly the commands associated with the proper Islamic organisation of society — were in fact aspects of Arabic culture which had nothing to do with 'pristine' Islam.[17] Islam, therefore was a religion that demanded of its followers 'faith', and it did not confine its followers to any form of social organisation. Ziya Gökalp's blueprint for the future — which never emerged as a completed proposal — was to draw out the latent Turkish culture of the Turkish nation, to establish a Turkish state based on it, to accept Western civilisation and to make Islam a matter of conscience, a private belief. A memorandum Ziya Gökalp had written for the Young Turks in 1916 concerning the role of Islam in Turkey was implemented by the Young Turks.[18] It led to the exclusion of the *Şeyhülislam* — the highest religious functionary in the Ottoman empire — from the cabinet, the separation of the religious courts from the Şeyhülislamate and their attachment to the ministry of justice; the placing of the administration of pious foundations under the authority of a member of the Cabinet; and the separation of the *medrese* from the Şeyhülislamate and their administration by the ministry of education.

With the defeat of the Ottoman empire in the First World War and the loss of the Arab lands a new situation arose. For all practical purposes Turkey now consisted of the Anatolian peninsula. Part one of the Islamic formula — its function as a link between Turks and

Arabs — could now be jettisoned. It is remarkable, however, that Mustafa Kemal did not immediately dispose of this formula when he was organising resistance against the terms of the treaty that were about to be imposed on Turkey. During the years when he was leaving this resistance movement, between 1919 and 1922, he was dependent on the sympathies of Muslims outside Turkey, and often used the theme of the unity of Islam. He also made use of it to mobilise the feelings of Anatolian religious notables against an Ottoman administration which continued to function in the capital as a virtual prisoner of the Allies. He took advantage of the prestige of the Caliphate at the time when, paradoxically — he was about to suppress it. But in both cases he had made up his mind very early concerning the Turkey he visualised in the future.

The Turkish republic and the New Nation

Atatürk's contributions are usually analysed in terms of his unique ability to bring about needed reforms. In this appraisal, he figures as the instrument of a great wave of progress leading to some predestined point. This image is thoroughly teleological, for it depicts him as outstanding not only in having been able to negotiate successfully a number of difficult passages to his own consciously set goals, but also because he 'fulfilled the requirements' of enlightenment thought. I believe this particular judgment to be somewhat simplistic but the appraisal also hinders us from placing Atatürk in a more 'sociological' context. The view which characterises Atatürk as a servant of progress is derived from a primitive picture of the inevitability of progress. It does not help us to locate him in the major social upheavals which have shaken the world in the last four centuries and which continue to do so with increasing violence. The full meaning of Atatürk's contribution only emerges when we relate his work to that of two key processes which subsume the momentous changes which marked post-feudal society, namely the multifarious new patterns of collective integration and the changing dimensions of the individual's personal integrative systems.

A new integrative system for the collective

Most Turkish and foreign scholars see the foundation of the Turkish Republic as the reorganisation — albeit a radical reorganisation — of a remnant of the Ottoman empire. In fact, the watershed appears not only in the radicalisation of the attitudes of the founding fathers of the Republic but in the very conception of the Turkish Republic as a nation-state. What happened was that Mustafa Kemal took up a non-existent, hypothetical entity, the Turkish nation, and breathed life into it. It is this ability to work for something which did not exist as if it existed, and to make it exist, which gives us the true dimensions of the project on which he had set out and which brings out the utopian quality of his thinking. Neither the Turkish nation as the fountainhead of a 'general will' nor the Turkish nation as a source of national identity existed at the time he set out on this task. He was distinguished from his more cautious collaborators by such a vision of the future and the will to make it materialise. 'Nation' and 'Western civilisation' were the two fundamental code words which provided the latent rationale for his project, and his attitude towards religion assumes coherence when we evaluate it from that vantage-point. The determination he showed in pursuit of an ideal of society is not contradicted by his great talent for temporising: what gives meaning to his tactical reversals is the project on which his mind was focused.

The sequence of events which eventually led to the secularisation of Turkey is well known and does not need to be related in detail. However, one characteristic of the way in which Mustafa Kemal tackled the issue from the very beginning shows the depth of his political talent and should not be overlooked as a foreshadowing of his policy of secularisation. We find this prefiguration of his political genius in his use of the concept of a 'grand' National Assembly as the source of political legitimation for the resistance movement. The Sultan-Caliph was theoretically invested with his power because he was the leader of that Muslim community — the Ottoman community — which held the most effective power in the Muslim world. Since the person occupying the position of Sultan-Caliph was now a prisoner of the Allied forces, he could no longer act as a free agent. The *millet*, the concept which originally referred to the various religious subdivisions of the empire, but in this particular case to the Muslim community, would re-establish its sovereign rights as the fountainhead of legitimacy. In fact, since the end of the nineteenth century *millet* had been used with increasing frequency to translate the word 'nation'. Its meaning was therefore ambiguous. It is as a consequence of this ambiguity that the body which had been assembled in Ankara as a representative assembly, and which had a strong clerical representation in it, passed Article 1 of the Provisional Constitution proposed in 1920 without any objections (20 January 1920). This article stated that sovereignty belonged without reservation to the *millet*. The ambiguity of the term allowed clerics to believe that what had been invoked were the rights of the community, whereas for Atatürk it was a preparation for invoking the sovereignty of the nation.[19] The Assembly had accepted the re-establishment of the primitive rights of the Muslim community, but by the same token it had accepted that the Assembly could legislate in matters both secular and religious in the absence of a Sultan-Caliph. Mustafa Kemal made sure that no one bearing these double attributes would ever emerge again.

From the image of the Sultan-Caliph as a prisoner of the Allies, the Ankara regime moved on to a new constitutional system where temporal power was effectively severed from the Sultanate.[20] This was followed by the abolition of the Sultanate on 1 November 1922, the proclamation of the Republic on 29 October 1923, and finally the momentous laws of 3 March 1924: this series of laws, all passed on the same day, abolished the Caliphate, made all education a monopoly of the state, and abolished the *medrese*. Religious affairs and the administration of pious foundations were thereafter to be directed by directorates attached to the office of the prime minister. In April 1924, religious courts were abolished. In 1925, mystic orders (*tarikat*) were outlawed. In 1926, the Swiss Civil Code was adopted, and the link between the *Şeriat* and criminal law was severed. In 1928, the constitutional provision which still mentioned Islam as the religion of the state was abrogated. The same year the latin alphabet was adopted.

Whenever a rationale was invoked for these moves, the reason given was that of 'the requirements of contemporary civilisation'. This may be followed in a number of speeches Mustafa Kemal made in the 1920s. One of the most concise statements of this rationale is found in the 1931 statutes of the Republican People's Party. The new regime had, from the start, rallied its supporters by establishing a political party within the Grand National Assembly, the Republican People's Party. This party eventually emerged as the only legitimate organ of political articulation in the Republic and the centre where the official ideology of the new republican regime was elaborated. The 1931 statutes of the Party stated that it stood for the principle of 'laicism', defined as a condition in which the state took no role in religious life since religion was 'a matter of conscience'. The text stated: 'The Party has accepted the principle that all laws, regulations and procedures used in the administration of the state should be prepared and implemented in order to meet the needs of this world and in accordance with the foundations of and the forms provided by science and technology in modern times.'[21] Party leaders later underlined the idea that they did not consider laicism to be synonymous with atheism (*dinsizlik*), since the performance of religious ritual (*ibadet*) was protected by the Constitution. In 1937 the principle of laicism was introduced into the Constitution, together with five other guiding principles of the Party — republicanism, nationalism, étatism, populism and reformism.

The history of laicism in Turkey and of its application is, of course, much more complex than this synopsis can suggest, but the meaning of laicism as a project is best highlighted not by a description of its practice as by its relation to the primordial goals of the republican regime. One of these was the need to find a principle of social cohesion for Turkish society and to devise a means of raising social consciousness among the Turks (*conscientización*). Insofar as Islam had been found wanting in both these respects, it had been rejected. As Islam no longer served these purposes, it had indeed become a matter for the 'private' consciences of Turks.

The consciousness of the new Turks was to be rooted in science ('Western civilisation') which Atatürk repeatedly mentioned as the source of all valid knowledge and behaviour. But then the matter was not so simple, because 'consciousness raising' aimed to elicit a set of characteristics which one expected the citizens of the new republic to possess. 'Science', as such, had no answer to questions regarding the building of national identity; nor did it tackle the issue of social identity, the orientation of the individual towards social ideals.

Two ideologies emerged in the 1930s which were expected to promote national identity: the so-called 'Turkish history thesis' and the 'sun-language' theory.

The 'Turkish history thesis' was built on the idea that Turks had contributed to civilisation long before they had been incorporated into the Ottoman empire. They had originated an urban civilisation in Central Asia from which many other civilisations had sprung. They had maintained their cultural identity even after becoming a minority in a multi-national empire. It was from this fund that an identity could be drawn for the citizens of republican Turkey. To a limited extent this thesis achieved its goal; Turks began to feel a new sense of their accomplishments as Turks, and pride in being a Turk did indeed develop whereas only five decades earlier the term Turk was still used as a synonym of nomad or peasant by denizens of the Ottoman empire.

The 'sun-language' theory was an attempt to rationalise a development which had been taking place in Ottoman literature since the middle of the nineteenth century, namely the increasing use of the vernacular instead of the flowery and allusive language of the Ottoman officials. The vernacular contained few of the Arabic and Persian roots that prevailed in 'officialese'. It was now proposed that 'pure' Turkish — i.e. Turkish which had not been infiltrated by the vocabulary and the grammar of other Middle Eastern civilisations — was an ancient language of central importance in the history of languages. It was claimed that many other languages had been built on this foundation and that one could find guidance for the reform of linguistic usage if one studied this early Turkish language. This was a difficult theory to sustain in the light of linguistic research; nevertheless, the practice of trying to reconstitute 'pure' Turkish did fire a number of Turkish intellectuals who devoted enormous energy to this task. To support linguistic reform became enshrined as an aspect of Kemalist radicalism, and this somewhat bizarre association between linguistic purism and republican radicalism had continued to our day when it was picked up by marxism. It is part of the means available to modern Turks to build for themselves a Turkish identity.

In retrospect, however, the most solid foundation for building a republican-Turkish identity seems to have been another, more solid, theory of society which provided a social ideology of Kemalism. This theory was solidarism, the official ideology of the French Third Republic. Solidaristic theorising had reached Turkey through Durkheim and through Ziya Gökalp, one of Durkheim's admirers. The theory was based on the thesis that there was no necessary conflict between classes in modern society. What was important was the way social institutions and the contributions of all professional groups made society a going concern. Industrial society could be kept in equilibrium by propagating a social ethic focused on the contribution of individuals and groups to society. In addition, Turkish solidarism offered a social program which envisaged that 'capital accumulated through the appropriation of surplus values on behalf of society' would be invested in 'industrial plants and large farms to be established for the benefit of society'.[22] Kemalist education propounded a theory of citizenship based on these principles. It was the businessman, the schoolmaster and the politician who, working together under the shield of solidaristic redistribution, were to make up an integrated Turkish nation. In more recent years, Kemalism may have lost much of its momentum, but its dream of a non-conflictual and at the same time redistributive society has continued to mark Turkish social thinking. This pattern has also appeared in the diffuse aspirations of its newly-mobilised population. It is also such an image of society which emerges from the thinking of the military group which tried in 1960 to re-establish a 'truly' Kemalist system.

The new Turkey and the individual

One of the key words in the ideological vocabulary of Atatürk was *istiklâl* (independence), but at the individual level this emphasis was paralleled by his use of *müstakil* (autonomous, free).[23] I have tried to show how the attempt to replace the traditional system — en bloc, so to speak — by a new one is a tendency which one observes in the generation which preceded that of Atatürk. I have also pointed out that Atatürk's policies of reform concentrated on the building of a new collective identity in the make-up of which religion was denied a role. But then, there also exists another basic aspect of his secularising reforms which aims to broaden the autonomy of the individual in society. Here Atatürk was working to liberate the individual from what he may have agreed to call the 'idiocy of traditional, community-oriented life'. Once again he was going well beyond the reforms of the *Tanzimat* statesmen. In view of the solid support which community culture found in Turkey, it may be said that he showed even greater courage in this field than in his actions within a more political context.

I believe that the drive that compelled him towards this goal was also a product of the dissonance created by his educational background. The peculiar form that this dissonance took was his disgust with the forms of social control which sprang from Ottoman folk culture. To provide an understanding of my use of such an explanatory model we must first consider the influence of Western political and social ideas on Atatürk.

Atatürk travelled outside the Ottoman empire for a total of three times, once to observe military manoeuvres in France, the second time as military attaché in Sofia, and the third time during the First World War in Germany. His knowledge of Europe was not limited to these contacts, but was nevertheless acquired primarily from the Turkish press which kept closely in touch with world events and which also followed scientific and cultural developments. A limited number of translations of the works of persons who were political theorisers of the era were also available to him. Atatürk read French and understood it well. In his library, preserved near his mausoleum, works of thinkers such as Rousseau do figure, and some have marginal annotations, but these probably date from the last years of his life. The consensus is that at the time he carried out his main secularising reforms he had a general knowledge of Western political systems, but that he was also dependent on the information he received from his colleagues (such as the minister of justice, Mahmut Esat Bozkurt) who had studied abroad.

How, then, can one explain the consistency of his secularising reforms? What gives us the feeling that there is a latent pattern around which they are unified? In particular, why does one feel this concerning his reforms dealing with the mystic orders, the rights of women, 'secularisation' of dress, and state control of education?

A hypothesis I would like to propose is that these secularising reforms are linked by the underlying common denominator of the liberation of the individual from the collective constraints of the Muslim community. To understand this, we have to look at the smallest operative unit of the community in the Ottoman empire, the *mahalle* or city quarter. In those times the *mahalle* was more than an administrative unit with somewhat arbitrarily drawn boundaries; it was a compact *gemeinschaft* with its boundaries protected by its own toughs and faithful dogs, and a setting within which much of the normal life of an average Ottoman citizen was shaped. It is here that primary education was undertaken, births were celebrated, marriages were arranged, and the last rites were performed for the dying. It was here that the mosque operated as a social institution bringing all inhabitants to hear what was expected of them. It was against the background of the *mahalle* that the authority of the paterfamilias was exercised and supported. And it was here that sometimes blood-money was paid; that the Islamic institution of morals-control wormed its way into drinking parties and gambling dens, and organised posses to surprise careless lovers; that the café — a communications centre — operated; that the first stamp was affixed by the prayer leader on a petition that was to travel on to higher authorities; and that local saints' tombs could be visited and living holy men dispensed their own kind of influence and justice. *Mahalle* rules were in fact quite flexible, but the flexibility operated behind a mask of decorum. It was quite inflexible with regard to overt mixing of sexes. Atatürk's reforms have an aspect which tried to replace the personnalistic ties and the hypocrisy that pervaded the *mahalle* morals-control by a set of rules which tried to obviate control and replace it by a system of regulations that gave the individual responsibility for his actions.

Atatürk's determination to wrest the individual away from folk control had an origin which, once more, is found in the new educational system. *Mahalle* norms were not particularly galling to someone who had spent his entire lifetime there; but for students who spent most of their time at school as boarders, school directives became more important. School directives, however, stressed a completely different type of control; the rationality of bureaucracy took over, and what had to be achieved was the revitalisation of the empire which was now dependent upon new virtues. *Mahalle* virtues were linked to the preservation of small groups. There was no use for them in the building of the nation-state. Religious morality was replaced by intellectual and military disciplines and once more Islamic ethics and commands related to the good of the community rose up as irrational restrictions with no purpose except the snuffing out of personality.

The school setting was not the only context in which community control and the specific values which came with it were being devalued. The devaluation of the *mahalle* was a cumulative process in which the rise of new ways of thinking about society also had a part. One of the indirect ways in which the *mahalle* ethos was devalued was that a new focus for the citizen's allegiance, 'society' (*cemiyet-i beşeriye*), began to appear in the writings of modernist intellectuals. This was a concept which differed from *devlet* (the state) insofar as it took in a number of social processes that were not subsumed under the heading of policy, power, coercion, rule and prestige, these being the primordial components of the concept of *devlet*. The family and the individual, both subjects of *mahalle* control, were sub-units comprised within the concept of 'society', and persons who wanted to reform 'society' also wanted to reform the family. 'Society' operated on the basis of free exchange of goods or services, and it therefore immediately condemned domestic slavery. The *mahalle*, on the other hand, accepted domestic slavery as a fact of life. Society was based on contract, and the *mahalle* operated on ascriptive bases; thus the *mahalle* began to appear as a fund of traditional values which were hampering the expansion of human personality.

At about the same time there began to emerge a rejection of the dress characteristic of the *mahalle*. Bihruz Bey, a super-westernised hero in one of the earliest Turkish novels, takes a walk in the park, sees his lower-class compatriots in baggy pants, and complains: '*Qu'est ce que c'est que ça? Est-ce que le carnaval est arrivé?*' But the revulsion against folk culture which was building up is best expressed by the writer Yakup Kadri Karaosmanoğlu, who was to join Mustafa Kemal in Ankara. One of Yakup Kadri's stories concerns a westernised Turk who is beaten up by *mahalle* toughs because he dares to wear a hat. On one occasion he describes the oppressiveness of folk culture as follows:

In this stagnant air, none of the atoms of which is moved by a melodious sound, in these squares, none of which is adorned by a figure, in these streets, the dust and the mud of which we daily brave, in the face of these people whose ears are deaf to any pleasantness, whose eyes are blind to any beauty, who squat at night in coffee houses with their coloured printed nightgowns listening to the tube of a gramophone vomit belly-dance tunes, I find the seeds of their sickness.

Yakup Kadri's complaint was that the *mahalle* ethos and intellectual climate killed creativity in Turkish writers. The same connection between *mahalle* as an amalgam of Islamic and folk culture and lack of creativity seems to have been made by Atatürk. Atatürk was very much of the opinion that baggy pants and the *fez* were part of a 'carnival'. Not only was his aesthetic sense offended but these clothes

symbolised the stranglehold of a folk culture where final legitimation had always to be obtained in terms of religious values, and
where both religion and man were therefore debased and corrupted.
Western society, which received its legitimation from science, was
much more open and therefore more inventive. It was only with a set
of rules that would enable the individual to escape from the suf-
focating folk values that creativeness could be encouraged. Two
policies were devised by Atatürk to this end: first, his secularising
measures, where the specific target was to destroy control, and secondly, his program of cultural westernisation for the Republic.

The individual in Atatürk's secularist reforms

The first view we get of Mustafa Kemal's attempt to liberate the
individual from community norms is the law of 3 March 1924 on the
'Unification of Education'. Not only did this law take education
once and for all out of the hands of the *ülema* but it opened the doors
for co-education and thus a completely new integration of the sexes
from the school years onwards. In fact, Atatürk's thrust to establish
women's rights may be conceptualised as a concentrated effort to
smash what to him appeared as the most stifling and dark aspect of
the *mahalle* ethos, namely the restrictions it placed on contacts
between men and women in the day-to-day routine of life. A large
area of the changes brought about by the adoption of the Swiss Civil
Code was concerned with the transformation of women's legal
status. Among these were monogamous marriages, equality of
status between men and women as heirs, and a number of provisions
concerning property management. This was followed in 1930 by the
granting of rights to women to vote and stand for election in local
contests (Municipality Law of 14 April 1930)[24] and by the right to
vote and stand for election in national elections in 1934.

Atatürk's many references to women working side by side with
men in the Turkish Republic created the climate that enabled many
Turkish women who had received education to enter professional
life. As a result, Turkey today has an enviable proportion of its professional cadres filled by women. The 'lifting of the veil', which was
never placed into a statute, followed from this development.

Once again, Atatürk's attitude towards the mystic orders (*tarikat*)
is related to his attack against stifling *gemeinschaft*. When one reads
the law of 1925 abolishing these orders, it is clear that what Atatürk
had in mind was to disallow the influence of local charismatic leaders
who were either notables with local political power or appeared as
ignorant and cunning figures exploiting the lower classes. Turks
would in future be ruled not by corrupt sheikhs but according to the
way set out by science. Their personality would not be determined by

the counsel of a religious mentor but by immersion in Western culture.

Atatürk and Western culture

To provide Turkish citizens with a new view of the world which would replace that of religion and religious culture, Atatürk sponsored a movement of cultural westernisation which he equated with civilisation. The alphabet was latinised partly to enable an easier access to works in Western languages. For a time, the performance of oriental music in public was banned. A conservatory was established in Ankara, where opera, ballet and Western polyphonic music were taught. Western-style painting was encouraged by the government which also subsidised the publication of a number of cultural periodicals in which the products of modern Turkish painting were presented. In 1926 a statue of Kemal Atatürk was unveiled in Istanbul: in a country where the interdict against reproducing the human figure had been publicly enforced, this called for considerable courage. Statues now appeared all over Turkey. Folk culture was rescued by making it a subject of study in the 'People's Houses' (community centres established in the 1930s with the aim of propagating culture in a Western mould), and including its motifs in the subjects taught there: Turkish culture was thus brought back to the fore without its outer rind of *mahalle* Islam. And although, in a general sense, the experiment in the westernisation of Turkish culture has had great success since the 1930s, this is the very point where a note of pessimism has to be introduced.

In the years following the death of Atatürk, and particularly after the institution of multi-party democracy in 1950, laicism was challenged by a number of groups. In fact, the principle had rooted itself sufficiently firmly never to be removed from Turkish constitutional practice. Even the Demokrat Party, which was often accused of having undermined laicism, kept the principle in operation. Nevertheless, the military intervention of 1960 was caused in part by fear that that party was encouraging religious obscurantism which would endanger the constitutional foundations of the Republic. Since 1960 religious currents have not abated; if anything they have become stronger, but the constitutional principle of laicism, upheld by a large segment of the Turkish intelligentsia, is still the foundation of Turkish constitutional law. What, then, is happening in Turkey? What is the meaning of the flood of Islamic publications, of the resurgence of *tarikat* and the growth of new sects, of the rise of a clerical party in parliament and of the muted streets during the month of Ramadan?

There is, first, a social context for the revival of Islam. Part of this is demographic: the population of Turkey is growing very fast, with enormous cohorts in the adolescent age groups for which ideology is so vital. In that sense Islam competes with marxism. But more important than the demography is 'social mobilisation', the ability of a much larger proportion of Turkey's population — due to the influence of the mass media — to change their environment or propel themselves into other roles. This is accompanied by a severing of traditional roots, leaving a vacuum to be filled. In this situation some of the limitations of the Kemalist experiment begin to emerge.

Mustafa Kemal's ideas about the society which he imagined as emerging on the ruins of the Ottoman empire were focused on the collectivity, and acquired their particular strength from this. They were also focused on the individual's liberation from the stifling *gemeinschaft* of the Muslim community. But a new 'collective conscience' and liberation from community influences were only two aspects of what Mustafa Kemal really wanted to achieve, namely the forging of a new identity for Turks. For this identity to crystallise around the new symbols of the Republic, the latter had to have a 'sensory component' with the ability to 'arouse feelings'.[25]

What we observe is that the symbols of Kemalism assumed this function for only a limited number of Turks. But, in addition, Kemalism did not understand the role played by Islam for Turks in the building of personal identity. After all, Islam had an aspect which addressed itself to man's being-in-this-world, to his basic ontological insecurity, which enabled it to fasten itself on to psychological drives. It is a truism, but still one worth emphasising, that Islam has become stronger in Turkey because social mobilisation had not decreased but on the contrary increased the insecurity of the men who have been projected out of their traditional setting. This insecurity is sometimes 'cognitive' and appears as a search for a convincing political leadership or a bountiful economic system. Here Islam assumes an ideological guise and competes with marxism. In many cases, the insecurity is deeper, more truly ontological, and Islam appears in its aspect of a cosmology and an eschatology.

The revitalisation of Islam in modern Turkey is a very complex occurrence part of which is structured at the personal level, part of which relates to the attempt to bring back the full glory of Islam, and part of which is political. It is a pity that positivism, which played such a large part in the elaboration of Kemalism, did not choose in its Turkish version to remember Auguste Comte's warning: '*L'Humanité se substitute définitivement à Dieu, sans oublier jamais ses services provisoires.*'[26]

NOTES

1. Halil Inalcık, *The Ottoman Empire X: the Classical Age 1300–1600*, London, Weidenfeld and Nicolson, 1973, 34.

2. Faik Reşit Unat, *Türkiye'de Egitim Sisteminin Gelişmesine Tarihi bir Bakış*, Ankara, Milli Eğitim Basimevi, 1964, 19.

3. *ibid.*, 38.

4. *ibid.*, 45.

5. *ibid.*, 14.

6. *ibid.*, 65.

7. Niyazi Berkes, *The Development of Secularism in Turkey*, Montreal, McGill University Press, 1964, 185.

8. Niyazi Berkes, *Türkiyede Çağddaşlaşma* Istanbul, Doğu-Batı Yayinlari, 1978, 234.

9. Abdurrahman Şeref, *Tarih Konuşmaları*, 1923; ed. Eşref Eşrefoğlu, 1978, Istanbul, Kavram Yayinlari, 158–9.

10. *ibid.*, 160.

11. Ahmed Ihsan (Tokgöz), *Matbuat Hatiralarim I 1888–1923*, I. *Meşrutiyetin, Ilânına Kadar 1889–1908*, Istanbul, Ahmet Ihsan, 1930, 28–30.

12. Roderic H. Davison, *Reform in the Ottoman Empire 1856–1876*, Princeton University Press, 1963, 13–14.

13. *op. cit.*, 125 ff.

14. M.A. Griffiths, 'The Reorganization of the Ottoman Army under Abdulhamid II, 1880–1897', unpublished Ph.D. dissertation, University of California, Los Angeles, 1966, 94.

15. Erring Goffman, *Asylums*, London, Pelican Books, (1968) 1978, 17.

16. Bernard Lewis, *The Emergence of Modern Turkey*, 2nd edn, London, Oxford University Press, X 1968, 236.

17. Berkes, *Türkiyede Çagdaşlaşma*, *op. cit.*, 435.

18. *ibid.*, 451.

19. *ibid.*, 493.

20. G. Jaschke, *Yeni Türkiye'de Islâm* (transl. H. Örs), Ankara, Bilgi, Yayınevi, 20.

21. *ibid.*, 96.

22. Niyazi Berkes (ed.), *Turkish Nationalism and Western Civilization: Selected Essays of Ziya Gökalp*, London, Geo. Allen and Unwin, 1959, 312.

23. For a text, see Ş.S. Aydemir, *Tek Adam: Mustafa Kemal*, vol. 3, Istanbul, Remzi Kitabevi, 1966, 473.

24. B.N. Sehsuvaroğlu, 'Atatürk Ilkeleri Işığında ve Bugünkü Türkiye'de Kadın Hakları' in *Atatürk Devrimleri I. Milletlerarası Sempozyumu Bildirileri*, 1974, 422.

25. Victor Turner, *The Forest of Symbols*, Ithaca, NY, Cornell University Press, 1967, 28.

26. Auguste Comte, *Catechisme Positiviste*, 2 edn, Paris, 1874, 378.

The modernisation of Japan and Turkey

Some Comparisons

TAKESHI HAYASHI

Introduction

For the Turks and for the Japanese, modernisation was not enforced from the outside through colonialism. In this sense, Turkey and Japan are different from other late-starting nations which were deprived of their independence and forced to accept humiliation at the expense of their endogenous culture, and were thus confronted with a serious identity problem. The fact that Turkey and Japan were able to maintain their political independence may have been a pre-requisite for genuine modernisation.

In general, the principle of national self-determination should be protected to the fullest possible extent in order for modernisation to be realised on a global scale, and irrespective of the population size of a group sharing a common culture, size having no bearing on the value of a culture. However, a problem which has to be confronted by cultural groups with very small populations which opt for modernisation, is that because of the universal nature of 'modernity', which has scale requirements, modernisation cannot work unless the group is of a certain size. Consequently, when a small-sized society opts for modernisation, there should be a full guarantee for its 'freedom to integrate' with other societies. If there is no advantage in enlarging the size of the society, the 'freedom to separate' should also be afforded.

Japan's rush towards modernisation was motivated by fear of colonisation by the Western powers. In the process it even adopted the nineteenth-century expansionist model and, as a result, deeply harmed not only the peoples of Asia but also itself. Japan has now learned that it must co-exist with other nations and that every nation, no matter how small, is equal. This attitude is clearly reflected in Article 9 of the Constitution, a pacifist declaration renouncing war as a means of resolving international disputes. In addition, Japan's attitude is based on its experience as the first nation to suffer the horror of atomic war. This is one of the conclusions that Japan has drawn from its trial-and-error efforts to modernise; in this sense, its

221

experience may be considered unique and somewhat different from the nineteenth-century Western model.

Japan's modernisation provides the model of a pacifist state with values of a new dimension. Not many Western nations have achieved this standard of modernisation. However, this does not mean that every nation has to set as its goal a uniform style of modernisation. It merely indicates the possibility of a wider range of options for various nations which at present are still striving to achieve modernisation based on the old nineteenth-century model. It would not be unrealistic to assume, moreover, that this model could stimulate the already modernised nations to reorient their growth strategies.

A foreign observer once commented that Japan is a nation characterised by the science and technology of the twentieth century, the economic philosophy of the nineteenth century, and the political system of the eighteenth century. This comment is not totally irrelevant, since for a latecomer to modernisation unbalanced development is inevitable. This might best be exemplified by the ideology of the leading political groups in society. For example, Turkish intellectuals who gathered around the *Kadro* in the early 1930s assumed 'a superficial combination of Marxism, nationalism, and corporatism'.[1] In other words, as Bernard Lewis commented,[2] their thought was a 'blend of ideas from Rome, Constantinople, and Moscow'. This strange combination of ideas, however incomprehensible to the objective eyes of outsiders, was to some extent an accurate reflection of the reality of Turkish society in its strivings for 'modernity', even if those affiliated with the *Kadro* were few in number and the group itself was a marginal one compared with the mainstream Kemalist movement.

The Republican People's Party, the vehicle of Kemal Atatürk's political ideology, adopted 'secularism, étatism, and reformism' as a systematic social and economic policy. These principles, plus the doctrines of 'republicanism, populism, and nationalism', formed together what was termed in 1931 the 'six arrows' policy. Compounded by the serious impact of the Great Depression of 1929, this platform expressed the understandable objectives of Turkey's modernisation process, although the political system then in existence should not escape criticism as an authoritarian regime exercising one-party rule. This system might have been a natural outcome, especially for a country where it cannot be proved that social and economic difficulties could have been overcome under a multi-party political system. Peter F. Sugar described this state of affairs as 'logical though naïve'.[3]

A case similar to that of the *Kadro* is Japan's *Shōwa Kenkyūkai* (Shōwa study group), founded in 1933 as a 'think tank' to Prince

Fumimaro Konoe (1891–1945), who became prime minister in 1937. Westernised liberal intellectuals had high expectations that he would be the first leader to block military fascism, but after failing to stop the Sino-Japanese war, he paved the way instead for the military regime's organisation of a nation-wide centralised movement leading towards total war. The Shōwa study group included a diverse array of intellectuals. Ideologically, the members were patriots, liberals and both radical and moderate socialists. Occupationally, they were university professors, journalists, military officers, high-ranking bureaucrats and businessmen. The study group lacked a real identity, and its members had only one thing in common: all of them recognised Japan's resignation from the League of Nations as a national crisis; Japan was then so isolated as a result of the Manchurian problem that in 1933 its demands were rejected by a vote of 42–1 at the General Assembly of the League. However, it is surprising that an important member of the Shōwa group, who played a significant role in the course of post-Second World War 'democratisation', stated that the group 'did not conceive of fascism as being bad at that time'; it was rather impressed by the criticisms of the European democratic powers made by pro-Nazi intellectuals.[4] This indicates that it was difficult for this group to identify fascism as such because it was often disguised as an agressive nationalism. This reminds us of the fact that fascism itself emerged as an outcome of the critical environment, both domestic and international, that prevailed, in post-First World War society.

This leads us to conclude that, for the late starters suffering from an unbalanced development, unless 'modernisation' as a value and as an ideal is integrated with nationalism, it does not translate into an actual nation-building programme. This in no sense means, however, that modernisation when coupled with nationalism can, *per se*, be justified. As was seen in Japan and elsewhere, unconditional nationalism always runs the risk of transforming itself into xenophobic chauvinism or self-centred ultra-nationalism.

The onset of modernisation

When comparing the modernisation of Turkey with that of Japan, the problem arises of how to determine the precise period in which modernisation began. In Japan this process got under way in the 1850s and particularly after the Meiji Restoration of 1868, when a systematic effort to modernise was made. In Turkey, one might take the view that modernisation started during the period of *Nizam-ı Cedid*, under Sultan Selim III (1789–1807), and if this is true, Turkey was half-a-century ahead of Japan. In order to examine the relevance of this statement, we will make a few comparisons.

Chronologically, the *Tanzimat* reformation (1839–76) coincided with the early Meiji period. However, the polities of the two countries at that time were different in nature: Turkey was part of the multi-ethnic Ottoman empire, while Japan was an independent nation-state. Not until victory in the war of independence led by Kemal Atatürk did Turkey succeed in building a nation-state. Turkey's modernisation developed with truly remarkable speed after 1923, owing to Kemal's powerful personality and leadership. But by this time Japan had already experienced its industrial revolution, and the transition from the steam engine to electrically-generated industrial energy was almost complete. Politically, Japan remained a monarchy in the true sense until the end of the Second World War in contrast to the Republic of Turkey, and women's suffrage was not granted until 1945. In this respect, the collapse of Japan's autocratic military clique after the Second World War may be compared to the dissolution of the Young Turk regime as a result of the Ottoman empire's defeat in the First World War.

In view of these factors, any resemblance between the Meiji Restoration and the *Tanzimat* reformation would be superficial. Turkey at that time was part of a great empire embracing many ethnic groups, and in which the Turkish population accounted for less than 30 per cent. In fact, it is doubtful whether the legacy of the *Tanzimat* reforms for Anatolia was of overwhelming significance, no matter how large the scale of the reforms, compared to those of the Meiji Restoration in Japan. Even though it was a preparatory step for 'modern' Turkey, *Tanzimat* seems only to have had a limited impact on the country at the time. It was not until after independence that the actual modernisation process led by Kemal himself began.

Objectively, the Meiji Restoration was only a small-scale reform undertaken by a nation-state incomparably smaller and poorer than the Ottoman empire. However, one might argue that because Japan was a small country, it was much easier for it to create a national consensus for modernisation. Moreover, it is possible that the real reason why Japan as a small nation was able to avoid being colonised once it had set its sights on modernisation is closely related to its geopolitical location at the farthest remove from the Western powers. The Turkish conditions were totally different in this regard, the Ottoman empire lying very close to Europe. In addition, it was a rich empire. Consequently, various components of the society such as the military, the administration, the culture, and the economy had to rely on an ethnic division of labour: it might have been impossible for this gigantic empire to maintain its unitary system without a differential structure. However, this type of division of labour, based on ethnicity, left each ethnic group in a decisively disadvantageous position after the empire went into decline. When the empire was divided, each ethnic group was economically deprived of the power to organise a nation-state on its own.

The élite, which foresaw this disintegration, hoped for the empire's rebirth and formed the Young Ottoman and the Young Turk movements. The latter group was attracted by such ideologies as Ottomanism, Pan-Islamism and Pan-Turanism until it finally came to believe in Turkish nationalism. The assertion of national identity and the theme of nation-building in the chaos that followed the decline of the empire and Western intervention must have been a laborious task, which only a leader with a powerful and charismatic personality could achieve.

This type of nationalism, which was nurtured in a severe international, political and military environment, did not exist in Japan. This fact might account for the emergence of the ideology of the Greater Japanese Empire, which simply imitated — and vaunted — the Western road to modernisation. It was not until after the Second World War that Japan's modernisation began to assume a 'national' character and to be recognised as inseparable from democratisation and demilitarisation. The experiences of Turkey and Japan have taught us that both great empires and imperialism are obsolete.

Industrialisation as the only solution

In both Turkey and Japan, those who initiated modernisation were a political and administrative élite who intended to transform their nations along Western lines. Reforms 'from above' characterised the approach of both nations to modernisation. In contrast to Turkey's ethnic diversity, which to some extent also characterised the Young Turks, the élite who led the modernisation in Japan were all Japanese without exception. But this does not mean that there was no dissonance or conflict within the Japanese élite. For instance, the majority of those who overthrew the feudal Tokugawa regime came from a few clans in western Japan, and all the important offices in the newly-established government were monopolised by them. Antagonism and resentment occasioned by their rule appeared in every form, the most severe being the civil war of 1877, the first major crisis of the new regime.

The Meiji élite were mainly from the warrior class (predominantly lower-ranking *samurai*). Because the ultimate objective of their political revolution was to protect their country from colonisation, it is understandable that the new government should have had a military and defence orientation from the beginning. Modernising Japan through enriching the nation and strengthening the military became their goal as a matter of course.

Ultimately, the burden of industrialisation was placed upon the shoulders of peasants who made up more than 70 per cent of the population, but after the frequent peasant revolts of the late Tokugawa/ early Meiji era, this class eventually came to accept the inevitability of industrialisation. However, it was only after the victory in the Sino-Japanese War (1894–5) that the new Meiji government attained stability and came to be regarded as better than the Tokugawa regime. The strong sense of political responsibility and service to the national interest entertained by the Meiji élite must have been the propelling force behind this success.

Industrialisation as a means of modernisation was initiated in Japan with the construction of warships. Faced with gunboat diplomacy, which demanded the opening of its ports for trade, the Tokugawa regime had no choice but to establish diplomatic relations with the Western powers. Although groups of warriors from various feudal clans were dissatisfied with the opening of diplomatic relations and resorted to desperate acts of exclusionism, they were quickly subdued by modern weapons. On realising that a battleship could not be cut down with a sword, they not only supported the opening of the ports but also earnestly desired modern armaments.

In Europe, industrial development started with mining, followed by iron manufacturing, shipbuilding and arms manufacture. Because Japan followed the reverse course, developing armaments first and then shipbuilding, iron manufacturing and lastly mining — it was natural that certain difficulties should have arisen. Although the technology for constructing large ocean-going wooden vessels existed in Japan in the fifteenth century, it was lost during the 300 years of Tokugawa rule which prohibited the construction of large vessels as part of the feudal regime's policy of isolation. In contrast to this, even though the scale was small, mining and metallurgical technology was preserved under the direct control of the Tokugawa government. This field progressed by leaps and bounds when the latest European technology, particularly in the form of drainage and ventilation equipment, was introduced. Moreover, the introduction of new metallurgical technology brought remarkable progress, making possible the utilisation of residues which were formerly discarded by indigenous techniques. Copper, in particular, ranked as one of the best export items in early Meiji Japan.

Even though traditional technology and skills were preserved in mining, the number of miners was insufficient to handle the newly-developed demand. In addition, traditional miners were bound by guild-type restrictions, and due to the legacy of the 'agriculture-first' principle of the Tokugawa regime, mining was regarded as a discreditable occupation. When modernisation efforts began, mining science and metallurgical technology were regarded as the most important fields of study in the newly-established Western-style college that later became the University of Tokyo. Surprisingly, many ex-warriors (the highest sector of the literate population) sought admission to these courses. This was probably due to the abolition of the ascriptive status of *samurai* after which only education and skills could lead to a new career. Nevertheless, it shows the severe competition for employment among the ex-*samurai* class, which made up about 10 per cent of the population.

The foreign engineers who led industrial development recommended that, in the interests of efficiency foreign businessmen be entrusted with management and that cheap but highly-skilled Chinese labour be imported. The Meiji government rejected this recommendation, which was rather unusual; furthermore, the Mining Act was promulgated in 1873, six years after the birth of the new regime, prohibiting not only mine development by foreign concerns but also the employment of foreign labour. In view of the fact that the Ch'ing dynasty controlled a nation incomparably larger than Japan, the new government may have feared that the introduction of Chinese labour could lead to a troublesome diplomatic problem. This Act took the lead in nationalising Japan's natural resources.

Although huge sums were invested in industrialisation at the outset of Japan's modernisation for military purposes, there were repeated failures such as that in the iron mills. The failures were mainly due to the direct and unadapted application of Western techniques to Japan, disregarding the differences in the quality of local ore and fuel; policy-makers who did not accept the opinions of experienced Japanese engineers must also be held responsible. Those who eventually put Japanese iron manufacturing on to the right track, and indeed played the crucial role during the modernisation process were not foreign engineers but Japanese ones. Iron mills in Japan were government-run after 1880 and were set up at different places (Kamaishi, Yawata, etc.); in 1906 production was stabilised, and the 'iron hunger' of the First World War finally made iron manufacturing profitable.

In Turkey, the basis of industrialisation was laid when iron manufacturing started in 1932. This coincided with the formulation of the first economic development plan. Consequently, production in various fields such as textiles, paper, sugar, chemicals, cement, and iron and steel showed a remarkable rate of growth. These industries constitute the most important sectors in the economic structure of Turkey today. The textile industry in particular has earned considerable profits as a main export item. Some of the Turkish iron mills, as well as many other factories in various sectors, have been subsidised by the government from the beginning. In Turkey the étatist organisation was the sole source from which experienced, skilled engineers were drawn. It is undeniable that étatism was of great importance to Turkish industrialisation.

The international environment in the early twentieth century was quite severe for colonised or developing nations. The great powers often got around commercial principles by cancelling contracts unilaterally or by refusing delivery depending upon changes in the world political situation. This severely affected the process of modernisation. The course pursued by both Japan and Turkey was the only possible response to the unstable international setting of that time. The iron and steel industry was supported by people who believed that iron manufacturing would lay the foundation of a modern state. On the basis of this motivation, incessant technological innovation was made in Japan, without which Japanese products would have been defeated in the price and quality competition with their European products.

Kemal Atatürk's achievement

The greatness of Kemal Atatürk lies in the fact that he created a new nation. By contrast, his superiority as a military leader — although he was able to win a war of national independence in face of enormous difficulties — was of secondary significance. Also, undeniably, he was a first-rate political leader, acute enough to foresee the coming era of national self-determination. But the truly difficult task was state-building after political independence. His achievement in this domain should therefoe be considered his greatest.

In the making of a national identity, Kemal had to stand against the Muslim concept of political identity which had been the legitimate basis of the polity of the Ottoman empire. The abdication of a sultan was not in itself a totally unprecedented event in Muslim political history; however, the implantation of a completely new political legitimacy was something altogether different. The enormous difficulty faced by Kemal at this time can be understood by anyone with some knowledge of Islamic ideology and Muslim political history. The abolition of the Sultanate and Caliphate created a political vacuum that could easily have produced chaos: and in order to fill it, an entirely new principle, i.e. nationalism, needed to be fostered with great urgency. Kemal was able to convince not only the insecure and suspicious masses but also the deeply critical élite of the necessity of modernising. He accomplished, so to speak, an ideological revolution. In this respect, although he was a charismatic leader, it is noteworthy that he never turned himself into a prophet.

In as much as 'revolution cannot be monopolised by one generation' (Gamal Abdel-Nasr), the evaluation of a revolutionary leader must also rest upon another criterion, namely the fostering of competent heirs. Kemal was equal to this task as well: proof enough of this lies in the fact that those who protected Turkey's national interests during the Second World War by adhering to a neutral position were Kemal's direct successors. Turkey joined the Allies in the final stages of the war only to secure its membership in the newly-emerging United Nations. By contrast, the Meiji élite seems to have failed to breed successors who could lead the nation along the right path. In 1925, a few years before Kemal called for 'republicanism, populism, and nationalism', the infamous Peace Preservation Law, which renounced the equivalents of these Turkish ideals, was enacted in Japan. This was a revised edition of the Police Security Act which had been promulgated in 1900 with the object of prohibiting freedom of speech and the right of assembly for political purposes. It is of immense value that Kemal left successors who, in the late 1940s, could change the dictatorship into a multi-party system when increased national political participation was deemed to be more in line with the national interest.

Political myth and religion in Japan

While attempting to overthrow the Tokugawa regime, the opposition leaders supported the Emperor, who had been entirely non-political, and helped him to act as the legitimiser of change. After the Restoration, the Emperor, who had had authority but no power, began to be politicised as a legitimate sovereign and leader of the state. With time, this ideology was intensified. A liberal scholar who objectively pointed out that, under a constitutional monarchy, the Emperor was nothing but a function of the state was indicted in 1935 on the grounds that his ideas were contrary to the spirit of the Peace Preservation Law, although the view he was expressing had been generally accepted in the academic community, and he had given lectures at the Imperial University of Tokyo. The basis for the politicisation of the Emperor lies in the political myth intentionally created by the Meiji government. The Meiji élite deified and mythicised the Emperor and created state Shintoism as the foundation of the new political legitimacy. This trend was later escalated by military fascists and fanatical xenophobes. In this way, the Meiji élite established an institution that ran contrary to the great accomplishment of Kemal. This was probably unfortunate even for the Emperor himself, who had been made powerless by those who used him; he was not freed of his fabricated divinity until after the Second World War, when he disclaimed it.

The government, from Meiji until the end of the Second World War, thoroughly indoctrinated the masses with this political myth through the national school system. The Japanese, confronted with the contradiction between the state political myth and Buddhist-oriented private life, astutely resolved the ambiguity by amalgamating the two religions. Ancestor worship and the Buddhist faith constituted a uniquely Japanese dualism in religious life. The Japanese of the present time still maintain this dualism in which state and public affairs are officiated by Shintoist rite and private matters by Buddhism, and it is not rare even today to find a small shrine in one corner of a big modern plant or on the roof of a skyscraper. It is there to ensure safety and prosperity. Even though state Shintoism was abolished after the Second World War, and religious freedom is now guaranteed, Shintoism has survived in the form of collective and communal religious rites. Concerning religious education, however, there is no demand that it be reintegrated into the public school carriculum.

Since secularism was one of the pillars of Kemal's doctrine, the future of religious education in Turkey is an interesting issue. It is to be noted that a comparative study on modernisation and religion in Turkey and Japan is yet to be attempted.

Modernisation at the grassroots

As has already been noted, the modernisation of Turkey is characterised by political success whereas that of Japan is characterised by success in economic growth, science and technology. In contrast to Turkey, 'a potentially rich country' whose resources were 'hardly even known when the republican government took power',[5] Japan had only the minimum resources needed to begin modernisation. None of Japan's resources were sufficient to withstand the intensification of international competition. Therefore, in order to catch up with the powerful advanced nations, Japan has made every effort to save the capital it has needed for investment. This has been done through the intensive gathering and meticulous examination of technical information. In other words, Japan tried hard to imitate advanced industrial techniques. The aim was to ensure the growth of domestic production and substitute Japanese goods for imported ones.

The process of industrialisation through imitation is complex; it is not simply a matter of equipment or plants, although these are of course indispensable. Scientific principles must be ascertained and applied to production; prior marketing research is also necessary.

Expressed in modern terms, products must be appropriate commodities. Moreover, an adequate supply of manpower and skills in operating facilities are a precondition for production. However, skills can be only gradually accumulated through practical experience, and during the period when manpower and skills were not yet sufficiently accumulated, Japanese entrepreneurs, many of whom had backgrounds as engineers, devoted themselves to a rational division of the production process into several stages. This made it easier for workers to acquire experience and skills, and so at last there appeared highly skilled workers who had mastered all the techniques required for each stage of production. This process also encouraged the creation of entrepreneurs of a new type. Thus, once manpower had been nurtured and skills accumulated, the production system was complete, and the stage of imitation was left behind.

Abstract, generalised theories and principles of industrialisation cannot be operative before each nation applies them to its particular situation by trial and error and transforms them into a concrete and appropriate production process. In Japan, it was light industry, i.e. spinning, weaving and food processing, that first underwent transformation as imported technology was adapted to fit endogenous industrial forms. Even if these products were of low quality by international standards, they sufficed as long as the domestic demand held up.

Japan had imported a massive quantity of Indian cotton products at the end of the nineteenth century. Superior quality was ensured in India, where the skills, accumulated over millennia through the workings of caste, were employed by the factory system. These skilled workers were paid better wages than Japanese spinning labourers; yet, in about ten years, Japan was able not only to catch up with India but also to supersede her. This is mainly because Japan was able to raise productivity through rationalisation of the production process by dividing it into several sub-stages. Japan challenged Indian-type skills. Thus, Japanese cotton products finally came to be competitive in the international market.

It was during this process that the number of small-scale indigenous cotton farmers began to recede in Japan as large-scale modern mills came to buy Indian raw cotton. Many farmers, especially in Western Japan, were hard-hit, because raw cotton had been an important source of side-income for them. However, out of this serious setback emerged diversified agricultural handicraft industries: shell buttons, which had previously been imported, came to be produced domestically, and subsequently the manufacture of metal buttons involving all the farmers of a village dominated the domestic market. The buttons also became an export item. This was made possible by the use of capital-saving manufacturing equipment and the training of skilled workers within a short period of time. But it cannot be denied also that the success of this industry was partly stimulated by the depressed state of farm finances.

Merchants often provided producers with information regarding the vicissitudes of demand, and this served as a stimulus for producers when they were considering innovations in production. At times, the merchants even became active themselves in the development of production technology. In these instances, commercial capital not only distributed the products but also supplied raw materials to the producers. The prototype of Japanese trading companies (*shōsha*) can be found here.

In the case of Turkey, a new type of entrepreneur and specialist emerged from the policy of étatism. The later a nation comes to industrialisation, the more significant becomes the role of the state, which is especially pertinent in reforming the infrastructure. In this relation, one should be reminded of the problems inherent in excessive reliance on foreign engineers and specialists, who tend to regard the model provided by their home country as absolute and are sometimes totally indifferent to the social and cultural systems of the country to which they were invited. Moreover, foreign specialists are handicapped in not always being provided with necessary data and have little access to the common knowledge of the people of the recipient-country. For instance, most of the fireproof stone buildings designed by foreign architects in the early Meiji period lacked special protection against earthquakes. Thus, there are hardly any such buildings left at present even though wooden buildings built by indigenous carpenters still survive. This example best illustrates the fact that the wisdom of the common people in the traditional culture should be carefully observed in the course of modernisation.

Concerning loans from abroad, Kemal Atatürk once stated that 'the shortest path to the loss of independence is to spend money one does not possess.' He must have been expressing this belief on behalf of the entire Turkish nation, which had suffered many bitter experiences under the Ottoman empire, yet he did not hesitate to obtain a foreign loan when Turkey needed it for a modernisation fund. He used it to improve the infrastructure, laying an essential foundation for the future.

The Japanese population in the first year of Meiji is estimated by present-day demographers (there were no accurate statistics at the time) to have stood at 35–36 million. Of the total population, over 75 per cent were farmers, and over 50 per cent resided in western Japan. The region west of Tokyo had a larger population and enjoyed better living conditions. The eastern and northern regions of

Japan could not afford double-cropping and because of this were less developed and poorer. In proportion to the land area (372,000 square km. as against Turkey's 780,576 square km.), Japan had too large a population — today more than 101 million as against 45 million in Turkey. This was the situation of the Meiji government when the government advocated two policies to be pursued simultaneously: one, to carry out industrialisation and the other to increase agricultural productivity. Because of financial restrictions, the government had to decide which policy should be given priority: the answer was industrialisation. Government investment amounted to 30 million yen between 1870 and 1880, of which 54 per cent was spent in 1878; and of the 1878 expenditure, 80 per cent was invested in railway installations and mining. Little was left for the farmer; indeed the success of industrialisation in Japan was supported by delaying agricultural growth. This problem surfaced after the First World War in the form of a series of tenant revolts. Those who participated in these revolts often held physiocratic ideas, and socialism also infiltrated the agricultural sector. It should be added that the very basis of the state-remodelling theory of fascism rested on an impoverished village society.

Although a great number of farmers were placed under hardship, agricultural productivity gradually increased all over Japan in this period — due solely to the efforts of agricultural leaders at the grassroots level. These were the people who actually implemented the policy which the Meiji government had set aside as of secondary importance: never progressive in ideology, the village leaders were only concerned with finding some means of increasing productivity in order to feed the increasing population. At that time, except in Hokkaidō, there was no room for the further development of new fields, and since farm land had been subdivided over the centuries, most of the farms were small in scale and scattered throughout the village; even the farms of larger landholders were the same. For this reason, leaders were keen on technological innovation and recognised the need for efficient irrigation facilities. They were capable of gathering adequate funds to obtain a small irrigation facility without government support.

The introduction of modern irrigation systems, however, caused the decline of customary irrigation practices, and as a result there were conflicts with neighbouring villages. It was the village leaders who provided the impartial mediation needed to resolve these problem; they also persuaded farmers to relinquish their irrigation rights which had been possessed by certain families for generations, so that communal irrigation for the benefit of all members could be established. The village leaders also had to be astute politicians and negotiators as they had to deal with both high- and low-ranking government agents. They were naturally affluent enough as farmers to be able to spare time for such voluntary tasks. However, to be wealthy was not enough. Unless they possessed superior agricultural skills, they could not gain the respect of farmers; furthermore, they had to be honest and impartial. Villages that had such leaders prospered, but those without could not even repair the village road adequately, and there was no harmony in the village. These village leaders influenced the government in the adoption of new agricultural policies. They also paid attention to the skills developed at government agricultural experiment stations. They were quick to try out a new strain in their own fields if they thought it feasible. These factors all contributed to the present high level of agricultural productivity.

Japanese 'modernisation', in terms of industrialisation and the making of a pacifist polity, has to some extent been a successful venture. But it cannot be denied that a series of new difficulties has already emerged at an advanced level in various fields.

NOTES

1. K.H. Karpat, *Turkey's Politics: the Transition to a Multi-Party System*, Princeton University Press, 1959, cited by Bernard Lewis in *The Emergence of Modern Turkey*, London: Oxford University Press, 2nd edn, 1968, 463.

2. Bernard Lewis, *op. cit.*, 464.

3. Peter F. Sugar, 'Economic and Political Modernization: Turkey', in Robert E. Ward and Dankwart A. Rustow (eds.), *Political Modernisation in Japan and Turkey*, Princeton University Press, 1964, 166.

4. Two years after the founding of the Shōwa Study Group, however, its members took an anti-fascist stand.

5. Peter F. Sugar, *op. cit.*, 165.

The Authors

FEROZ AHMAD is professor of history at the University of Massachusetts in Boston. A specialist in twentieth-century Turkish history, his publications include *The Young Turks* (1969) and *The Turkish Experiment in Democracy: 1950–1975* (1977).

KORKUT BORATAV is associate professor of economics at the Faculty of Political Science, University of Ankara. He has published numerous books and articles on Turkish economic history, including *Étatism in Turkey* (1974, in Turkish).

VLADIMIR I. DANILOV is Chief of the Turkey section at the Institute of Oriental Studies of the USSR Academy of Sciences in Moscow. His main publications are *Middle Strata in Turkey's Politics* (1968) and *Seven Thousand Kilometres around Turkey* (1975, in Russian).

S.N. EISENSTADT is professor of sociology at the Hebrew University of Jerusalem and formerly Dean of the Eliezer Kaplan School of Economics and a professorial fellow of the Truman Research Centre of that university. He is the author of many books and articles, among them *The Political Systems of Empires* (1969), *Tradition, Change and Modernity* (1973) and *Revolutions and the Transformation of Societies* (1978).

TAKESHI HAYASHI is councillor at the Institute of Developing Economies in Tokyo, and United Nations University Project Co-ordinator on 'Technology transfer, transformation and development — the Japanese experience'.

ENVER ZIYA KARAL is professor of history at the University of Ankara and President of the Turkish Historical Society. He has published numerous books and articles on the history of the Ottoman empire and the Turkish republic.

ALI KAZANCIGIL is the associate editor of the *International Social Sciences Journal*, Unesco. Before joining Unesco, he was an assistant professor of political science at the Middle East Technical University, Ankara, and the special correspondent in Turkey of the French daily *Le Monde*. He has worked and published on issues related to the state, North-South relations and Turkey's political system and foreign relations.

ŞERIF MARDIN is professor of sociology and former Dean of the Faculty of Administrative Sciences at the Boğaziçi University, Istanbul. He has been a visiting professor at several U.S. and British Universities and has published extensively on the history of political ideas and socio-political analyses of religion and ideology, including *The Genesis of Young Ottoman Thought: a Study in the Modernization of Turkish Political Ideas* (1962) and *Religion and Ideology* (1969, in Turkish).

ERGUN ÖZBUDUN is professor of constitutional law and politics and Director of the Institute for Middle Eastern Studies, Faculty of Law, University of Ankara. A member of the Executive Committee of the International Political Sciences Association, he has published numerous books and articles on political regimes and social change, political parties and electoral issues, including *Social Change and Political Participation in Turkey* (1976), and co-edited *Electoral Parties in the Middle East: Issues, Voters and Élites* (1980).

DANKWART A. RUSTOW is distinguished professor of political science at the City University of New York. He has published extensively on comparative politics, the Middle East and Turkey. His books include *The Modernization of Japan and Turkey* (ed., with R. Ward, 1964), *A World of Nations: Problems of Political Modernization* (1967), and *Middle Eastern Political Systems* (1971).

Index